Dementia: walking not wandering

Fresh approaches to understanding and practice

Edited by Mary Marshall and Kate Allan

JOURNAL OF DEMENTIA CARE

Dementia:
walking not wandering
Fresh approaches to understanding and practice
Edited by Mary Marshall and Kate Allan

First published in 2006 by
Hawker Publications Ltd, Culvert House, Culvert Road, London SW11 5DH
Tel 020 7720 2108, fax 020 7498 3023
www.careinfo.org

British Library Cataloguing in Publication Data
A catalogue record for this book is available from the British Library
ISBN 1 874790 68 X

Designed by Andy Jackson • andy@designersolutions.co.uk
Printed and bound in Great Britain by Pims Digital, London
Cover photograph from Liquid Library, www.liquidlibrary.com

Hawker Publications publishes *The Journal of Dementia Care* and *Caring Times*.
For further information please contact Hawker Publications at the address above or visit www.careinfo.org

Also published by Hawker Publications:

Making a difference – An evidence-based group programme to offer Cognitive Stimulation Therapy (CST) to people with dementia
By Aimee Spector, Lene Thorgrimsen, Bob Woods and Martin Orrell (2006 ISBN 1-874790-78-7)

Assistive technology in dementia care Edited by John Woolham (2006 ISBN 1-874790-83-3)

The Safe at Home project – The effectiveness of assistive technology in supporting the independence of people with dementia in the Safe at Home project (2006 ISBN 1-874790-77-9)

The handbook for care assistants – A practical guide to caring for elderly people (Sixth Edition)
Edited by Lynne Phair and Sue Benson (2000 ISBN 1-874790-69-8)

Food, glorious food – Perspectives on food and dementia. Edited by Mary Marshall (2000 ISBN 1-874790-71-X)

Dementia topics for the millennium and beyond Edited by Sue Benson (2001 ISBN 1-874790-64-7)

Care homes and dementia Edited by Sue Benson (2001 ISBN 1-874790-57-4)

Improving dementia care (A resource for training & professional development)
Training pack by Buz Loveday, Tom Kitwood and Brenda Bowe (Revised edition) (2000 ISBN 1-874790-38-8)

Person-centred care Edited by Sue Benson; Introduction & concept Professor Tom Kitwood (2000 ISBN 1-874790-54-X)

Care to communicate – Helping the older person with dementia Jennie Powell (2000 ISBN 1-874790-48-5)

Openings (Dementia poems and photographs) John Killick & Carl Cordonnier (2000 ISBN 1-874790-49-3)

ASTRID (A social & technological response to meeting the needs of individuals with dementia and their carers)
Edited by Mary Marshall (2000 ISBN 1-874790-52-3)

The care assistant's guide to working with people with dementia
Edited by Sue Benson (2002 ISBN 1-874790-70-1) £13.50

Design for dementia Edited by Stephen Judd, Mary Marshall, Peter Phippen (1998 ISBN 1-874790-35-3)

You are words (dementia poems) Edited and introduced by John Killick (1997 ISBN 1-874790-32-9)

The new culture of dementia care Edited by Tom Kitwood and Sue Benson (1995 ISBN 1-874790-17-5)

This book is dedicated to all of us who will have dementia, in the hope that we will be able to walk outside and feel the rain on our faces.

Mary Marshall and Kate Allan

Acknowledgements

This book began with a grant from the Scottish Executive to the Dementia Services Development Centre at the University of Stirling which enabled Kate Allan to set to work recruiting the first group of contributors. We are most grateful to the Executive. Without their help this book would never have got off the ground. The production of this book has been a long slow process for a number of complicated reasons and we want to thank our contributors for their chapters and for their patience as we put it together. They all share our commitment to a more considered approach to this term 'wandering' and we hope they are proud of the book we have finally published.

We also want to thank three people who worked very hard on the text: Sue Benson and Catherine Ross at Hawker Publications and Marion Munro when she was publications secretary at the Dementia Services Development Centre at the University of Stirling. John Killick also deserves thanks for his help with the editing.

The photographs (and one painting) which make this book such a treat to look at are by Keith Ingham, Rosas Mitchell, James McKillop, Tony Price, Kirsty Bennett, Eileen Richardson, Sue Benson, Laura Benson. We are most grateful to them too.

Mary Marshall and Kate Allan

The publisher and editors would like to thank, most warmly, the following authors and publishers for permission given to reprint material:

Bryson B (1995) Notes from a small island. London: Transworld.

Chatwin B (1987) *The Songlines*. London: Picador.

Craig D (1987) *Native Stones*. London: Secker & Warburg.

Davis R (1993) *My journey into Alzheimer's disease*. Amersham-on-the-Hill: Scripture Press Foundation.

Hillman J (1999) Paradise in walking. *Resurgence magazine*. Issue 197, www.resurgence.org

Holloway R (1996) *Limping towards the sunrise*. Edinburgh: Saint Andrew Press.

MacCaig N (1966) *Surroundings*. Chatto and Windus (The Hogarth Press Ltd) London.

Stephenson L (2000) Walking with Beth. *Alzheimer's Society newsletter*. August.

Contents

Contributors

KATE ALLAN trained as a clinical psychologist and worked in adult and older adult mental health services before joining the Dementia Services Development Centre at the University of Stirling in 1998 as a researcher exploring communication with people with dementia. Her interest in walking dates from an MPhil project looking at the subject, and this eventually led to her editing a collection of papers about walking into the first DSDC book on the subject, published in 1994.

PAUL BATSON works for Avon & Wiltshire Mental Health Care Partnership NHS Trust as a drama therapist in the Department of Old Age Psychiatry at Victoria Hospital, Swindon, UK.

KIRSTY BENNETT is a registered architect in Victoria (Australia) who has specialised in designing for older people and people with dementia for 15 years. This has included being responsible for the briefing, design, documentation and contract administration of a range of nursing home and hostel projects in many parts of Australia. She is currently working as an architect for the Uniting Church in Australia.

CHRISTINE CALDER is a resource worker in Social Work Resources at South Lanarkshire Council (UK), based within the Older People's Services Management Team. She has a range of remits in relation to service developments for older people and is lead officer in the development and delivery of assistive technology services within the council.

DENISE CHASTON qualified in 1984 as a registered mental health nurse. She is a clinical nurse specialist working with people who have young onset dementia and their carers/partners. Her commitment to involving users in service development and other aspects of their care has been heavily influenced by personal experience.

CLAIRE CRAIG is an occupational therapist who has worked for a number of years with people with dementia. She is particularly interested in how the arts can support the individual with dementia and promote person-centred communication. She is a keen walker.

HELEN CRAWLEY has worked in the field of human nutrition for 20 years – in government, the NHS, teaching and research. She researched and wrote the 1998 VOICES report, *Eating well for older people with dementia*, and lectures on the importance of good nutrition for people with dementia.

MARY DIXON is a social worker with more than 25 years experience in working with older people. She has contributed to several publications and has a particular interest in the formulation and development of new services.

BRENDA DUNN is a senior physiotherapist who has worked with the Care Homes Training Team in Glasgow, Scotland for more than five years. The multi-disciplinary team provide training as well as offering professional assessment and problem-solving support. The team's remit covers care homes for the elderly within the Greater Glasgow Health Board area.

ANN FERGUSON has worked for Age Concern Scotland for more than 23 years during which time she has developed extensive experience and knowledge of issues affecting older people. Several years ago she began specifically focusing on elder abuse and now manages Age Concern Scotland's national elder abuse project.

FIONA FOWLER works at the Dementia Services Development Centre (DSDC) at Stirling University, Scotland as the training and education officer. She spent 12 years in regulation for various councils and has lectured in health and social care studies at Peterborough College. Her background is in social care as a manager of both residential and day care provision for older people.

FAITH GIBSON is an emeritus professor of social work at the University of Ulster. She has long been interested in exploring how the past influences present behaviour in dementia and also in applications of reminiscence and life review. Her publications include *Reminiscence and recall* and *The past in the present: Using reminiscence in health and social care*.

HEATHER HILL has worked as a dance therapist for 20 years and has come to specialise in working with people with dementia. She completed her PhD in 2005 on 'Barriers to person-centred care in dementia'.

ROSALIE HUDSON is a registered nurse and an associate professor, School of Nursing, University of Melbourne, Australia. She has published articles in nursing and theological journals on subjects of spirituality, palliative care, dementia, pastoral care and ethics at the end of life. She has co-authored two books on death and dying and edited *Dementia nursing: a guide to practice*.

IAN JAMES is a clinical psychologist and works at the Centre for Health of the Elderly at Newcastle General Hospital, UK. He is also a research tutor on the doctorate course in clinical psychology, University of Newcastle. He used to work at the Newcastle Cognitive Behaviour Therapy Centre before specialising in dementia. Much of his work is informed by this prior experience.

JOHN KILLICK has been working full-time on communication work with people with dementia for the past 11 years. He has written or co-authored a number of books on the subject, including *You are words: Dementia poems*, *Openings: Dementia poems and photographs*, and a CD of him reading poems, all published by Hawker Publications. He also lectures, broadcasts and runs workshops in the UK and abroad. He has a part-time consultancy at DSDC, University of Stirling, looking at the use of the arts in the field of dementia.

RHONDA KNIGHT is senior lecturer in the Faculty of Health and Social Care at the University of the West of England, Bristol, UK. Her teaching interest s the care of the older person, especially the person with dementia. She is a registered nurse, who previously worked in an acute medical setting specifically for people with dementia. She is a part-time PhD student at the University of the West of England researching eating and drinking from the perspective of the person with dementia.

TRISHA KOTAI-EWERS has pioneered creative writing work with people with dementia in Australia over the years. She has spoken at conferences and published articles and chapters on the work.

DONALD LYONS is director of the Mental Welfare Commission for Scotland. An old age psychiatrist, he worked within NHS Glasgow and has wide clinical and managerial experience in the care of older people with mental health problems.

LORNA MACKENZIE is a challenging behaviour nurse specialist, Newcastle Challenging Behaviour Service, Centre for the Health of the Elderly, Newcastle General Hospital, UK.

MARY MARSHALL (emeritus professor of the University of Stirling) retired recently after over 30 years of work with and for older people as a social worker, researcher, lecturer and voluntary organisation manager. She was inspired by the social approach to dementia in Australia in 1982 and this became the focus of her work. She has written and edited several books on dementia care including *Food, glorious food* with Hawker Publications.

WINNIE MANNING is an old age psychiatrist who currently works in Lanarkshire, Scotland.

GILLIAN McCOLGAN is a sociologist and research fellow at the University of Stirling. Her PhD work was an ethnographical study in a private nursing home where research informants were people who had dementia. Her continuing interests are in ethics in research, relationships and social support, with a particular interest in companion animals as social support and assistance animals in everyday life.

JAMES McKILLOP was diagnosed with dementia in 1999, but his troubles started years before then and built up. After taking some time to get over the diagnosis, he returned to life by getting person-centred help from Alzheimer Scotland and Turning Point Scotland. He promotes the cause of people with dementia and acknowledges the support of those who helped him on his journey.

MARION MUNRO was the publications secretary of the Dementia Services Development Centre at the University of Stirling. While in this post she completed a part-time degree in English Studies. She undertook much of the preparatory background work for this book. She is now the information officer for Waterwatch Scotland.

ROSEMARY ODDY trained as a physiotherapist. After gaining general experience in the UK and abroad, she worked for 27 years with the Leicestershire mental health service where she developed a special interest in people with dementia and pioneered ways of promoting their mobility. She has now left the NHS and lectures at home and overseas, sharing her ideas and experience with colleagues and carers. She has written many articles on the subject of mobility in dementia care and in 1998 her book *Promoting mobility for people with dementia: A problem-solving approach*, was published by Age Concern, England.

JANET PRICE is a keen walker – in the hills, through backstreets and along the urban walkways of whichever city she is living in. She has never owned a car. Now retired from a life-long career in education and having completed all 284 of the Scottish munros*, she is exploring the remoter parts of Scotland including ancient long-distance routes. *Scottish hills over 3000 feet in height, defined originally by Hugh Munro in 1891 as having the status of separate mountains as compared to subsidiary tops.

MELANIE REID joined *The Scotsman* in 1980 as graduate trainee. She became women's editor in 1984. Between 1987 and 2000 she was associate editor at the *Sunday Mail*. She subsequently joined the *Express* as a columnist before moving to *The Herald* in 2001 where she is assistant editor and columnist.

TRICIA ROE is the administrator for the Newcastle Challenging Behaviour Service, Centre for the Health of the Elderly, Newcastle General Hospital, UK.

MALCOLM STEPHENSON is a challenging behaviour nurse specialist, Newcastle Challenging Behaviour Service, Centre for the Health of the Elderly, Newcastle General Hospital, UK.

GRAHAM STOKES is consultant clinical psychologist at South Staffordshire Healthcare NHS Trust, head of mental health at BUPA Care, honorary teaching fellow in the Department of Health Studies, Coventry University, honorary lecturer in the Department of Social Policy and Social Work, and honorary tutor in the Department of Psychology, University of Birmingham. His interests are neuropathology, neuropsychology and the understanding and resolution of challenging behaviour in dementia. He has been instrumental in the development of person-centred approaches to care.

FIONA TAYLOR was the unit manager for the residential home described in her scenario. In the absence of Scotland's Adults with Incapacity Act 2000, she used the guidelines from the Mental Welfare Commission on the use of restraint to draw up the protocol for ethical use of equipment in this case discussion. She is now a senior development officer for North Lanarkshire Council, Scotland, and her role is mainly about developing services for older people and people with dementia. She completed an MSc in dementia studies and her area of research is 'The uses and limitations of assistive technology for people with dementia'.

ROSEMARY TAYLOR is a carer for her father who has vascular dementia, and at the same time supports her mother in her caring role. She is a planning and performance manager, where part of her remit is care of the elderly, including project management of a dementia review.

ALISON THOMSON is a nurse officer with the Mental Welfare Commission for Scotland. She previously worked as a senior nurse and ward manager within NHS Borders and has wide experience in the care of people with dementia.

STEPHEN WEY is senior occupational therapist (OT) with Leeds Community Mental Health Teaching Hospitals NHS Trust, UK. He works on an assessment and treatment ward for people experiencing dementia but this article also draws on his experience working in the Leeds Community Treatment Team – a specialist intensive home treatment/support team for people experiencing dementia in Leeds. He qualified as an OT in 1993, before which he spent much time working in mental health in a variety of settings, including as a nursing assistant on wards for people with dementia and also learning disabilities. He has a degree in behavioural sciences.

PAM WILSON is a community psychiatric nurse with the Mental Health for the Elderly team based at the Borders General Hospital, Melrose, Scotland, which she joined after leaving West Port Day Unit.

A normal, enjoyable activity

1

1.1 Introduction

by MARY MARSHALL

This book grew out of an increasing awareness of the paradox that walking is normal and healthy but when people with dementia do it, it is pathological and labelled 'wandering'.

Clearly, there are issues of safety and quality of life in some of the walking of people with dementia, but we have to ask ourselves whether the response of those in dementia care is always one which treats people with dementia as fellow citizens. Would we refer to walking in any other group of people as 'wandering'? Is this term helpful? Does it promote a holistic and considered response?

Our aim in putting this book together was to promote more reflective use of the term 'wandering'. We hope this collection of papers encourages readers to think carefully before using the term and to focus more on why people with dementia walk. If we know why, we might be better able to come up with constructive and helpful responses which improve the quality of life of the person and their friends, family and staff who care for them.

The papers are divided into several sections. This division is somewhat arbitrary since there are a lot of shared concerns (such as the need to look for reasons, which is either implicit or explicit in most papers) but we hope it is helpful.

Why, where and how we walk

Clearly, *walking for enjoyment* is where a book like this should start, so in this first section you will find a quote from a book by David Craig and two personal statements. One is from Chris Smith (Lord Smith of Finsbury) who is the President of the Ramblers Association, and one is from Marion Munro, the secretary who did all the supporting work on this book.

Finding the *reasons for walking* is clearly a major theme of the book. John Killick provides some voices of people with dementia and he reflects on walking and communication. Ian James and his colleagues propose a detective approach: more Columbo than Sherlock Holmes.

Graham Stokes provides a rich collection of possible reasons. Melanie Reid provides a controversial view of why her mother walked out of her care home. The PROP group of people with dementia make some suggestions from their own experience and a short piece about Bill describes an unexpected explanation.

Medical aspects follow on from the previous section. Winnie Manning looks at several medical reasons why people with dementia might wander, including depression and sleep deprivation. An extract from Lee Stephenson tells the story of Beth and the consequences of her medication.

Three authors write about *specific settings*: Rhonda Knight about acute hospitals, Pam Wilson about a day

hospital and Brenda Dunn about care homes with special attention to the chairs people sit in. There are particular challenges when people with dementia walk a lot in all three settings.

Confinement can be a consequence of 'wandering'; this needs very careful consideration of the sort provided by Donald Lyons and Alison Thompson. Trisha Kotai-Ewers describes walking with a lady who felt confined, and in her paper on abuse Anne Ferguson suggests that this is one way of looking at some of the responses to apparently meaningless walking. The section concludes with a quote from Bruce Chatwin's book *Songlines* about the Aboriginal people of Australia who sing the songs of their ancestors when on 'walkabout'.

A *focus on the past* is another recurring theme. This section starts with a reflection from Rosemary Taylor about her father, followed by an erudite paper from Faith Gibson referring to historical literature about walking as well as the significance of the past in the present walking of people with dementia. Janet Price, in her personal piece, refers to literary writers who walked a lot.

James McKillop provides an unsettling reflection on his mother who has always walked a lot – this story of Mary shows how very important the past can be. Fiona Fowler gives an account of a woman who needed to walk about with a briefcase because she had done that in her past work. James Hillman goes right back to Adam and Eve in reflecting on walking in the past.

Movement is a section about the importance of moving about to stay healthy and socially integrated. Rosemary Oddy most usefully links exercise and cognition and provides advice on how to help people with dementia to keep moving. Heather Hill tells us how dance can help.

Support and therapy

Staying safe and healthy begins with a challenging story from Mary Dixon about a woman who walked ceaselessly for no apparent reason. Staff ensured she ate enough and her feet were looked after, but they were unable to provide her with safe outside space. This leads on to authoritative pieces from Helen Crawley on food and Kirsty Bennett on design. Christine Calder and Fiona Taylor provide some stories on how technology can help.

The book concludes with two very positive sections. In the first, on *walking as therapy*, Stephen Wey talks about George and how his problematic walking became part of his therapy. James McKillop tells us how his brain functions less well when he cannot walk for a spell.

The final section is about *walking with*. It begins with Claire Craig's story of Edith, with whom she walked and from whom she learned a great deal. Gillian McColgan reminds us of the importance of animals associated with walking. Rosalie Hudson reflects on spiritual aspects, including the fact that walking is part of all religions. Pilgrimages, for example, have always been part of the Christian tradition. Paul Batson describes silent walks with Gordon, in which Gordon was able to demonstrate a kindness each time. The book concludes with Richard Holloway's suggestion of walking as contemplative prayer.

This book could have grown and grown. A day seldom passes when someone has not told me stories or shared concerns about people with dementia and walking. The book provides a rich and diverse set of papers to promote reflection and debate, but there is need for a great deal more.

1.2 Perspectives on 'wandering'

by MARY MARSHALL

This chapter aims to put the spotlight on the phenomenon of 'wandering' in people with dementia in order to stimulate more care and reflection in the use of this widely-accepted but very non-specific term.

It draws on some perspectives on 'wandering' from books written for carers and professionals in a range of fields involved in dementia care. Many of the books cover several of the perspectives but emphasise some more strongly than others.

Inevitably, the perspectives also overlap. The aim is not to impose some spurious classification but to ground the rest of this book in mainstream current thinking.

The perspectives might usefully be characterised as:
• inevitable
• restraining
• challenging
• classification
• communicating
• healthy.

Inevitable

Thomas and O'Brien (2002), in a textbook of old age psychiatry, list a series of symptoms of dementia: cognitive, non-cognitive and behavioural. They include wandering along with agitation in a group headed 'overactivity'. They claim that all overactive behaviours tend to become more common with increasing severity of dementia. Szwabo (2002) in a chapter on the role of nursing in an old age psychiatry textbook, suggests that "as dementia progresses, symptoms can worsen" and she includes wandering as a symptom of dementia. Sano and Weber (2003) claim that wandering is likely to occur at some point in the disease.

The notion that wandering is inevitable is widely accepted. Davies (2004), a nurse on a psychogeriatric unit, undertook a study of management approaches on her ward in a hospital within the Powys Health Care NHS

Trust. In her opening paragraphs she states: "One of the most important of behavioural changes in dementia is wandering" (p4). It is tempting, but not correct on the basis of this small sample of current textbooks, to assume that it is the medical textbooks which are embracing a medical model of dementia. By this I mean attributing behaviour solely to brain damage with the implication that there is nothing that can be done about it beyond keeping the person safe. In this small sample, the geriatric medicine and nursing textbooks addressed the social and environmental determinants as well.

The emphasis on wandering as an inevitable consequence of dementia with dire consequences is most dramatically illustrated by some American textbooks. They provide a perspective not seen in the UK, which is what one might call the 'shock/horror' presentation. Even the title of the book by Silverstein et al (2002) has a tragic feel: *Dementia and wandering behaviour: Concern for the lost elder.*

This is a book which, from the start, emphasises the traumatic and dangerous aspects of wandering. Words like 'frightening' and 'emotionally wrenching' occur in the first paragraph of the introduction. The numbers of people with dementia living in their own homes are described as a social policy time bomb and wandering as the behaviour which has alerted professionals to the ticking of this time bomb. Figures are given which show, for example, that seven out of ten people with dementia will wander and become lost.

There is an emphasis on the inevitability of wandering as well as its profoundly awful consequences, with phrases like, "wandering is a major hallmark of dementing illness, and as such it cannot be ignored" (p4). Wandering is seen as part of a process which involves "multiple interacting factors, including biomedical changes in the brain, lifelong patterns of coping with stress and environmental stimuli".

There is a tendency to use very dramatic statistics, such as those quoted in Turkington and Galvin's (2003) *Encyclopaedia of Alzheimer's disease*, in which they claim that 60 per cent of patients with Alzheimer's disease will wander and become lost during the course of the disease.

In a textbook for social workers, Tibbs (2001) describes a scenario where the social worker is 'threatened' with the coroner's court by anxious GPs, relatives, home carers and others. Fear of what might be said in court or by the media makes a preoccupation with risk very understandable, but not the best foundation for coming up with rational, person-centred solutions.

Clearly I do not, in this chapter, want to pretend that wandering is not a source of great stress and strain for relatives and friends who feel responsible for the person with dementia. When your relative with dementia walks away and gets lost it is every bit as traumatic as losing a child. Many relatives are not physically fit enough to accompany the person with dementia and they suffer many hours of anxiety about the person's ability to return home, or they prevent them going out by locking the door and then they experience the anger and frustration that results. Relatives often find it inexcusable when care homes and hospitals lose people with dementia. It is experienced as almost a breach of trust: "I trusted you to look after my vulnerable husband and you let him get lost." The point here is that by focusing primarily on the inevitability of wandering and the dangers that then arise, there is a sense of helplessness and a possibility that we lose sight of the individual with dementia.

Restraining

Silverstein et al (2002) point out that increasing concerns about autonomy and self-determination will arise. They therefore look "at ways such as the Alzheimer's Association's Safe Return Program to emerging, high tech personal technologies which can help people with dementing illness remain safe".

Among other things Molloy and Caldwell (2002) recommend a medical alert bracelet inscribed 'memory loss' or 'Alzheimer's'. The focus on safety can imply the use of all sorts of procedures and equipment from systems and technology to restraint by confining the person to a bed, chair or place.

There are many texts which provide guidance on the proper legal and ethical use of restraints and other limits to freedom. In a textbook for social workers, Marshall (1996) draws attention to the issues of abuse and restraint.

She asserts that there are circumstances when restraint is necessary and she draws on RCN guidelines (1994) in stressing the need for a clear written protocol in these circumstances which lists what the problem is, what has been done to solve it, why the decision to restrain was made and by whom, when it will be reviewed and by whom.

There are always fine judgements to be made in dementia care about the limits of autonomy. There are also fine judgements to be made about what is restraint. Davies and her colleagues (2004), for example, tried several perhaps unexpected techniques on her hospital ward, which included the use of a mirror on the door and disguising the door handle with a tea towel or pillowcase.

The Mental Welfare Commission for Scotland has published (2002) a most useful set of principles and guidelines to assist when "consideration is being given to the use of physical restraint and other limits to freedom".

It starts with a set of principles emphasising the seriousness of limiting freedom and the importance of assessment and the search for alternative approaches. The book then covers direct physical restraint, direct mechanical restraint, locking the doors, tagging, video surveillance, passive alarms, and medication.

Much of the text relates to people who wander. The commission has subsequently published special guidance on the use of technology such as tagging and tracking devices for people who wander (2005).

Since restraint is often linked to the risk of falls, it is worth mentioning here the figures on falls in older people. This is a serious matter. The English National Service Framework for Older People (DOH 2001) estimates that approximately 400,000 older people will visit an accident and emergency department each year as a result of a fall and many will die from the complications which arise.

Restraint is, however, not usually the answer. Stumpf and Evans (1998) have shown that restraining people increases the incidence of falling.

Challenging

Most of the professional textbooks include wandering in a section on challenging behaviour. Few of them have a whole chapter about it. Hudson's textbook for nurses (2003) is an exception, with a chapter by Lai and Arthur.

Lai and Arthur (2003) take the view that wandering is not just one behaviour but a group of behaviours. This is a useful reminder that the behaviour described as 'wandering' has at least two very different presentations. In simple terms, people with dementia often walk a lot and can cause carers and paid staff a lot of anxiety. Generally speaking this is when they walk outside and are no longer able to continue and return safely.

Another form of constant walking can be seen in people who are always on the move in long-term care settings. Other people with dementia, staff and relatives can be disturbed and even distressed by these people. It can be particularly disturbing when they are clearly trying to leave but are prevented, usually by locked doors. Martino-Saltzman et al (1991) have suggested that this can be classified as *direct* (straight to a destination), *random pacing* (back and forth between two points) and *lapping* (circuitous movement revisiting points sequentially along a path or track).

In a textbook for psychologists (1996) Stokes addresses the problem of definition. He suggests that wandering is a determination to walk:

• with no or only superficial awareness for personal safety (eg an inability to return, impaired recognition of hazards); or
• with no regard for others (eg in terms of time of day, duration, frequency or privacy); or
• to excess, thereby disrupting essential adaptive behaviours (eg eating, sleeping, resting).

He states that "wandering is indexed by single-mindedness that is unresponsive to persuasion" (p607).

Jacques and Jackson (2000), in a book for doctors generally, classify behaviour as positive and negative, by which they mean that behaviour which is intrusive and demands action is positive, and behaviour which is quiet and withdrawn is negative. They put wandering into the positive group, and warn that people with 'negative' behaviour can be neglected.

The textbooks vary in specifying action to be taken. Thomas and O'Brien (2002) may be demonstrating their perception of the role of old age psychiatry by limiting their intervention to drugs: "Several drugs may help such behaviours and, while low dose anti-psychotics are the most widely prescribed, carbamazepine may also be helpful" (p517).

Most other textbooks suggest that management first requires an understanding of causes. All textbooks point to multiple causes. Lai and Arthur (2003) provide three: biomedical, psychosocial and person-environment interaction.

The biomedical cause relates to the location and extent of brain damage. The psychosocial perspective usually lists factors like those in Allan (1994):

- continuation of lifestyle patterns
- occupation
- leisure
- response to stress
- anxiety/sadness/anger
- boredom
- need for toilet
- pain
- loss of navigational skills
- faulty goal-directed behaviour
- need for exercise
- form of communication
- desire to leave.

If the person-environment interaction is the cause, wandering usually results from difficulties with the environment such as getting lost, struggling with inadequate light, too much heat or a response to noise. Other medical factors such as physical or psychiatric illness and the side effects of medication can also be neglected by books which focus on brain damage.

Fulmer *et al* in a textbook for geriatricians (2000) use the classification of Chou *et al* (1996) of the causes of assaultive behaviour and expand it to include other disturbing behaviour such as wandering. This classification groups causes into three categories: patient factors, environmental factors and caregiver factors. Their section on caregiver factors emphasises the value of an informed understanding of dementia and techniques to manage challenging behaviour. Lai and Arthur (2003) say:

> It should never be assumed that wandering is 'aimless'. Rather, it is likely to be purposeful in some sense, and skilled nurses should

assess every person from a physical, psychosocial and environmental perspective in an attempt to determine the likely causes and appropriate interventions. (p73)

Classification

Cantley (2001) has edited a handbook for a range of professionals. One author, Maria Parsons, says that constant walking or 'wandering' behaviour often causes concern to families and formal carers. She quotes Allan's assertion (1994) that careful and systematic assessment may reveal explanations and provide different options for intervention. Bond (2001) in the same book takes a different sociological view. He suggests that we all need to classify events and experiences for practical reasons in order to manage them. He uses the way we classify people who wander as problematic as an example. This is an important perspective for this book, which is trying to urge a more careful use of the word.

Two aspects of this labelling of people who wander as problematic need to be considered. One is the lack of clarity about what is meant by wandering and the tendency to include a range of behaviours, all of which involve walking. Another is grouping them all together as problematic without asking: problematic for whom? Chapman, Jackson and MacDonald (1999), in a textbook for care staff including nurses, emphasise that a first step in understanding challenging behaviour is to determine for whom it is a problem.

The Alzheimer's Society (2000) advice sheet entitled *Walking about or 'wandering'* puts these complex professional uncertainties into simple language:

> There are many reasons why some people with dementia feel compelled to walk about or leave their home. It is important to think about why the person might be doing this so that you can find ways to deal with the situation. Any approach you choose should, as far as possible, preserve the person's independence and dignity.

The advice sheet lists many reasons for walking: feeling lost, loss of memory, continuing a habit, boredom, energy, pain and discomfort, response to anxiety, searching for the past, a task to perform and confusion about time.

Communicating

One way of looking at challenging behaviour is to suggest that it is a means of communicating. This may be particularly relevant for people with dementia, many of whom have difficulties making themselves understood verbally. Molloy and Caldwell (2002), in a book for carers, say "people often wander because they cannot express their needs" (p134).

In a sense this overlaps with an approach which emphasises the need to understand the causes of wandering. People with dementia may be trying to tell us what is wrong by walking. This is very far from the underlying notion of aimless walking.

The Collins Dictionary defines wandering as: "To move or travel about, in, or through (a place) without any definite purpose or destination."

It is almost always clear that the behaviour of people with dementia who are wandering is not aimless; it may be risky and it may be difficult to understand but it is not aimless. There is very little professional literature which addresses wandering from the point of view of communication, but this may change with a burgeoning interest in communicating with people with dementia.

The realisation that people with dementia have preferences and views and wish to share them is a relatively recent one. Goldsmith's book (1996) was a milestone in taking stock of this issue. Allan and Killick have since produced very influential texts (Killick & Allan 2001; Allan 2001; Allan 2002).

We should also reflect on what we, the professionals, communicate in labelling people with dementia who walk as 'wandering' or 'wanderers'. Walking is, after all, a normal activity. We all walk to go somewhere, to think more clearly, to explore, to escape, to relax, to loosen stiff joints, to ease indigestion, to enjoy different textures beneath our feet, to stimulate appetite and so on. The reasons people with dementia wander, listed by Lai and Arthur above (biomedical, psychosocial, personal/environmental), is a way of classifying the same reasons, except that by biomedical they mean brain damage rather than simply related to the working of the brain.

We need to ask ourselves why we need to pathologise a normal behaviour. I would like to suggest several reasons:

• Because we are concerned about risk

This is perfectly understandable especially in our blame culture of care, and because we care about vulnerable people coming to harm. However, we do have to ask ourselves whether the use of the label 'wandering' meets our needs more than those of the person with dementia.

• Because we keep people in abnormal places

People with dementia may need to walk a lot to cope with the kind of places in which we provide long-term care, and we may need to label this walking pathological in order to cope with our own emotional pain at confining them and providing less than optimal environments.

• Because we feel better if we see the behaviour as part of a disease

The medical model with its emphasis on brain damage can relieve us of guilt because it implies that we are not responsible for the behaviour of people with dementia. The disability or social model on the other hand implicates our interactions with the person with dementia and the care we provide.

Kitwood and Bredin's (1992) person-centred care implies that we should feel guilty for the malignant models of care we provide. We can protect ourselves from emotional pain if we believe that challenging behaviour is a result of brain damage rather than a response to how we care or an attempt to communicate.

• As a shorthand

Wandering is a shorthand way of describing various sorts of walking behaviour in people with dementia. It is not used with other groups of people. It is generally negative and non-specific. Being labelled 'a wanderer' is a negative label, which actually tells us very little. If we used the term 'a walker' we would have to provide more explanation about what we meant. Mrs A is trying to escape by walking out of the doors all the time; Mrs B is an energetic walker who is always on the go; Mr C walks because there is nothing else to do – and so on.

The use of the term underlines the belief that people with dementia are different from the rest of us. We may need to believe this because we are afraid of dementia, we are embarrassed by people with dementia or because we need to justify what we do to people with dementia. It is a way of communicating a whole lot of things besides a description of behaviour.

Healthy

Some of the professional literature on wandering mentions that walking is healthy (for example, Lai and Arthur) but this is seldom recognised in the heavily problem-focused literature. Wandering is almost always seen as negative and to be prevented or discouraged. Yet all literature on healthy ageing stresses the importance of exercise. We may need a change of mindset, which this book is keen to encourage. Lamb in Grimley Evans (2000) states, for example, "The benefits of physical activity and exercise in later life are protection against disease, promotion of health and prevention of disability".

This chapter has drawn from textbooks for professionals likely to be involved in dementia care, to show how the term 'wandering' is interpreted. It has proposed six approaches and suggested that some of them detract from the need to see each person with dementia as a complex and unique human being.

References

Allan K (1994) *Wandering*. Stirling: Dementia Services Development Centre.
Allan K (2001) *Communication and consultation: Exploring ways for staff to involve people with dementia in developing services*. Bristol: The Policy Press.
Allan K (2002) *Finding your way: Explorations in communication*. Stirling: Dementia Services Development Centre.
Alzheimer's Society (2000) *Walking about or 'wandering'*. London: Alzheimer's Society.
Bond J (2001) Sociological perspective. In Cantley C (ed) *A handbook of dementia care*. Buckingham: Open University Press.
Cantley C (2001) *A handbook of dementia care*. Buckingham: Open University Press.
Chapman A, Jackson G, MacDonald C (1999) *What behaviour? Whose problem?* Stirling: Dementia Services Development Centre.
Chou KR, Kaas MJ, Ritchie MF (1996) Assaultive behaviour in geriatric patients. *Journal of Gerontological Nursing* 22 30-38.
Davies C (2004) *The management of wandering in older people with dementia*. Powys: Powys Health Care NHS Trust.
Department of Health (2001) *National service framework for older people*. London: Department of Health.
Fulmer T, McDougall G, Abraham I, Wilson R (2000) Providing care for elderly people who exhibit disturbing behaviour. In Grimley Evans et al. *Oxford textbook of geriatric medicine* (2nd edition). Oxford: Oxford University Press.
Goldsmith M (1996) *Hearing the voice of people with dementia*. London: Jessica Kingsley Publishers.
Grimley Evans J, Williams TF, Beattie BL, Michel J-P, Wilcock GK (2000) *Oxford textbook of geriatric medicine* (2nd edition). Oxford: Oxford University Press.

Hudson R (ed) (2003) *Dementia nursing: A guide to practice*. Melbourne: Ausmed Publications.

Jacques A, Jackson G (2002) *Understanding dementia* (3rd edition). Edinburgh: Churchill Livingstone.

Killick J, Allan K (2001) *Communication and the care of people with dementia*. Buckingham: Open University Press.

Kitwood T, Bredin K (1992) *Person to person: A guide to the care of those with failing mental powers*. Essex: Gale Centre Publications.

Lai C, Arthur D (2003) Wandering. In Hudson R (ed) *Dementia nursing: A guide to practice*. Melbourne: Ausmed Publications.

Lamb SE (2000) 'Exercise and lifestyle'. In Grimley Evans *et al Oxford textbook of geriatric medicine* (2nd edition). Oxford: Oxford University Press.

Marshall M (1996) *I can't place this place at all: Working with people with dementia and their carers*. Birmingham: Venture Press.

Martino-Saltzman D, Blasch BB, Morris RD, McNeal LW (1991) Travel behaviour of nursing home residents perceived as wanderers and non-wanderers. *The Gerontologist* 31(5) 666-72.

Mental Welfare Commission for Scotland (2002) *Rights, risks and limits to freedom*. Edinburgh: Mental Welfare Commission for Scotland.

Mental Welfare Commission for Scotland (2005) *Safe to wander? Principles and guidance on good practice in caring for residents with dementia and related disorders where consideration is being given to the use of wandering technologies in care homes and hospitals*. Edinburgh: Mental Welfare Commission for Scotland.

Molloy W, Caldwell P (2002) *Alzheimer's disease*. London: Constable and Robinson.

Parsons M (2001) Living at home. In Cantley C (ed) *Handbook of dementia care*. Buckingham: Open University Press.

Royal College of Nursing (1994) *The privacy of clients: electronic tagging and closed circuit television*. Issues in Nursing 25. London: Royal College of Nursing.

Royal College of Nursing (1999) *Restraint revisited – rights, risk and responsibility*. London: Royal College of Nursing.

Sano M, Weber C (2003) Psychological evaluation and non-pharmacological treatment and management of Alzheimer's disease. In Lichtenberg PA, Murman DL, Mellow AM (eds) *Handbook of dementia*. New Jersey: John Wiley & Sons Inc.

Silverstein NM, Flaherty G, Tobin TS (2002) *Dementia and wandering behaviour: Concern for the lost elder*. New York: Springer Publishing Company.

Stokes G (1996) Challenging behaviour in dementia: a psychological approach. In Woods RT (ed) *Handbook of the clinical psychology of ageing*. Chichester: John Wiley & Sons Ltd.

Strumpf NE, Evans LK (1998) Physical restraint of the hospitalized elderly: Perceptions of patients and nurses. *Nursing Research* 37(3) 132-137.

Szwabo P (2002) The role of nursing. In Jacoby R and Oppenheimer C (eds) *Psychiatry in the elderly* (3rd edition) Oxford: Oxford University Press.

Thomas AJ, O'Brien JT (2002) Alzheimer's disease. In Jacoby R and Oppenheimer C (eds) *Psychiatry in the elderly* (3rd edition) Oxford: Oxford University Press.

Tibbs MA (2001) *Social work and dementia*. London: Jessica Kingsley Publishers.

Turkington C, Galvin J (2003) *Alzheimer's disease*. New York: Facts on File, Inc.

1.3 Enjoyment of walking

by CHRIS SMITH, DAVID CRAIG AND MARION MUNRO

I began walking when I was a teenager at school in Scotland, and I discovered the wild and windswept hills and glens of the Highlands, and found – a little to my surprise – that I really enjoyed it. The exercise was hard, and sometimes the conditions were miserable, and frequently you'd come back from a day out thoroughly soaked, but somehow the triumph against adversity was something to relish, deep down. And often of course there were the most glorious days of far-reaching views and golden sunlight and deer gathering on the slopes and perhaps even an eagle up amongst the clouds.

I've spent a lifetime since, tramping the mountains and moorlands, climbing all the 3000-foot mountains in Scotland, walking the Pennine Way, and even exploring abroad to exotic places like California or Spain. And I've never lost that youthful enthusiasm I first had. I still feel a bit of a thrill as I put my boots on in the morning and set off for a good walk. And I especially treasure this sensation because I have too few opportunities these days to do it. The busy political life of Westminster holds you too much in thrall. But the best antidote of all is to stand on a mountain ridge with the wind blowing around you and half the country spread out around you. It really does help to put things in perspective.

It's also something that can be enjoyed throughout your life. A couple of years ago I was coming down from the summit of a mountain up in the Torridon area of the north-west of Scotland, and coming up towards me was a man who looked remarkably sprightly despite his advancing years. He told me this was his way of celebrating his eightieth birthday, that very day. I just hope that I have his energy and agility – and enjoyment – when I get to that age!

You don't need to climb the high mountains, either. Walking can be good for you and, much more importantly, fun in virtually any setting. On most days when I go to and from the Houses of Parliament I try to walk through the Embankment Gardens in the heart of London: a short walk, but a real oasis of flowers and greenery in the bustling heart of the capital city. It's a far cry from the Highland ridges, but it's walking too, and it's a real pleasure.

Chris Smith

"Yet nature has enthralled me since I first staggered about waist-deep in the heather hills of Aberdeenshire. I wanted always to immerse myself in the wilderness, the beyond-the-civilised, the steep slopes and the blue or grey skylines angling up beyond the suburbs and beyond the farmlands. Nature was the lovely element, the countryside was where we went whenever we were free, and this was renewed when our children had come into the world and needed the nourishment of getting to know whatever was outside our own city limits.

We walked the green trods through the dales of Yorkshire, we climbed the mountains and combed the beaches of Wester Ross and the Hebrides, and then the whole thing leafed again, renewed and refocused itself, by taking to the steepest, least frequented parts of the country – the crags. It was as though I had grown another pair of eyes, or a special limb – one that reached up compulsively, curled round edges, fitted itself onto the rough, far-out ends of things.

Even if you walk out into the wilderness there is still a layer of artefact between yourself and nature – the sole of your boots. But to climb is to be intimate with the very stuff of our habitat, to smell its minerals (the struck-match odour of split rock or rock in a heatwave), to imitate the lie of it in the twisting and flexing of your muscles, to relish its most durable elements through the nerves of your fingerends.

One of Engel's most fundamental insights has always been for me the motto I would choose if I was allowed just one. "Practically," he said about Lancashire work-people who had dispensed with religion, "They live for this world and strive to make themselves at home in it". We can't actually make ourselves at home on the crags (although a friend of mine spent three weeks on the North America Wall of El Capitan, writing his novel in the morning and climbing in the afternoon). But when I sit on a six-inch ledge with my feet dangling above a two hundred-foot drop, the hart's tongue fern and dwarf hawthorn a few inches from my eyes, the air smelling of moss, wood-pigeons clattering out of the tree-tops down below, then at least for a time I have grafted myself back into nature, and the sense of rightness achieved, or regained, is unmistakable."

David Craig (1987) Native Stones
London: Secker & Warburg

Many of us enjoy being out of doors, particularly when it brings a welcome break to our daily routine. Besides the physical benefits of walking I have often found it affects my mood in a positive way. Stress can be reduced simply by taking a brisk walk; a walk which can offer an opportunity to get thoughts into perspective and relax the mind. Walking is therapeutic for me especially in the winter months when my mood can be a bit low due to lack of daylight.

A place where I love to walk is around a man-made loch within the grounds of the University of Stirling. It is a beautiful walk, which clearly marks the changes in the seasons. It stimulates the mind and the senses in many ways. Even on the darkest of days if I just take time to look around me and reflect on the environment I can always find something to smile at.

The spring months are beautiful as new life appears along the walk. The rhododendrons and azalea bushes provide an abundance of bright colours. Ducklings and cygnets are among some of the wildlife that can regularly be seen on this walk. In summer I have a favourite bench where I sit under a large oak tree at the water's edge, close to a little wooden gate that leads off into a large meadow filled with daisies and buttercups. It is a little respite for a few minutes, which really breaks up a full day at work.

The autumn brings many changes to this walk. The narrow path becomes softer underfoot and copper leaves provide a satisfying crunch with every step. Bird sound is a constant companion at any time of the year. In winter the landscape changes dramatically. A day of hard frost turns this familiar walk into a winter wonderland; swans descend at a great speed on to the frozen loch and gracefully slide along the ice. Little birds peck around for food and some manage to find a little thawed edge to swim in.

There is so much to enjoy in nature, distinctive seasons and a sense of being alive and at peace with the world, even if just for a few moments. The freedom to roam, to stroll or on energetic days to power walk is one I hope I never take for granted.

I am reminded often of a humbling experience a few years ago. My elderly mother-in-law, a very frail lady, had spent her entire life living in the West Highlands of Scotland. Her childhood had been spent in a very rural area, built up around a slate quarry, on the edge of the ocean, nestling under majestic cliffs. I watched one summer's day, eyes brimming with tears, as she painfully walked barefoot over a shingle beach just to put her feet in the water once more.

Marion G Munro

Reasons for walking

More than a mile: encounters with people walking

by JOHN KILLICK

Reasons for walking in life are manifold: to get somewhere, to keep healthy, to exercise the dog, to explore your environment, as an accompaniment to conversation (the words 'walking' and 'talking' do not chime by accident) – that is just the start of a list. If *we* do any of these things it is not a topic for comment. Yet if someone with dementia wants to walk, we immediately start questioning their motives. With dementia we tend to pathologise even the most commonplace human activities.

That is because we do not understand, and cannot bear to remain in ignorance. This may be partly because we are in a caring role and genuinely need to find out what is going on so that we can offer appropriate help. But surely it is just as likely that we are succumbing to the depressingly familiar mindset that attributes every word and deed of the person with the condition to their confusion. This is a cruel and unwarranted prejudice.

Q If you met someone with dementia walking round a unit or ward or house and they said to you "I'm going round the bend", would you think:
a) that they were showing insight into their impending madness? or
b) that they were announcing their intention of turning the corner?

Here is something that someone in a nursing home said to me as we proceeded along a corridor together:

> "When you've gone round there and round there (but not up there!) and round there and round there and back again, you've gone more than a mile!"

As a statement of fact this was an exaggeration, but an entirely reasonable one. The unit was a large one, the corridors were long, and prolonged walking was repetitive and tiring.

Differences

There is a big difference between going for a walk round urban streets or in the park or in the countryside, and settling for an indoor environment that is necessarily restricted in its opportunities. It may have seemed like a mile to this woman, and that is an emotional rather than an intellectual observation. Despite the drawbacks, she carried on walking in the unit and one can only speculate on the needs that it fulfilled.

One of these might be to keep active in the face of routine which was predominantly sedentary. She may, of course, because of short-term memory loss, have been unaware of the repetitive nature of her perambulation and therefore still retained a hope of fresh prospects (though she did remember, we must observe, that one of the options before her led to a dead end, and she seemed to know that a full circle was possible).

It strikes me as the statement of someone who is making the best of limited facilities. She appeared reasonably cheerful as I disengaged and she continued on her way.

Q If you met someone with dementia and they said, as they walked, "I do as I do because I do as you say" would you think:
a) they were talking riddling nonsense? or
b) they were expressing a need to conform?

Here is something that a woman said to me as we sat in a lounge watching some of the other residents walking in the corridor, and leaving the lounge area to join them. It seemed a formally exact speech so I made it into a poem:

On the move

Take yourself back to the first time
you saw them doing it. Hither and thither
and thither and thither.
It seems definitely not just
absentmindedly. It seems as if
people have something on their mind.
Going A to B to C to D to E…
They seem to be so restless.
I think to myself they must get
awfully tired. There seems to be
an awful lot of movement.
It doesn't strike you at first.
But then everybody's doing it.
It is really rather shattering,
because you've been surprised
by others doing it, and then you find
that you are doing it yourself!

The whole description of the walking process here is informed by the concept of development and change. Time passing is a reality to this speaker, and she moves in the piece from an awareness of the process she is observing, through contemplation of possible reasons for the behaviour, to the gradual realisation that she is participating in it too.

She makes a number of very interesting remarks. Early on, she rejects the idea that such movement is meaningless (so, by implication, she would not go along with the use of the term 'wandering').

She also employs the word 'restless', which suggests that, for whatever reason, people are finding it difficult to settle. The description of being drawn into involvement without consciously making a decision to do so implies a certain helplessness.

The picture of a number of people progressively entering into a ritual by a kind of osmosis is both mysterious and attractive. Social conformity may play a strong part in it. It is often the case that where a number of people with dementia are gathered together and walking starts, not everyone will walk alone: people pair up, sometimes holding hands, and even small groups form. This mirrors variations in gregariousness found throughout society.

Q If someone with dementia was searching methodically in a corner of a room would you think:
a) that they were out of their mind? or
b) that they had lost something?

In the following text, which I have arranged poetically because its repetitions seem to impart a structure to the piece, the person was stopping and starting in the ways indicated by the statements.

On the other side

I'm just going round to see what's round the corner…

I've lived here twenty-five weeks in the city,

up and down the language, twice up and down…

I'd better just have another look…

I'll tell you if you can understand the language.

And I'm talking, talking all the time…

I'm just off to see if it's changed at all…

I didn't know if you would understand,

with you living on the other side…

I'll just see if it's all right over there…

Young girls wearing white on the other side

of their dress getting married…

I'll just see if I can get far enough along…

The poem is framed by five remarks delivered on the move, which all refer to looking for something. While delivering these the person was crossing the room or walking along the corridor peering intently at aspects of the environment and exploring surfaces with their hands.

The other comments were made when pausing from searching and standing still to reflect on experience. The five remarks indicate a lack of familiarity with or certainty about what was to be found. Anxiety is expressed that things may turn out to be different from expected. The other four statements also seem to proceed from a state of puzzlement. The person finds it difficult to accept that they can be helped because they doubt that they can make themselves understood. The word 'language' occurs twice, and they seem reluctant to accept that words can still work for them. In this piece the activity of walking and the idea of communication are strongly linked.

I should like to suggest that the very act of walking can be considered a form of communication. Sometimes it might best be described as self-communicating. When we go for a walk in the street or the park we are interacting with our environment. This includes people and animals we may meet.

Greater need

Much of the walking of people with dementia can be considered in this way. But maybe there is a greater need for some people with the condition to make physical contact with aspects of their environment because the capacity to verbalise is being lost. To prove to yourself, and to others, that you are still alive could involve movement taking the place of talk.

Giving people who are confined within institutions opportunities to explore different settings may be an important way in which we can help them to maintain their functioning as human beings.

Q If you found you had been locked in an unfamiliar house with long corridors would you:
a) make strenuous efforts to leave? or
b) give up and go to sleep?

Some people in dementia units, I have found, are reacting to being confined by searching for an exit. I have observed them move from the main door to any other door that may lead to the outside world (a fire door for example), taking in many other doors on the way.

Driven by anxiety, and the understandable resentment of being confined for the first time in their lives, they rattle at doors, and implore anyone going in and out to take them with them. One man I spent over an hour with, attempting to help him become reconciled to his lot, in the end turned angrily on me: "You're no use to me, Killick, you don't have a key!" And he resumed his imploring of staff to have compassion upon him.

In one home where I worked I was introduced to a younger woman with dementia who was exhibiting what were described as 'problem behaviours'. From early morning to late at night she walked the corridor, examining the doors wherever she went. She could hardly even be persuaded to sit down and take a mouthful or two of food at mealtimes.

The activity only ceased when she fell into bed exhausted at the end of the day. I attempted to befriend her by walking with her. She moved at such a furious pace that I barely kept up and had to rest every 15 or 20 minutes. I gradually learned that her life had been an isolated one; she had lived in a big house and had made few close relationships.

Living in close proximity to so many strangers, in an environment designed to make full use of every space, was so alien to her that her every thought and ounce of energy was devoted to getting away. Walking as flight has never been illustrated more dramatically. It took many weeks for this woman to be persuaded to slacken the pace, and this was achieved by patiently building bridges between her and the other residents. As she gradually came to see them as unthreatening, and actually made friends with one or two, she began to live life less frenetically. On my most recent visit to the home she greeted me warmly, introduced me to some of her companions, and we went out together like two friends taking time for a walk and a chat.

Q If you were on a vigorous walk and suddenly realised that you were singing at the top of your voice, would you:
a) be embarrassed and stop at once? or
b) be pleased, and invite others to join in?

Here is something that happened to me in a nursing home. A man I had got to know well had taken to walking in the garden which formed the central courtyard of the home. On this occasion he began singing loudly, which startled many of the residents. I went outside with another visitor to the home to watch and listen to him. He was singing opera but attempting all the parts, high and low. He paused before us to sing out with all the gestures.

Then he broke off abruptly saying, "It's time we did some work. We're here to work and not to sing". He moved off, but almost immediately began singing again. When he came round again he stood before us and sang, recitative-style, making up his own words:

> He's got the love.
> He's one of the best.
> Wonderful chap.
> One of the best.
> He knows what to do.
>
> Yes, John, terrible tie.
> Get rid of the blasted thing!
> But you're a wonderful man.
>
> So don't rush. Don't stop.
> Don't stop being beyond us.
> Because that's what we need.

He continued walking and singing for nearly half an hour. Then he moved inside the unit. As he came round the corner at one end of a corridor I timed it that I entered at the other end. I began singing too.

We walked towards each other both singing at the top of our voices. When we met we linked arms and danced and sang together for a while. Suddenly he stopped. "Why are we doing this?" he asked. "Because we want to" I answered. We roared with laughter, linked arms again and went dancing on.

This story illustrates how walking can be ancillary to other activities, like talking, or in this instance, singing. Without the exhilaration provided by fast walking I doubt very much whether this man would have begun to sing. I heard him sing on a number of other occasions, but never when it was not accompanied by vigorous exercise. His recitations were a necessary form of release for strong emotion, and I often saw tears roll down his cheeks while he sang. He was a man who was very conscious of his limitations, and frequently appeared depressed. One day he said to me:

> "I'm not like you. You can see and do
> everything. I don't know what I'll be doing. I'm
> just an ordinary character, not like you."
> "You're a really nice man," I replied.
> "Nice man's not much on its own. Far better
> to be nice man and what you've got," he said.

Yet when he strode out and sang what was in his heart, he was a man transformed – free, vibrant and expressive. Walking was his time for integration, for wholeness.

To offer any generalisation at the end of this brief piece seems presumptuous. As with so many aspects of dementia we are only at the beginning of finding answers, of exploring possibilities.

But I am sure of one thing: that in our efforts to provide a fuller life for those with the condition, purposeful activity (which is what walking is) must play a part, and may hold one of the keys to interpreting what people are trying to tell us about their experiences and needs.

WALKING AND GRIEF

Many people, like CS Lewis, walk a lot when they are suffering from grief. In *A grief observed*, his moving account of his grief following the death of his wife, he describes how the sheer physical activity helped: "I do all the walking I can, for I'd be a fool to go to bed not tired". Walking itself may help ease the pain. For CS Lewis, it was also walking outdoors in the familiar landscape which slowly began to raise his spirits. It had clearly been a source of pleasure before his marriage and he comments: "Today I have been revisiting old haunts, taking one of the long rambles that made me so happy in my bachelor days. And this time the face of nature was not emptied of its beauty and the world didn't look (as I complained some days ago) like a mean street. On the contrary, every horizon, every stile or clump of trees, summoned me into a past kind of happiness, my pre-H. happiness." People with dementia may be unable to tell us that they are grieving, and that this is the reason that they need to walk. CS Lewis' book is essential reading for anyone wanting to understand the pain of grief: *Lewis, CS (2001) A grief observed. New York: Harper Collins.*

Mary Marshall

Dealing with challenging behaviour through an analysis of need: the Columbo approach

by IAN JAMES, LORNA MACKENZIE, MALCOLM STEPHENSON AND TRICIA ROE

This chapter outlines a therapeutic framework that is currently used by the Newcastle Challenging Behaviour Service (James *et al* 2003a,b). This service is a community team, which works in homes (residential, nursing, continuing care, EMI, ESMI), assisting staff and carers to deal effectively with people with dementia who are exhibiting challenging behaviours (CBs).

In keeping with a number of other services (Cohen-Mansfield 2000), the Newcastle team examine CBs in terms of people's needs. In this sense, people's needs are seen as the features that drive their behaviours. Adopting this approach enables the therapist to side-step the thorny issues of defining and labelling CBs, because the behaviour is not the main focus of the analysis.

Using this 'needs framework', therapists are required to function like detectives, finding the clues that allow them to identify people's needs. This chapter presents a framework for improving therapists' detective skills. In most circumstances, they will be working alongside staff and other carers, who will also be trying to understand the person with dementia's behaviour.

It is therefore important that they try to work collaboratively. As well as the staff being important sources of information, collaborative work can help them to gain a better understanding of the person's behaviour. Greater understanding might also prevent the reinforcement of any biases or misattributions staff might be holding. For example, one staff member said: "Before we looked at the situation together, I used to think that he followed me all the time because he knew it wound me up".

Teamwork

Good teamwork should normally occur across all the different phases of the therapy (assessment through to intervention). The collaborative process gives the staff a greater sense of ownership of the therapy, making any therapeutic strategies more likely to succeed. In order to promote such collaboration, the Newcastle team favour a 'Columbo' type of sleuthing rather than a Sherlock Holmes style. We think the informal and disarming style of Columbo is more suited to engaging the help of staff than the rather condescending manner of Holmes.

The framework presented below concentrates a great deal on the individual with dementia, but this focus is not exclusive. It is important to remember that contextual features (staff communications, environmental aspects) are paramount in determining the way a person expresses his or her needs in a particular setting (Innes 2000). This chapter will address CB in terms of both the residents and the staff. The final section of the chapter will illustrate the framework through a case example.

The needs perspective

The Newcastle service has adopted this framework because the 'needs perspective' engenders a more positive and proactive way of seeing someone's situation. The needs perspective also allows staff and therapists to identify and empathise better with the person's situation. Thus it clearly gives staff the opportunities to reflect on what their own hypothetical needs would be if they were in a similar situation to the person with dementia.

In the past, when staff were confronted with 'difficult to manage behaviours' from a person with dementia, their main focus would often be the action component of the challenging behaviour. However, on reflection, it is evident that the behaviour of the person is often a poor indicator of what they are attempting to communicate. For example, someone's 'wandering' might be a reflection of them trying to communicate discomfort; alternatively, it might arise from a desire to explore, be due to boredom and/or frustration, or many other possible reasons. Cohen-Mansfield (2000) suggests that one should see a behaviour as a strategy employed by the person to communicate his or her needs.

She suggests that in order to understand what is driving the person to act, one should gather clues from the person's background as well as observing their behaviour closely.

The process of gathering data to help understand the person's experience is called conceptualising; this term is used widely in the therapeutic literature (see James 1999). Using the detective analogy, the conceptualisation process is equivalent to the clue-gathering stage. In many respects the conceptualisation process is very similar to detective work. For example, during an investigation, a detective would usually try to establish each person's 'motives' – the equivalent of our search for a 'need'.

In the case of Columbo, he would examine both background features and events that occurred just prior to the murder. He would review each suspect's personality, their circumstances, abilities, means, possible triggers, and whereabouts and activities during the time of the incident. He would gradually piece together a coherent story based on the clues available, and then finally come up with his hypothesis.

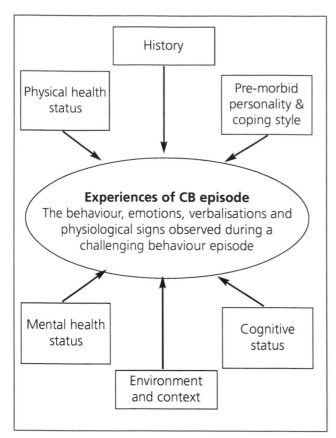

Figure 1: Factors used to conceptualise a person with dementia's challenging behaviour

The model for conceptualising challenging behaviours

Currently there are a number of conceptual models for understanding a person with dementia's behaviour (Kitwood 1997; Cohen-Mansfield 2000; James 1999, 2002). The framework presented in Figure 1 (above) borrows heavily from Kitwood and from cognitive behaviour therapy. The framework involves obtaining two types of information:

(i) background features, and
(ii) the experiences occurring during the CB episode – these are the verbal and non-verbal signs displayed by the person during the challenging episode.

By putting these two types of information together, one is in a stronger position to accurately identify the person's need.

Description of background features

Kitwood suggests that in order to understand and empathise with a particular person's perspective, one should look at five key factors: the person's history, premorbid personality, physical health status, cognitive status, environment. To these features we have added a sixth factor concerned with 'mental health status'. Here is a description of these features.

History: Information about the person with dementia's past is helpful in establishing a good therapeutic relationship with them. Knowledge of the person's life story, important relationships, skills, losses and so on are often helpful in putting the person's needs and behaviours into a developmental context. It is noteworthy that aspects of a person's long-term and procedural memory (memory for music, dance etc) often remain relatively preserved in many of the dementias. Therefore a knowledge of the person's previous abilities may be helpful in establishing a rehabilitation programme.

Personality and coping style before dementia: Despite dementia often being described as a process in which a person 'loses his personality', it is important to appreciate that a person's personality will be apparent throughout many aspects and phases of the condition. Individuals, even those with severe dementia, will want to express lifestyle preferences (accommodation, religious practices, food, sexual orientation).

While some of the personality 'changes' will be related to the changes in brain pathology, others will be associated with psychological factors. For example, owing to the emerging sense of vulnerability, a person with dementia may become more emotional and seek more physical attention.

Coping strategies are important to assess because these are the methods utilised by the person throughout his life to cope with different situations. Important clues about the person's abilities to deal with their current situation can be obtained from examining how they coped with difficulties in the past. Interestingly, the current difficulty might reflect the fact that, due to dementia, the person is no longer able to use a familiar method of coping (for example, dealing with stress by going for a walk).

Physical health status: Dementia tends to be an illness of old age, and hence it often occurs within a context of declining physical health. It is important to note that many challenging behaviours are related to pain and physical discomfort. Indeed, Cohen-Mansfield reports that many CBs occur during staff/resident interactions (eg toileting, transfers, washing), with pain being one of the key triggers in such situations.

Mental health status: The prevalence of mental health problems is such that it is important to acknowledge their potential influence. Difficulties the person had before developing dementia may well interact with current problems to produce affective (mood) disorders. Changes in brain pathology may also result in the emergence of psychiatric disorders.

Cognitive status, including type of dementia: Cognitive impairment is a feature of dementia. Clearly, the nature of the deficits produced by the impairments must be taken into account when trying to understand the person's experience of his world. However, it must also be noted that affective problems, which are often observed in people with dementia, may exacerbate the cognitive diffi-

22

Table 1: Emotions, themes and their relationship to challenging behaviours

Emotion	Theme	Coping or response strategy employed by the person with dementia	Possible challenging behaviours
Anxiety	Person sees self as vulnerable; doesn't believe he/she can cope; things seem chaotic	avoidance; reassurance seeking; worrying; ruminating; self-distraction via excessive activity	over-activity; trailing others; repetitive screaming or excessive activity
Anger	Person believes he/she is being abused/misused intentionally; must react to protect him/herself and self-esteem	physical aggression; shouting; escape from situation using force; high assertiveness	outbursts of temper; hitting; scratching; biting; pinching; verbal aggression
Depression	Person sees self as inadequate, worthless; there is no point in trying as he/she is helpless and things are hopeless	withdrawal; lethargy; apathy; resignation	inactivity; non-compliance

This table relates emotions to challenging behaviours via themes and coping/response strategies. As one can see, it is often the coping strategies that subsequently become labelled as the challenging behaviours. Emotions are dynamic. For example, typically, excessive anxiety can lead to aggression. Both chronic anger and anxiety can lead to depression, especially when the person's coping strategies prove ineffective (eg as one person with dementia said, "There's no point in shouting or trying to avoid the situation, they take no notice of me in here").

culties (eg both depression and anxiety reduce concentration, memory and problem solving skills).

The medication used to treat various conditions may also interfere with cognitive processing.

Because each form of dementia is associated with changes in different cortical and sub-cortical areas, each one tends to have its characteristic profile. The progressive dementias also have varying temporal and developmental profiles (Pieroni & Mackenzie 2001).

Environment, including interpersonal context: When someone has dementia, the quality of the environment becomes intrinsically linked to their level of well-being. This is due to the fact that the memory deficits, problem-solving difficulties, orientation problems and so on, often result in their becoming more reliant on environmental and interpersonal support (Knocker 2002).

Description of experiences of the CB episode

In normal circumstances, one is able to determine whether someone is feeling OK by simply asking them. Where possible, this is a very important way of gaining information about a person's current state of well-being. However, with people with dementia, it is sometimes not feasible to use this straightforward strategy.

In such cases, one can gain valuable information from observation and analysis. The following features are key aspects to attend to when one observes a particular CB episode: analyses of a person's behaviour, thinking, verbalisations, physiology and emotions.

Behaviour: As we are assuming that the behaviour is a strategy employed to enable the person with dementia to obtain something they need, a careful analysis of the

behaviour is required. Performing a proper functional analysis of the behaviour – what it is; its triggers; the consequences; where and with whom it does and doesn't occur and so on – will give a much better chance of determining what the person was trying to achieve by employing the behaviour.

Verbalisations: A person with dementia's verbalisations (what they say) may not always be coherent; nevertheless, it is important to take account of them. A functional analysis in terms of their nature (shouting, screaming), content (words spoken), triggers, volume and length is an important exercise to undertake.

Thoughts: It is very difficult to assess someone's current thinking when he or she has severe dementia. However, if it is possible to get some information regarding the person's thoughts, this is very helpful. Most of the clues about the person's thinking come from monitoring what they say.

Physiological state: It is important to monitor the person's physiological status. One can observe whether they appear anxious, lethargic, highly excited or aggressive. All of these observations are key in determining the person's current experience. This information is useful in helping to identify the person's emotional state, which in turn gives one a clue to their well-being.

Emotions: Emotions are dynamic features, and in the space of a few minutes someone can change from feeling happy, to being either sad or fearful. Unfortunately, it is quite common for people with dementia to get distressed for extended periods of time.

In order to help the person recover from this state, it is

useful to assess the exact type of distress they are experiencing. The three most common forms of emotional distress are: fear/anxiety, anger, and depression. Each of these forms of distress has characteristic themes associated with it. Hence, if a person is believed to be experiencing one of these emotions, it is helpful to examine the relevance of the themes. For example, when someone is experiencing anxiety, he will typically see himself as being vulnerable, and unable to cope with the demands of the situation. In contrast, someone with depression will perceive himself to be inadequate, worthless and see his situation as being hopeless (Beck 1976). In the case of aggression, the person will perceive himself as having been intentionally abused or misused in some way.

Once you have a better understanding of the person's experiences and themes, you are more likely to be able to make sense of the person's actions (see Table 1). Relevant questions also become apparent. For example, if a person is observed to be anxious, you could ask: What is making them feel vulnerable? What could we do with the environment to make it seem less chaotic and more manageable? (see James & Sabin 2002).

Working with carers and staff

In order to be confident that one has identified the needs of the person with dementia, the therapist must collect information from a wide range of sources. Key informants are usually family and staff, as they are able to provide information about background issues and the specifics of the CB episodes. It takes skill to gather this information in a sensitive and helpful manner from carers (Ballard *et al* 2001; Knocker 2002).

Using the Newcastle framework, there is a great emphasis on establishing a good, collaborative working relationship with the staff and other carers. As outlined previously, the 'Columbo' approach is preferred to a more didactic style.

To this extent the conceptualisation of a person's CB is routinely carried out as a joint project, requiring the therapist's attendance at staff and carer meetings. In the Newcastle Challenging Behaviour Service we have found the following guidelines useful when working in care homes:

1. Enlist the staff's help in collecting the information. Support them in doing this, because developing a conceptualisation is usually a new approach for most of them. Clear guidance from the therapist ensures that the staff are generating and identifying usable information from the appropriate sources.

2. Once sufficient data has been collected, it is recommended that the therapist organises a brainstorming session in order to describe and conceptualise the person with dementia's CB. It is also helpful to clarify the goals of the session, which are usually:
   (i) to generate hypotheses regarding the needs of the person with dementia
   (ii) to explain how the person's behaviours might relate

to their needs (eg when the identified need is believed to be loneliness, one is then required to explain why the person is communicating this through aggression)
   (iii) to identify what pieces of information are still required in order to have a better understanding of the situation (eg GP notes, medical files).

3. The style of the meeting should be friendly, open and interactive. The therapist should actively encourage staff to participate, especially seeking the views of the care assistants who do the majority of the hands-on care.

This approach, although undoubtedly time-consuming, provides staff with an overview of the person, relating their present situation to the past. It also provides a sense of ownership with respect to the staff, thus the conceptualisation becomes the shared property of the group (ie the staff, family and therapist). As such, the subsequent interventions that are developed from the conceptualisation are also jointly owned. As a result of this team approach, the interventions usually have a better chance of being implemented appropriately, and hence succeeding.

Before illustrating the needs framework with a case study, we should point out that when people are referred to the Newcastle Challenging Behaviour Service, they will receive an intervention package, which will generally include staff training (James *et al* 2003 a,b). In the case of someone referred for 'wandering', this will involve a review of the positive and negative aspects of this activity (Table 2).

Case example: Winnie

This case provides an example of the Newcastle approach being used to help understand a person with dementia's needs and behaviours. The first stage of the framework was to generate a conceptual model, derived collaboratively with the help of the staff and family. This was then used to develop some practical and feasible interventions.

Winnie was a 73-year-old widow who was referred because of complaints that she was 'wandering aggressively' on the ward and being aggressive towards fellow residents and members of staff. Winnie had Alzheimer's disease, with particular deficits in her memory and spatial

Table 2: Review of the positive and negative aspects of walking/wandering	
Positive features	**Negative features**
- A healthy and enjoyable activity	- Fatigue
- Enhances communication	- Cause of sore feet
- Increases orientation	- Result in weight loss
- Helps to prevent pressure sores	- May result in dehydration
- Helps bowel activity	- Increase risk of falls
- Increases appetite	- May result in inter-personal conflict with residents and/or staff
- Allows expression of choice and control	- Person may get lost if finds a way out of building
- Relieves boredom	

orientation abilities. She had been admitted to the inpatient unit two weeks previously after suffering a series of falls in her neighbourhood. On the last occasion she had been found walking on a nearby housing estate, very confused and with a badly bruised hip and eye. She explained that she was lost and had been trying to find her way home. The staff stated that she was a very nervous woman, and someone who seemed to prefer her own company. She disliked groups of people, and it was difficult for the staff to get her into the communal room for meals and activities.

More specific information about her background was put together under the following headings:

History: Winnie was from a working class background, but went to grammar school. She felt different from the other pupils, seeing herself as a second-class citizen. She married at 20, and was a housewife throughout her married life. Her husband was far more outgoing than her, and it appears that his social skills compensated for her difficulties. This feature became most apparent when her social network collapsed following his death. She had one daughter, with whom she maintained a good relationship. Her daughter had been doing her shopping for the last five years.

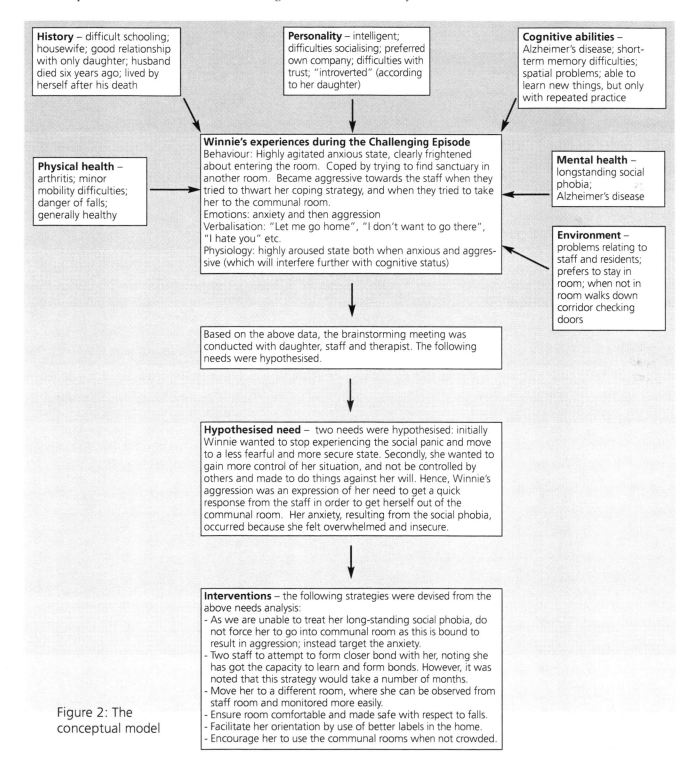

Figure 2: The conceptual model

History – difficult schooling; housewife; good relationship with only daughter; husband died six years ago; lived by herself after his death

Personality – intelligent; difficulties socialising; preferred own company; difficulties with trust; "introverted" (according to her daughter)

Cognitive abilities – Alzheimer's disease; short-term memory difficulties; spatial problems; able to learn new things, but only with repeated practice

Physical health – arthritis; minor mobility difficulties; danger of falls; generally healthy

Winnie's experiences during the Challenging Episode
Behaviour: Highly agitated anxious state, clearly frightened about entering the room. Coped by trying to find sanctuary in another room. Became aggressive towards the staff when they tried to thwart her coping strategy, and when they tried to take her to the communal room.
Emotions: anxiety and then aggression
Verbalisation: "Let me go home", "I don't want to go there", "I hate you" etc.
Physiology: highly aroused state both when anxious and aggressive (which will interfere further with cognitive status)

Mental health – longstanding social phobia; Alzheimer's disease

Environment – problems relating to staff and residents; prefers to stay in room; when not in room walks down corridor checking doors

Based on the above data, the brainstorming meeting was conducted with daughter, staff and therapist. The following needs were hypothesised.

Hypothesised need – two needs were hypothesised: initially Winnie wanted to stop experiencing the social panic and move to a less fearful and more secure state. Secondly, she wanted to gain more control of her situation, and not be controlled by others and made to do things against her will. Hence, Winnie's aggression was an expression of her need to get a quick response from the staff in order to get herself out of the communal room. Her anxiety, resulting from the social phobia, occurred because she felt overwhelmed and insecure.

Interventions – the following strategies were devised from the above needs analysis:
- As we are unable to treat her long-standing social phobia, do not force her to go into communal room as this is bound to result in aggression; instead target the anxiety.
- Two staff to attempt to form closer bond with her, noting she has got the capacity to learn and form bonds. However, it was noted that this strategy would take a number of months.
- Move her to a different room, where she can be observed from staff room and monitored more easily.
- Ensure room comfortable and made safe with respect to falls.
- Facilitate her orientation by use of better labels in the home.
- Encourage her to use the communal rooms when not crowded.

Mental health status: Winnie had long-standing social phobic tendencies, which resulted in her finding social situations very difficult. Since the death of her husband six years ago, her anxieties had worsened. She was diagnosed as having Alzheimer's disease five years ago.

Physical health status: Following a history of recent falls, she had extensive bruising to her face and body. She also had arthritis in her hips and knees, resulting in some mobility difficulties.

Environment: Before admission, Winnie had lived by herself in a bungalow and received help from a social services carer and her daughter. On the ward she was reticent about mixing with the other patients and the staff, preferring to stay in her room. However, because she was at risk of further falls she was encouraged to stay in the communal rooms. She would often be found wandering the corridors, attempting to find her own room.

Cognitive abilities: Winnie had problems with her short-term verbal memory and spatial orientation. This was causing difficulties for her remembering the layout of the ward. The high level of anxiety she experienced was reducing her problem-solving capacity further, making her appear more confused.

Personality prior to dementia: Winnie was an intelligent person who had always liked to have tight control over her affairs. She found social situations difficult, had few friends, and tended to distrust people.

Person's experience of CB episode

This aspect examines the current features, the details of what Winnie was experiencing during the distressing episodes. Hence, it involved an analysis of the behaviour, verbalisations, physiology and emotions associated with the CB.

The specific assessment of the problem revealed that her 'challenging behaviour' took two forms:

(i) walking up and down the corridors, trying to gain access to different rooms. She also often shouted as she walked – initially her verbalisations would be about wanting to go home (eg "Let me go home", "My husband will be waiting for his dinner"). After a period of time, she would start becoming abusive (eg "I hate you all", "Let me out or I'll give you such a crack")

(ii) throwing herself on the floor – this happened regularly during visiting hours, and the staff interpreted the action as attention-seeking behaviour.

The assessments revealed that both of the disruptive behaviours occurred most frequently when staff tried to place her in one of the communal rooms (eg the TV room or dining room). The behaviours worsened during visiting times. It was interesting to note that when she was in the communal rooms by herself there were few problems.

When she did shout, or throw herself on the floor, the staff's reaction was to use a time-out procedure. This usually meant taking her to her room, where she often calmed down quickly.

The two emotions observed were anxiety and anger; the anxiety usually precipitated the anger. For example, one of the staff said that she was like "a scared rabbit who would suddenly turn nasty". From the description of emotional themes provided previously, it appeared she was moving from a state of insecurity/vulnerability to one of feeling abused/misused when confronted by the staff.

The conceptual model

Figure 2 attempts to summarise the main features of the conceptualisation. This was produced via a brainstorming session held with the staff and Winnie's daughter. It suggests that typically, when staff place Winnie in one of the communal rooms, she experiences a high level of anxiety (probably relating to her social phobia – at this point she has a need to feel more secure). She attempts to cope with the anxiety through avoidance, by seeking refuge somewhere else on the ward. This strategy is reflected in her wandering and checking of doors. After a while, she becomes agitated. The agitation turns to aggression when staff continually try to re-direct her to the communal room.

Looking initially at the anxiety, it was necessary to examine her fear in terms of its themes. To do this, we needed to answer the question: What was making her feel vulnerable?

The same process was carried out with respect to the anger. For example, we asked: What was giving her a sense of being controlled/misused? What was she identifying as the source of this over-control?

Further work also needed to be done to understand the impact of the time-outs (ie when she was taken to her room). The first important thing to note was that the assessment procedure revealed that taking her back to her room was probably reinforcing her disruptive behaviour.

Indeed, the sense of relief she got from leaving the crowded room was serving to maintain her aggressive actions. Thus the time-out strategy needed to be amended. The interventions were then based on this conceptualisation, and developed in collaborative brainstorming sessions with the staff.

Interventions for Winnie

Owing to her long-standing social phobia, it was decided not to force Winnie to stay in crowded rooms against her will. She was encouraged to go to her room whenever she felt anxious. This prevented confrontation with the staff and thus reduced her levels of anger.

Because she was spending more time in her room, she needed to be helped to feel comfortable there. This was done by asking her daughter to bring in small pieces of furniture from home, and to mount photographs of her family on the walls. Her daughter also told us that Winnie was a great fan of the local radio station, and so her radio was brought in from home. To promote her ability to make choices concerning her movement around the ward, better signposting and labelling was used on the ward.

To further improve her orientation, Winnie was moved into a different bedroom (a room nearer to the staff room to facilitate informal observation) which she could find more easily. Her name was put on the door of her room in large writing on a piece of cardboard in her favourite colour (orange). To prevent her becoming totally isolated as a result of our intervention, she was regularly encouraged to come to the communal room, particularly when it was less crowded. Despite a clear reluctance to do this initially, over time she became bolder and would sometimes come to the room to watch her favourite television programme.

The staff also thought it would be a good idea to try to develop better relationships with Winnie. The aim was to build trust between her and two members of the staff. It was noted that this would have to be done gradually, due to her memory problems and her high degree of mistrust of others.

This approach proved successful in two areas, firstly in terms of Winnie's behaviour and secondly in terms of the attitude and skills of the staff. Winnie was no longer aggressive, and despite further deterioration in her cognitive status, her quality of life improved greatly. Despite continued social difficulties within group settings, she became much more secure in one-to-one interactions with staff. In terms of the impact on the staff, it was evident that they became far more aware of the importance of identifying people's needs and emotions.

It is relevant to note that the work undertaken with Winnie has generalised to other individuals on the ward. Indeed, with new referrals from this ward many of the staff have demonstrated greater self-reflection and a real enthusiasm to engage in a collaborative approach.

Conclusion

This chapter has presented a framework that is currently being used within a clinical service. The framework has been designed to provide a way of understanding the experiences of a person with dementia who is displaying a challenging behaviour, which can be seen to work. At its heart is the goal of trying to conceptualise the needs of the person with dementia. In order to do this, information is obtained about the challenging episode and relevant background features. A collaborative process, involving staff and therapist, is used to gather the information, devise the conceptualisation, and develop the interventions. Such teamwork is deemed crucial to the success of the programmes of care used in these settings.

References
Ballard C, Lowery K, Powell I, O'Brien J, James I (2000) Impact of behavioural and psychological symptoms of dementia on caregivers. *International Psychogeriatrics* 12(1) 93-106.
Ballard C, O'Brien J, James I, Swann A (2001) Training carers in behavioural management skills. In Ballard C, O'Brien J, James I, Swann A (eds) *Managing behavioural and psychological symptoms in people with dementia*. Oxford: Oxford University Press.
Beck AT (1976) *Cognitive therapy and the emotional disorders*. New York: International University Press.
Cohen-Mansfield J (2000) Use of patient characteristics to determine non-pharmacologic interventions for behavioural and psychological symptoms of dementia. *International Psychogeriatrics* 12(1) 373-386.
Hope R, Fairbairn CG (1990) The nature of wandering in dementia: a community based study. *International Journal of Geriatric Psychiatry* 5 239-245.
Innes A (2000) *Training and development for dementia care workers*. London: Jessica Kingsley.
James IA (2002) The treatment of distress in people with severe dementia using cognitive-behavioural concepts. In Benson S (ed) *Dementia topics for the millennium and beyond*. London: Hawker Publications.
James IA (1999) Using a cognitive rationale to conceptualise anxiety in people with dementia. *Behavioural and Cognitive Psychotherapy*, 27(4) 345-351.
James IA, Powell I, Kendell K (2003a) The castle and the know-it-all – access to the inner circle. *Journal of Dementia Care* 11(4) 24-26.
James IA, Powell I, Kendell K (2003b) A cognitive perspective on training in care homes. *Journal of Dementia Care* 11(3) 22-24.
James IA, Sabin N (2002) Safety seeking behaviours: conceptualising a person's reaction to the experience of cognitive confusion. *Dementia: The International Journal of Social Research and Practice* 1(1) 37-46.
Kitwood T (1997) *Dementia reconsidered*. Open University Press. Buckingham
Knocker S (2002) The right mix of ingredients: working alongside staff. In Benson S (ed) *Dementia topics for the millennium and beyond*. London: Hawker Publications.
Pieroni K, Mackenzie L (2001) How can we know what it's like? *Journal of Dementia Care* 9(3) 12.

The authors would like to thank Ian Powell and Dr Kathryn Featherstone for their intellectual and clinical contributions to the work described in this chapter.

Bill

Bill had been admitted to a rehabilitation unit where only a few of the patients had dementia. For the first few weeks in the unit he wandered at night into a female patient's room, which caused her a great deal of stress and alarm.

The staff on the unit thought his behaviour to be a cause for concern. One of the senior nurses decided to explore what might be the reason for this nocturnal wandering and discovered that it did indeed have meaning for Bill. He was actually seeking out a clock.

Bill wanted to know the time when he woke in the night and went to the nearest room that he knew had a clock in it. Once the staff got Bill a clock of his own, the 'wandering' ceased.

2.3 We walk, they wander

by GRAHAM STOKES

Wandering "is often one of the first symptoms that gets an individual living in the community into trouble, or puts him or her in danger" (Burnside 1980). Rabins *et al* (1982) reported that 40 per cent of family carers found wandering to be a troublesome problem. For some carers the strain can promote a range of coping strategies as extreme as physical restraints and chemical control (medication and alcohol), as well as provoking aggressive reactions (Dodds 1994). Yet, what does wandering mean? Is it even a symptom of dementia?

Most reports of the prevalence of wandering in dementia are flawed by the lack of both a clear definition of the behaviour and a reliable method of assessment. As a result, it is possibly the most misused label employed in dementia care. We can, however, bring clarity to the concept by considering the following definition (Stokes 2000):

> Wandering is a single-minded determination to walk that is unresponsive to persuasion with either:
> a) no or only superficial awareness for personal safety (eg an inability to return; impaired recognition of hazard) or
> b) no apparent regard for others (eg in terms of time of day, duration, frequency or privacy) or
> c) no regard for personal welfare (thereby disrupting the essential behaviours of eating, sleeping, resting).

This behavioural definition distinguishes between wandering with risk (a) and wandering as nuisance (b) as well as interpreting walking as wandering if the behaviour is 'to excess' (c) even though there is no risk or disturbance to others. The final element of the definition accommodates the finding that following entry to a secure care setting to live alongside others who rarely, if ever, respond, a person can be allowed to walk or pace the building hour after hour because their wandering does not give rise for concern.

The absence of risk or nuisance should not, however, generate complacency or inertia to the point where the pursuit of understanding and resolution is deemed unnecessary.

Without this definition, the behavioural characteristics listed below (some of which are common to those established in the community survey of Hope & Fairburn 1990) may attract the label of 'wandering' as soon as a person with dementia walks. The restrictions on activity that may follow can in turn result in a sedentary lifestyle and

actions that may even contravene basic human rights (Mayer & Darby 1991). Without doubt, the equation to avoid is that if wandering means they are walking, then walking must equal wandering. For if this is the case, as soon as a person ventures out of a chair then it will be interpreted as wandering and action taken to prevent or limit movement.

All people must be allowed to walk. To be able to do so is a fundamental human need. From the moment we are months old a child is on the move. First on their tummies, then crawling. Eventually we share their joy at being able to stand, to be followed by protective concern as they totter precariously clutching onto furniture to prevent a tumble. Then having mastered walking, the need to run.

We all need to walk. It is a fundamental human expression to not only walk, but also to stroll, ramble and roam. Didn't Wordsworth wander "lonely as a cloud"? Was Lee Marvin the only one "born under a wandering star"? The need to walk, which may at times reflect the motivation to satisfy a multitude of other needs, does not end with a diagnosis of dementia.

Could it be that we are too quick to see the desire to walk as wandering when there is no evidence of unacceptable risk, nuisance or suggestion that the behaviour is detrimental to welfare? 'Wandering' is a construct which invariably says as much about the tolerance of others, building design and interior layout as it does about the behaviour.

The person with dementia is motivated by a need to walk; cognitive impairment (eg storage deficits, confusion, impaired reasoning) may compromise that motivation and influence the outcome, but the perceptions of others cannot be excluded from the analysis (Albert 1992; Sayer 1994).

Behavioural characteristics

Once the behaviour is defined, the behavioural characteristics describe 'what the behaviour looks like' – in other words, what the person actually does. In practice, a person's behaviour would be described in terms unique to them and their circumstances: a process known as pinpointing.

Research over recent years has, however, yielded broad descriptive categories of many behaviours that challenge us, including wandering. These actions can take place outside or indoors, or result in an attempt to go outside. It is undeniable that the type of behaviour and its location will influence whether carers see the behaviour as 'wandering' or not. These categories include:

- pottering with purpose (busying themselves)
- following behaviour (walking behind or hovering around others)

- apparently aimless walking
- pacing or restless movement
- comfortable remnants (pursuing tasks from the past)
- trailing or tracking a significant other (clinging to a carer)
- searching for their past (going home, going to work, seeking young children)
- attachment behaviour (when apart, seeking the proximity of a person or place that represents security)
- over-appropriate functional or comfortable behaviour (appropriate goals, excessive frequency)
- exit behaviour (persistent efforts to 'get out')
- place disorientation (getting lost within a building)
- walking with no or little awareness of hazard in pursuit of an appropriate goal
- appropriate functional or comfortable behaviours, inappropriate time.

The behavioural definition and characteristics constitute the operational definition – a description that precisely details the behaviour in question. This approach enables us not only to carry out meaningful assessments and thereby challenge imprecise and possibly inappropriate labelling, it helps us move on from just understanding the nature of the action to an appreciation of the explanation. Fine-grained descriptions of a person's behaviour can yield clues that give us insight into reason and cause.

Why might it be happening?

The motivation to walk is varied, and so the same must apply to wandering. Hence, wandering does not constitute a coherent syndrome. Instead it is best to interpret the different types of wandering as each having their own explanation.

A person who 'potters with purpose', is unlikely to engage in 'exit behaviour' or 'trailing and tracking', for each are the behavioural consequences of different motivations. Unless needs change, other wandering 'characteristics' are unlikely to appear. While there is a rich tapestry of underlying motivations, research across a range of care settings has yielded the following possible explanations.

Separation anxiety

When in the company of another whose presence provides reassurance and peace of mind, all is relatively well for the person with dementia. Unfortunately, as that other person lives their life, they move around the house, or go out.

Deterioration in the person with dementia's ability to store information means that he or she does not recollect where the other person has gone or how long they have been away, or retain any message that they will return. The person is simply absent. Separation anxiety motivates some people with dementia to cling to this other person ('trailing and tracking').

If the person with dementia is removed to another setting in order to give their partner respite from the suffocating pressure of being 'trailed', they may seek the whereabouts of this significant other ('attachment behaviour') in order to meet their need for security.

Confusion

Memories from long ago become a restored reality for the person. This results in attempts to find someone or something which is unobtainable now because it resides in the past. Searching for young children, going home and seeking deceased loved ones, usually parents or a spouse, are commonly observed.

The person's determination to search for their past arises from conviction and desperate need for peace of mind. To us their walking is directed towards an inappropriate goal, but that is not how it is feels to them.

Habits of a lifetime

People with dementia may engage in actions that are continuations of what they once did but are now inappropriate to context, for example, walking around at night 'securing' the residential unit before going to bed. These 'comfortable remnants' may be related to parenting, occupation or home life.

Emily would spend her days walking around the unit making circular hand movements. On occasions, she would stand over a table or face a wall and perform the action. Disconcertingly she sometimes walked up to others and performed the action. Were these bizarre, meaningless movements? The staff, familiar with her history, knew otherwise. Emily had worked for over forty years in a textile mill. Her job had been to feel the cloth and, if she felt a snag, she would pull it through. Her behaviour was a testimony to her occupational self – conduct at variance with her current circumstances, but not without meaning. Of course, if nobody had known Emily and her past, the interpretation of her wandering might easily have led to the opinion that she was displaying a troublesome symptom of dementia.

Living life

As a person carries out the practical tasks of daily life and pursues comfortable behaviours (which might include the pure enjoyment of walking), this pursuit of the need to be oneself may be intrusive.

Memory deficits, time disorientation and poor judgement may result in the person becoming a nuisance if the task is carried out with inappropriate frequency (for example, watering houseplants throughout the day; visiting the post office hour after hour; checking to see if the front door is closed).

They may cause concern if they are no longer able to appreciate danger or know that they will become lost. The challenge to others may be that the motivation is inappropriate at the time chosen ('appropriate goal, inappropriate time'). Examples would be going to the shops when they are closed or attempting to walk in the garden during the hours of darkness. This explanation integrates the effects of cognitive impairment with the knowledge of a person's uniqueness and their subjective appreciation of a life to be lived.

Physical discomfort

Because walking can ease discomfort, and even distract us from our suffering, a person with dementia may start to walk around. As they are unable to articulate a reason for their excessive activity, we see apparently aimless or restless movement. We don't see their need to be pain-free.

Coping with stress

To pace is a stress response ('the caged animal', 'the expectant father') so in settings that are often mysterious and maybe even threatening, is 'restless pacing', especially at night, so surprising? To gain relief from worry some people go for a walk when they are troubled. We may see apparently aimless wandering, and not observe or recognise the person's need to be free from anxiety.

Mr Bryan would spend his days pacing the corridors. Agitated, he would engage with no one. If approached he would walk away. On many occasions he would walk through the lounge paying no heed to anyone, and try in vain to open the French windows that opened to the garden. Unfortunately for Mr Bryan the garden was insecure so the doors were always locked. Often he would bang on the glass in frustration. He was seen as disruptive and a risk to himself.

The care staff had not been told that Mr Bryan, once a successful businessman, had never suffered fools gladly, nor could he tolerate weaknesses in himself. He had coped with his dementia in the early years by avoiding others and isolating himself in the garden, where he would work for hours without a break. He would say that 'out there', pointing to the garden, 'I don't fail'. That was not so, but his errors and misjudgements were not readily apparent to him, and nobody was around to say he was doing wrong. In the company of people he felt awkward. He would forget names, fail to recognise people he should know, lose the thread of conversations and, most embarrassing of all, he would repeat himself. Caught in the crossfire of words, he would walk out. People were averse to him, not because he was shy, but because he had insight into what were for him intolerable failings.

As Mr Bryan deteriorated he responded to his failing powers by withdrawing from social contact. Now in care, he found himself having to endure the presence of people every waking moment. It did not matter that there was little conversation to avoid, or that the absence of insight meant that his failings were now no longer acknowledged. He simply found people intimidating. He was driven to leave their

presence. Yet, whenever he reached a door or the entrance to the garden a sense of confinement rather than arrival was experienced. While the home provided a safe environment, it cannot be said that his care was consistent with Mr Bryan's needs. Stokes (2002) describes the tragic conse-quences of Mr Bryan's frustration-related anger.

Failure of navigation

An inability to store new experiences or recall previously learned information will result in a person becoming lost within a building as they try to locate, for example their bedroom or the toilet ('place disorientation'). Does the building help a person with dementia meet the need to find their way and avoid the distress of being lost and bewildered?

Boredom

A basic human need observed at the beginnings of life is to be occupied. If this was not so, why would parents place mobiles above the cots of their new-born babies? Inactivity motivates a person with dementia 'to do'. As they walk around busying themselves their actions are purposeful, even though the observed actions may be bizarre, for example, gathering, moving furniture, manip-ulating objects. While their wandering may be a nuisance to us, 'pottering with purpose' is a source of contentment. If their 'pottering' is reminiscent of known patterns of behaving, then it is categorized as a 'comfortable behaviour', possibly an historical remnant.

Loneliness

The person with dementia who lives alone may leave their home to meet their need for human contact. The motiva-tion is not inappropriate, the challenge is they do not appreciate the risks involved ('walking with risk toward an appropriate goal'), it is the wrong time of day ('appro-priate behaviour, inappropriate time') or the appropriate purpose is repeated to excess ('over-appropriate behaviour'). In communal settings, it is not that they are isolated, but 'being alone in a crowd' motivates them to walk around in an effort to find a friendly face to be with. This may result in 'following behaviour'.

Curiosity

A hunger that characterises the human condition is the need to know. A person with dementia may search their environment for meaning and answers. Their world is often strange and at times beyond comprehension. Their quest to find out can result in others interpreting their behaviour as 'apparently aimless walking', 'exit behaviour' or 'place disorientation'.

Fear

In a place that resonates with unfamiliarity, or when faced with the strangeness of others, those with dementia may feel so unsafe or frightened they have to leave ('exit behaviour'). Alternatively, they may roam around unsuc-cessfully seeking a reassuring face ('attachment *behaviour' or 'searching for their past'). Disorientation may add to their fear.*

John was 57 when he was diagnosed with probable Alzheimer's disease. There had been increasing concern over recent years as his concentration and memory let him down and his job as a machine operator proved beyond him. With hindsight the work stress he experienced five years earlier was most likely the start of his dementia.

John had always been a most pleasant and gentle man. As his dementia progressed this is how he remained. His wife would talk about his engaging, self-deprecating personality and how he would think of others and give help or support whenever needed. Sadly his speech skills were soon to be lost, yet he understood more than he could articulate. He still enjoyed friends and family coming to visit. There was always a ready smile and a warm welcome.

Then everything had changed. Problems with perception and recognition indicated that John was now affected by visual agnosia. He struggled to recognise his own mirror image. One day when out with his family, he and his son used a public lavatory. His son turned to see his father trying to wash his hands in a urinal. He was quietly sobbing for he knew he was doing something wrong, but he couldn't work out what.

As summer turned into autumn and the dark evenings drew in John was tormented by his reflection in the windows and the television screen. For John it was not his reflection he was seeing, but strangers appearing for no reason. He would point, wave his arms, scowl and shout at them, 'Go, go away!' But if you shout at your reflection, what does it do? It shouts back. He would race over to the windows and, still shouting, bang on the glass. Efforts by his wife to lead him away and console him were met with aggressive resistance, actions fuelled not by a wish to harm, but more likely motivated by a need to protect her from these hostile 'strangers'. He may have seemed a different person, but he actually remained her devoted husband.

As the weeks passed she found it more and more difficult to cope with his agitated, aggressive behaviour. Increasingly to her John appeared a stranger, not the man she had known and loved for years. He was still that person, but he was now a frightened and tormented man trying to survive in a world we can hardly comprehend. She asked for respite.

In the care home he would pace the corridors, shouting and screaming. There were too many windows. He refused to eat, would push staff away and would often be found agitatedly trying to open the baffle-locked front door. Were these symptoms of disease, or evidence of emotional anguish?

Soon his wife could take no more and John entered a nursing home. There have, however, been no distressing consequences; John lives in relative tranquillity. He is still has problems with perception and recognition, but the care plan reflects his unique needs. He spends much of his time in either his bedroom or a small lounge. In both rooms there are neither mirrors nor televisions, and the curtains are always closed. With no reflections he is no longer tormented by strangers. John will sit quietly for long periods. Whenever possible a nurse will spend time with him. When his wife visits John often sparkles in her company. The care plan does not describe ways to 'manage the challenge' of John's agitated wandering and aggressive behaviour; instead, it has as its principal goal the meeting of his need for peace of mind. With a true understanding of both his dementia and his subjective experience, John's care plan meets that need.

Avoidance behaviour

A person who is unable to voice their complaints may seek to escape from unpleasant environmental 'noise' to meet their need for quiet and solitude. Sitting by the meaningless stimulation of a television, having to endure age-inappropriate background music or the calling out of others can understandably result in people trying to get out and becoming lost, or apparently walking without purpose once the motivation to walk has been forgotten.

Perseveration

Damage to the brain's frontal lobe, causing perseveration (repeating activities), may be a direct cause of a person's walking to excess. This means that their actions are not under voluntary control.

Malcolm, a 50-year-old man with probable Pick's disease, does very little other than walk continuously around his home. He has a set route that he follows; through the lounge, along the hall, through the kitchen and back into the lounge. Having completed his circuit many times, he will sit for moments before getting up and starting again.

Mirroring

We observe certain residents in care who will leave their chairs to follow another person, for no other reason than that person started to walk. 'Mirroring' results in 'following behaviour' and is possibly motivated by the security found in the 'herd instinct'.

One person, insecure and not knowing, sees another leaving and follows them (because by taking the initiative to go elsewhere, that first person appears to be dominant and knowing).

Spatial agnosia

Spatial agnosia will make it so difficult for a person to find their way round, even in buildings known well, that they will end up lost as they try to identify 'landmarks' that make sense.

Sundowning

Agitated, seemingly purposeless pacing or determined

exit behaviour may occur at the end of the day. Often known as 'sundowning', this may be the consequence of cellular destruction producing diurnal rhythm disturbance (see Stokes 2000). On the other hand it may have psychological roots.

From our earliest years we became accustomed to departing at the end of the day. We went home from nursery, school, college and work. Triggered by both internal and external cues, the person with dementia may start to move around in early evening, as the need to depart to somewhere safe and familiar becomes all-consuming.

Fragmentation of experience

People with dementia have only a limited capacity to store information and hence they find it difficult to remember their intentions and goals. They may get up with a task or plan in mind – to get something to eat, to find the toilet, to look out of the window – then forget what they intended to do, leaving them wandering aimlessly with no apparent motive.

Given the variety of reasons that motivate us to walk, it is hardly surprising that the same richness of motivation underpins a tendency to wander.

No longer can it be said that a person with dementia wanders because – they have dementia! So, is wandering one of the psychological and behavioural symptoms of dementia, as described by Finkel *et al* (1996)? If by this it is meant that wandering is the result of brain pathology, the answer is most often no. In most instances wandering coexists with dementia. As people act out their needs, their cognitive impairment (the consequence of pathology) may result in them unwittingly walking with risk, nuisance or to excess. The dementia pathology is not the direct responsible agent, it is the psychology of the person that drives the behaviour. This is the focus of our involvement.

Behaviour that challenges us possesses function or meaning. Identify the function and often we observe the communication of need (Stokes 1996). Hence we are faced neither with problems to manage nor symptoms to contain, but rather needs to be met. For example, we can unintentionally create insensitive and, at times, harsh care environments that require people with dementia to live by a different set of rules from that which governs our own lives.

Staff often expect residents to sit in chairs for hours on end under fluorescent lights, with nothing to do, in lounges that have an odour of urine in the air, next to others who wet and soil or scream and shout.

When people provide us with testimony that they do not like where they are, by trying to leave, some staff are likely to say, "They're wandering again" and degrade their legitimate disquiet to the status of a symptom of a disease!

From managing challenge to meeting need

To ensure that we do not lose sight of person-centred values, it is advisable to communicate the challenge of wandering in the language of need, rather than assuming that the meaning and motivation behind the behaviour are accepted by all. A social worker ought not to refer a man to a day centre because he wanders around following his wife. Instead, attention should be given to his anxieties and the insecurity that motivates the behaviour. In turn, the understanding this gives carers should influence how they relate to a man who is likely to be even more distressed by the separation and in desperate need to feel secure.

Needs can be seen as challenges restated in positive terms. For example, 'Mr Reyes gets lost' can be rephrased as 'Mr Reyes needs help to find his way around the home'. Describing a challenge in the positive terms of a need places us on the road facing in the right direction, looking towards goals to be set and potential to be released. As Perrin (1996) states, we have progressed from a lifeless statement to a working statement of intent.

The way to move away from negative expressions to a positive restatement is to first identify the probable reason for the behaviour, and then couch the explanation in the language of need. For example, the behaviour is wandering, the characteristic is 'pottering with purpose', the likely cause is boredom, and the need is 'to be occupied'. Similarly, the characteristic is 'pacing', the probable cause is tension and anxiety, and the need is 'to be calm'. Or, the characteristic is 'exit behaviour', a possible cause is a history of walking for enjoyment, and the need is to 'be oneself'.

We cannot resolve wandering, we can only resolve the reasons for such behaviour. In contemporary dementia care our interventions are concerned with finding ways to help the person meet their needs. Our actions must be person-centred, not prescribed by rules or routines, and should most certainly not resonate with a need to contain and control.

References
Albert SM (1992) The nature of wandering in dementia: a Guttman Scaling analysis of an empirical classification scheme. *International Journal of Geriatric Psychiatry* 7 783-787.
Burnside IM (1980) *Nursing care of the aged* (2nd ed). New York: McGraw-Hill.
Dodds P (1994) Wandering: a short report on coping strategies adopted by informal carers. *International Journal of Geriatric Psychiatry* 9 751-756.
Finkel SI, Costa E, Silva J, Cohen G, Miller S, Sartorius N (1996) Behavioural and psychological signs and symptoms of dementia: a consensus statement on current knowledge and implications for research and treatment. *Review of International Psychogeriatrics* 8 (Suppl. 3) 497-500.
Hope RA, Fairburn CG (1990) The nature of wandering in dementia: a community based study. *International Journal of Geriatric Psychiatry* 5 239-45.
Mayer R, Darby SJ (1991) Does a mirror deter wandering in demented older people. *International Journal of Geriatric Psychiatry* 6 607-609.
Perrin T (1996) *Problem behaviour and the care of elderly people.* Bicester: Winslow Press.
Rabins PV, Mace HL, Lucas MJ (1982) The impact of dementia on the family. *Journal of the American Medical Association* 248 333-335.
Sayer RJ (1994) *The management of wandering in nursing and residential homes: is there a role for occupational therapy?* Unpublished report, School of Health and Social Sciences, Coventry University.
Stokes G (1996) Challenging behaviour in dementia: a psychological approach. In Woods, RT (ed) *Handbook of clinical psychology in ageing.* Chichester: John Wiley.
Stokes G (2000) *Challenging behaviour in dementia.* Bicester: Winslow Press.
Stokes G (2002) Behavioural, ecobehavioural and functional analysis. In Stokes G, Goudie F (eds) *The essential dementia care handbook.* Bicester: Speechmark.

2.4 It was my mother's choice to die, and no one is to blame

by MELANIE REID

A little over a year ago, if you had asked me what self-deliverance meant, and the taboo which surrounded it, I don't think I would have understood. Now I do.

My mother's slide into vascular dementia was very modest and quiet. Everything she did was a bit like that. She came from the generation which said you devoted yourself to your husband, you put yourself second, you made sure he was looked after before you even thought about yourself. She was independent, quietly determined and enormously resourceful.

My mother was born in 1916 and did a degree in maths and mathematical physics at Queens University, Belfast. It was a rare subject for a woman of her generation. She became a maths teacher. When war broke out, she joined the WRNS and was, because of her background, seconded to the Telecommunications Research Establishment at Malvern, where she became one of the team who developed radar. During this time, she met and married my father, another member of the team. She became an expert in centrimetric radar, which was a key factor in winning the war. She regularly went up in Walrus and Swordfish aircraft to gather data.

Career as carer

After the war, she had a 60-year career as a carer to my father. She was dedicated and brave at that, too. She absorbed two dreadful blows in her life: my father lost his hearing after the war, and was then permanently disabled in a road accident in the early 1970s. She devoted herself, some would say martyred herself, to caring for a deaf, frustrated, angry man. She just thought he was wonderful.

He got more unreasonable as he got older and, just at a time when she herself needed peace and quiet, she was increasingly required to calm him and pour oil on troubled waters. His tantrums exhausted her. Unsurprisingly, she developed very high blood pressure.

When she was about 83 she suffered her first stroke. She briefly lost her power of speech and one side of her face dropped; then within a month she seemed back to normal. Looking back, I can now see it was the beginning of vascular dementia. Superficially, she continued to hold it all together, protecting him, cooking, ironing. But she grew more withdrawn, quieter; in a way you couldn't put your finger on, this warm, gentle person who still centred all our lives became more shadowy. I didn't understand because I didn't know anything about vascular dementia. I reckon now she had more mini-strokes, unnoticed by any of us. She had a near-fatal brush with pneumonia, which dragged her down. Then, in 2002, she started to decline noticeably. She and my father came to live next door to me, and I became a carer for both of them.

Melanie Reid, centre, with her family – her mother is second right.

In 2003 I believe she had another stroke, again undiagnosed. She just wanted to lie in bed and sleep. My father, always a bit of a domestic tyrant, got annoyed with her because she wasn't getting up and caring for him. I tried to call a doctor but she said no, she didn't need one. "I just feel lazy," she said. "Don't make a fuss." She got better but became a strange mixture of sharp and very woolly, as if pockets of her brain were shutting down. She had always done the Daily Telegraph crossword every day of her life; she stopped doing them. Books sat on her lap, the pages open, unread. She pretended she was fine.

One night she turned to me, when she had got very muddled, and said, "Oh dear, this is dreadful. You will remember me the way I used to be, won't you?" How could I patronise her when she could say things like that? I knew she knew. She knew I knew.

Change in dynamics

Another interesting thing happened in the dynamic of her relationships. For years the doormat, she suddenly started getting angry with my father's bossiness, which had increased with her befuddlement. She wanted to get away from him, a repressed urge which I believe she had had all her life. Much to my father's anger, she kept trying to leave the house at strange times. She said she was looking for her mother. She wanted to go home. "I don't want to be with him. I want to escape. I wish I wasn't here," she told me.

We live on a farm, and one night I found her stumbling down the farm track in the dark, wearing a jumper over her nightie. As I took her back to bed, she expressed similar frustrations: "Oh I wish I could catch pneumonia again, and this time I would die," she said. We fitted deadlocks to the doors and hid the keys; she would stand banging on the windows. "I don't like this boat. I want to get off," she said. In between times, she would hold quite normal conversations.

My father, now to all intents and purposes stone deaf, got more and more frustrated with her when she could no longer make the effort to communicate with him. Eventually, after an incident when he pushed her on to the floor one night when she defied him, the social workers – and God bless Stirling Council, incidentally – insisted she be taken into emergency care on grounds of her own safety.

She was in the home for about three weeks before the final, great escape. It was a super place, used by the council, friendly staff, a little shabby, a bit like home. My mother still had some lucid moments. She accepted she was there because my father couldn't cope. But I knew she hated being there and, fiercely independent as ever, a desire for release still drove her. She escaped once, out the front door, down on to Callander High Street. Because of her behaviour the management, at great expense, fitted an alarm system on every door in the big rambling Victorian building. Every door in the house, that is, except one, the storeroom door downstairs in the basement.

One Wednesday afternoon, the care home manager was doing a crossword with the ladies in the living room. "Here's the clue," he said. "First batsman, six letters." No one knew the answer. There was silence. Then my mother's quiet voice from the corner declared: "Opener". Pockets of her brain, it seemed, were still working. That night she was put to bed. Her physical condition had by this time deteriorated steeply. Her heart was failing. She had massive oedema in both her legs – the fluid was leaking though the skin. She was becoming incontinent. She could barely shuffle with a stick, but I believe she planned her escape like a secret agent and what she managed to do, given her physical frailty, was incredible.

Freedom

What I am now going to tell you about her movements is what I have pieced together from the procurator fiscal (Scottish court officer), the police and the care home manager.

She got out of bed, carefully avoiding the pressure pads which would alert the night staff. She made the bed and put on her dressing gown. She left her room and she entered a rabbit warren of basement corridors, and somehow, in the dark, managed to clamber into a room

used as a store cupboard. She negotiated her way across the room and somehow managed to locate the one and only external door which, when they installed the alarm system, they had not wired up. She managed to open it in the dark.

Given her physical condition, I consider these acts to be the equivalent of a fit, young SAS soldier carrying out a succcessful hostage rescue against fairly insurmountable odds. Maybe it felt that way to her too, in the early hours of the morning, when she first felt the rush of cold air on her face.

She set herself free into the night: a soaring spirit, delighted in the end, I am sure, to find release. And so she died.

It was minus 5 degrees, the ground was white with hoar frost. She always said she never wanted to be a burden to anyone, and now she didn't have to be. I believe she died happy knowing that she had got her wish. Even now, I find it impossible to express my admiration for the courage she needed to do what she did; nor can I fully express my sense of pride in her. I am certain she knew clearly what she was doing, just as I am sure she was aware of the terrible physical ailments closing in on her.

The aftermath, as you can imagine, was pretty ghastly – for us, but especially for the poor care home. The morning shift found my mother lying in the garden, just outside the door, at 7am when they came on duty. Efforts were made to resuscitate her, which appalled me when I heard, but that's an issue for another day.

The staff went into a spasm of panic; naturally it became a police incident. Her body was taken for post-mortem and a report was sent to the procurator fiscal. They did not release her body for days. Tabloid newspapers arrived at the care home trying to do one of those "old lady freezes to death" stories. A posse from the Care Commission arrived in town, six guns at the ready. I can honestly say I didn't have time to grieve because I was too busy trying to convince everyone that it wasn't neglect; it wasn't an accident; it was a calculated act.

Self-deliverance

I knew in my heart she had got what she had wanted for months. This was the meaning of self-deliverance. Never for a minute did I doubt that she had intended this to happen. I knew pockets of her brain were still operating. I knew she knew the physical horrors closing in on her. I knew she had strong beliefs about not hanging on and being useless and a burden to her family.

Instinctively, her whole family was aware that she had done what the Native American elders used to do: they would, when their time came and they were holding up the progress of the tribe, drop back and be left behind, happy to die alone under the stars. We were unanimous in this reaction.

When I phoned my sister to tell her, she said simply, "I'm so proud of her." My poor deaf father, whom I could only inform by writing it down, that dreadful morning, kept the piece of paper I had written on and proceeded to show it to everyone who came to visit him, repeating, "Dear brave soul" over and over again.

Baroness Warnock put it perfectly when she said, last December, that she thought that the very old and frail should slink away, like elephants, to die quietly. That's what my mother believed. It was absolutely typical of my mother to do an act of ultimate selflessness: to creep off and get out of the way.

She was a rational, practical, no-fuss type of person. Just because she had dementia does not mean her character had changed. Why, then, given that strength, those guts, are old women like my mother treated as demented empty vessels and denied all self-determination? Why do we, culturally, cease to treat old people with dementia as individuals and instead regard them as some generically stupid mass? What was so wrong about crediting my mother with the courage and initiative to do what she did deliberately?

In the wake of her death, I tried to express that, but rapidly came to realise that I was talking an alien language. The weight of all the institutions I encountered was against me. Everyone was of the opposite view – everyone, from the police to the procurator fiscal to the Care Commission to the press, assumed that no self-will was involved, that she must be the victim of neglect. They wanted someone to blame. Several people wanted me to sue. This, I suppose, is the taboo of self-deliverance. It's just not allowed to speak its name.

The aftermath

I'm just so sorry that self-deliverance happened on someone else's watch and not mine, because of the trouble it caused them. The impact on night staff in the care home was awful to witness. They were good, simple people on a minimum wage who were literally terrified of the consequences which might befall them. They sobbed in my arms with relief when I said I wasn't angry with them. I wore myself out trying to protect them, but nobody wanted to listen, nobody considered their feelings. Several of them left their jobs, their confidence shattered. Coincidentally, a good friend of mine, a lawyer, once acted for a care home which was being sued after one of its inmates did something similar. She said it was the most upsetting case she had ever had to deal with. I can understand why.

The procurator fiscal found no evidence of wrongdoing by the night staff – a little carelessness, perhaps, but nothing remotely neglectful or criminal. Nothing that would have changed the outcome. Nevertheless the care home was ordered by the Care Commission to change its procedures and increase its staff/patient ratios, thereby probably incurring extra costs for the residents. But what does a regulatory body exist for, if not to justify its existence?

It seemed so very, very wrong, and so very unfair.

Mary Warnock caused a lot of shock and horror when she suggested that old people might even have a duty not to hang around. One of the things that would motivate her, she said, was that she couldn't bear being such a burden on people you loved. She said she didn't see what was so very wrong about sacrificing yourself for the sake of your family when your quality of life has gone. "I don't see what's so horrible about not wanting to be an increasing nuisance," she said.

And neither do I, not now, not after what I have experienced with my mother, because she put those sentiments exactly into action. She, like the elephants or the Native Americans, crept off to die.

But the problem which we have to address is that we live in a society which, as I have said, is institutionally unable to cope with this. We live in a society which wants to resuscitate those elephants. We live in a society spending millions upon millions of pounds creating over-regulated prisons where the elderly are denied any self-determination or freedom of choice.

How can we be sure that demented people who 'wander' are not in fact seeking that very thing: a form of self-deliverance? How can we be sure that it's not some instinct driving them to find a quiet place to lie down and die? And next question – this is the crucial one – how can we be so sure we have the moral right to stop them achieving that? How can we build institutional care and protection for old people which also allows them freedom?

Institutional cowardice

Readers in Scotland will remember the fire in the nursing home in Uddingston, Lanarkshire early in 2004, in which 14 elderly residents died of smoke inhalation. As a result, a new wave of care home regulations have been brought in, among them the insistence on a locked door policy. Safety inspectors apparently found 'potential fire hazards' at more than three-quarters of care homes for the elderly in Scotland.

Following this, the newspaper I work with, *The Herald*, highlighted the case of Margaret O'Riordan, an 86-year-old woman who died, say her family, as a result of the new closed-door policy. Shut in her room, deprived of human contact, of smiles and waves from people passing, she told her relatives she had lost the will to live.

But every time anything happens, the authorities react by shutting down freedoms, turning the elderly into virtual prisoners, removing their quality of life. No one seems prepared to credit old people, or people with dementia, with any space to make decisions about their own lives. I don't blame the individuals who work for these organisations, but the cumulative effect is that authorities these days are motivated by self-justification; by watching their own backs, not by any sense of what is right for the service users. The set-up is one of institutional cowardice and arrogance.

No one in power is wise enough to rise above the madness of this risk-averse approach and say that keeping old people like caged animals "for their own safety" is absurd, inhuman and a form of abuse in itself. No one seems to examine the statistics. No one assesses the fact that there have been no other major fires in nursing homes, buildings already subject to some of the most rigorous health and safety requirements in the western world. No one looks at the relatively tiny number of residents who die after escaping from care homes and contrasts that with the massive majority who remain safe within. Instead, at the least excuse, freedoms are curtailed more and more.

And no one, it seems, is bright or radical enough to devise some sort of waiver: so that old people or their relatives, on entering a home, might sign a declaration acknowledging that they are consciously choosing freedom rather than imprisonment; that they are going to live in a warm, relaxed, homely environment, and will not sue in the event of an accident.

The wonderful thing, if you like, is that my mother managed to get over the wire. Had she not, she might still be alive, bedridden, devoid of any quality of life, enduring a purgatory of physical decay and mental torture. She freed herself from that and she freed her family from having to watch it. In 40 or 50 years' time, I hope that I am half as brave, and that I likewise can avoid becoming a burden on my son. I hope I have the choice, and I bet there are many of you who feel the same.

But it all depends on those who legislate care regulations. Will they have the courage to leave the door open for us?

2.5 Interviews with members of the PROP group

by DENISE CHASTON

The PROP (People Relying on People) Group is comprised of people in the Doncaster and south Humberside area who have young onset dementia, and who meet in their own premises for various social and support activities. The service users were asked to give their views on the issue of walking, and met together as a group and worked through a semi-structured interview process. Relatives were interviewed on an individual basis.

The views of users

We asked users to answer this question: Do people with dementia walk with or without a reason? Their feedback is summarised below.

GF: When people with memory problems are walking or wandering around it is because they are trying to do things they did when they were working – trying to be normal like people that do not have the memory problems. For example I watch RS [another user] spending his time outside in the garden [at the activity centre]. Sometimes he is working and sometimes he is just walking around. I think he does this because he used to be a very important person at his work and he wants to feel the same as he did then.

MA: I sometimes feel lost and that I am in a place that is not known to me, so I walk to find my home or somebody that I know.

GF: Yes, I did this when I went to the airport, I came out of the toilet and didn't know where I was. All I wanted to do was walk and get away.

BC: I am always being told to sit down by my partner. I have always been busy in my home and at work; I find myself sitting down and looking for things. My partner says I am fiddling and interfering.

CB: I often walk because I don't like noise and I just need to get away for some peace and quiet. I prefer the peace and quiet. My wife gets upset because she worries about me getting lost and does not like me going out on my own. I get upset with her as I think she is treating me like a child.

MZ: I think that people with memory problems are walking with a purpose. It makes you feel good when you are doing activities similar to when you were at work. I'm sure that some health care workers forget that we were once of use to society and that walking is related to some past activity. This used to be a thing of mine when I was working in this field. I'm sure that when people with memory problems are walking they are also dealing with their feelings of loss in terms of memory and status. I know that's what I do.

The views of carers

Throughout the interviews with carers, there was a common theme: all felt that wandering or walking was a challenge to them and that this was something they were unable to deal with. They said that they would consider the use of medication to control the wandering, and had concerns about safety.

They were asked to consider the users' activities prior to the onset of their memory problems.

One said, "My wife was always busy both at work and at home." Similar comments followed from the other carers.

After exploring this further, the carers agreed that walking could be linked to previous activity or employment. However, they still felt that safety was the main concern and priority.

Further information about the PROP group can be found obtained from the Young Onset Dementia Team in Doncaster and South Humberside, tel: 01302 709149.

Medical aspects

3.1 Medical aspects of walking

by WINNIE MANNING

The focus of this chapter is the medical aspects of walking in people with dementia. In some cases the activity is associated with risks and distress, and medical intervention is needed. Research has been done in this area looking at causes and associated factors. Different terms are used in this research, but many of them involve the word 'wandering'. Since this is the term used commonly in the medical literature, I will refer to wandering throughout this chapter so that the treatment and causes discussed retain context and meaning.

Wandering is common in dementia. It is associated with increased risk of falling and of becoming lost, which in itself can have very serious consequences. Wandering can result in the person being over-sedated or restrained. It is described by many carers as a problem and may contribute to a person being placed in long-term care (Burns *et al* 1990). It is therefore important that appropriate interventions are made. In general these interventions are non-pharmacological but in some instances medication can be useful.

Wandering can be the result of many different factors and occurs in varying circumstances. In other words it is a symptom, not an individual condition, and therefore there is not one treatment which is successful in all cases. A number of psychiatric illnesses common in dementia, which are amenable to treatment, are associated with wandering. In a study of wandering behaviour in people with dementia living in the community, Klein *et al* (1999) found that moderate to severe depression, delusions, hallucinations and sleep disorder were associated with wandering. They also found wandering to be more likely in those with a diagnosis of Alzheimer's dementia, and with increasing severity of dementia. A study by Cohen-Mansfield and Werner (1999), looking at predictors of non-aggressive agitated behaviour, also implicated depressed mood and severity of dementia in wandering.

There are no treatments for wandering in itself; however, treatment of underlying causes such as those identified above, may help to reduce this behaviour. Therefore we will look at the treatment of:

• Alzheimer's dementia and worsening dementia
• depression
• delusions and hallucinations
• sleep disorder.

Alzheimer's and worsening dementia

Currently-available medications can help slow the progression of dementia and improve some of the associated behavioural problems.

A number of drugs (acetylcholinesterase inhibitors) have been licensed for the treatment of Alzheimer's dementia.

There is evidence that Alzheimer's dementia results in brain damage which lowers levels of the brain messenger acetylcholine. These drugs help to increase acetylcholine. They are useful for the treatment of mild to moderate dementia, and can improve behavioural and psychiatric symptoms as well as cognition. They have been shown to be useful in treating apathy, hallucinations and agitation (Cummings *et al* 1998). They may have a beneficial effect on wandering behaviour by decreasing some of the factors which contribute to it.

The limitations are that they are not licensed for use in other dementias or in severe Alzheimer's disease. There have been studies to indicate the benefit of their use in treatment of neuropsychiatric symptoms of dementia with Lewy bodies (McKeith *et al* 2000) and studies are being done on their effects in vascular dementia, so this may change. In most cases these drugs are prescribed only by specialists. They are not effective for everyone, they can have side-effects such as agitation, and they are expensive.

In March 2005 the National Institute for Clinical Excellence (NICE) published an Appraisal Consultation Document following their most recent review of the use of anti-dementia drugs. In it they state that cholinesterase inhibitors are not indicated for the treatment of mild to moderate Alzheimer's disease given the results of their cost-effectiveness analysis. Many objections were made to this document, and further consultation continues in 2006. Meanwhile the drugs are available as treatment.

Depression

Treating depression may be of benefit to associated wandering. Depression is common in elderly people and significant depressive symptoms may be present in 30 per cent of people with dementia. As there is evidence of under-treatment of depression in elderly people (Margallo-Lana *et al* 2001), this is an area that needs careful assessment and treatment. Assessment may be difficult in people with more advanced dementia as they may not be able to communicate how they feel.

Careful attention should be paid to changes in behaviour, appetite and sleep pattern. Carers can provide helpful information, and the person's past history may indicate a tendency to depressive illness. Specialist assessment can be helpful if there is uncertainty about the diagnosis.

There are many safe and effective antidepressant medications available. The antidepressant effect is not immediate. Antidepressants need to be continued for a long period of time. Some authorities suggest that this should be for at least one year after depressive symptoms have improved, and possibly for life (Anderson *et al* 2000).

Antidepressant medications may have anticholinergic side-effects, though newer ones tend not to. Acetylcholine is a brain messenger involved in memory and drugs with anticholinergic side-effects (eg dry mouth, urinary retention, blurred vision) interfere with the actions of acetylcholine. Antidepressants also vary in their sedative properties and their tendency to affect blood pressure. Some antidepressants can also cause agitation and nausea.

Depression needs to be treated but, given the possibility of side-effects, treatment needs to be carefully monitored. In instances where sleep is very disturbed, sedative side-effects may be found to be beneficial especially if the medication is just given at night.

Delusions and hallucinations

Psychotic symptoms such as delusions and hallucinations occur in about 10 per cent of those who have a diagnosis of dementia. They can cause great distress and also contribute to wandering. Antipsychotic medications are useful in the management of psychotic symptoms in dementia and remain the treatment of choice.

Psychotic symptoms can be very distressing to both people with dementia and carers and there is some evidence that those with psychotic symptoms have an accelerated rate of cognitive decline. Psychosis needs therefore be treated promptly.

However there are side-effects which must be kept in mind as they can be as distressing and disabling as the psychotic symptoms themselves.

There has been evidence of over-prescribing, particularly of antipsychotics, in elderly people (Margallo-Lana et al 2001; McGrath & Jackson 1996). Clearly this is something we need to avoid.

Parkinsonian side-effects and motor restlessness (akathisia) are common and particularly pertinent to a discussion on wandering. Akathisia is described as an inability to stay still; people often report 'restless legs' and a need to keep walking. Parkinsonian side-effects result in tremor, rigidity and slowing of movement. These types of side-effects can compound the difficulties of wandering.

There are many different types of antipsychotic drugs. The newer ones, referred to as atypical antipsychotics, are less likely to cause these side-effects. In dementia with Lewy bodies there is sensitivity even to these. Treatment of psychosis in those with dementia with Lewy bodies is extremely difficult, though there is evidence that treatment with anticholinesterase drugs may be helpful (McKeith et al 2000).

Concerns have also been raised recently regarding increased risk of stroke when using atypical antipsychotics in people with dementia.

The Committee on Safety of Medicines issued guidance in 2004 that risperidone and olanzapine should not be prescribed for treatment of behavioural disturbance in dementia, though risperidone could still (it advises) be used for treatment of acute psychosis.

The US Food and Drug Administration (FDA) has stated that atypical antipsychotics are not approved for the treatment of behavioural disturbance in dementia, and it may extend this warning to typical antipsychotics (2005).

Sleep disorder

Sleep disorder is common in the population as a whole but more so in those with dementia. Chen et al (2000) found 43 per cent of patients had clinically significant sleep disturbance. When this is accompanied by wandering, a person who previously lived at home may end up in care. Sleep disorder may be the primary problem.

There are many non-pharmacological interventions that can be tried, for example, aromatherapy, reducing stimulants such as caffeine, and having a milky drink at bedtime. These may not be sufficient to solve the problem and unfortunately there is no consensus on the best pharmacological intervention. Treatment is often based on clinical experience. A Cochrane review (2005) on this topic has been completed recently and should prove helpful.

Sleep disturbance may also result in, or be a result of, psychiatric illness. Depression, for example, is often associated with disrupted sleep, classically in the form of early morning waking. Finding and treating an underlying cause is clearly useful.

Drugs used to treat insomnia include antipsychotics, sedative antidepressants such as trazadone, and benzodiazepines. These can be very effective, benefiting the sufferer and relieving carer stress. As always, great care is required when prescribing medication to elderly people. Some of the difficulties associated with antipsychotics and antidepressants have been mentioned.

Benzodiazepines are also not without side-effects; they can lead to tolerance and dependence if used long-term. This can result both in increasing doses being required for effective treatment and withdrawal symptoms if medication is discontinued. The drugs may cause over-sedation, or paradoxical excitement can occur in older people.

Use with care

I have described some conditions which can co-exist with dementia, and can be treated. Wandering can also occur without evidence of these conditions being present. Although medication is sometimes used anyway, it might not be beneficial. Drug treatment can be a useful intervention for wandering if properly targeted.

However, this must be done cautiously as medications can worsen the situation or indeed be themselves part of the problem. For instance:

- Elderly people in general are more likely to suffer side-effects of medication, because of changes in metabolism with age. Those with dementia may be even more sensitive.
- Dementia with Lewy bodies (DLB), a subtype of dementia which may account for as many as 20 per cent of all people with dementia, is associated with even greater sensitivity to antipsychotic medication (McKeith et al 1992).
- Medication with anticholinergic side-effects may make confusion worse in an elderly person. These side-effects are caused by most antipsychotic medications and some antidepressants as well as some non-psychiatric medications.

These factors, coupled with the fact that people with dementia may not be able to give informed consent to treatment, mean that great care must be taken in prescribing medications.

This should not result in the exclusion of medication as an option altogether. Medications can be valuable tools in reducing suffering and improving quality of life. They need to be prescribed with care to older people, making sure that ongoing assessments review response and need. Risks and benefits of treatment have to be carefully weighed. Dementia is a progressive and changing illness and medication may not be a constant requirement. Stopping medication for a period of time may be helpful in deciding if it is still needed. These so-called 'drug holidays' are very useful.

Conclusion

In general, first line treatment of wandering should be non-pharmacological. There are many interventions, discussed elsewhere in this book, which are beneficial. Understanding the cause is particularly important. Wandering may be associated with underlying factors such as depression and psychosis, sleep disturbance and severe dementia. There are drug treatments for these which can be helpful, though care is required in their prescription.

References

Anderson IM, Nutt DJ, Deakin JFW (2000) Evidence-based guidelines for treating depressive disorders with antidepressants: a revision of the 1993 British Association for Psychopharmacology guidelines. *Journal of Psychopharmacology* 14 3-20.

Burns A, Jacoby R, Levy R (1990) Psychiatric phenomena in Alzheimer's disease. *British Journal of Psychiatry* 157 72-96.

Chen JC, Borson S, Scanlon JM (2000) Stage-specific prevalence of behavioural symptoms in Alzheimer's disease in a multi-ethnic community sample. *American Journal of Geriatric Psychiatry* 8(2) 123-133.

Cohen-Mansfield J, Werner P (1999) Longitudinal predictors of non aggressive agitated behaviours in the elderly. *International Journal of Geriatric Psychiatry* 14 831-844.

Committee on Safety of Medicines (2004) Atypical antipsychotic drugs and stroke: Message from Professor Gordon Duff, Chairman.

Cummings JL, Cyrus PA, Bieber F, Mas J, Orazem J, Gulanski B (1998) Metrifonate treatment of the cognitive deficits of Alzheimer's disease. Metrifonate study group. *Neurology* 50 1214-1221.

FDA Public Health Advisory (2005) Elderly deaths with antipsychotics in patients with behavioural disturbances. Web file from www.fda.gov/cder/drug/advisory/antipsychotics.htm

Forbes D, Morgan DG, Bangma J, Peacock S, Pelletier N, Adamson J (2005) Light therapy for managing sleep, behaviour and mood disturbances in dementia. The Cochrane Database of Systematic Reviews, Issue 2, No: CD003946.pub2. DOI: 10.1002/14651858.CD003946.pub2

Klein DA, Steinberg M, Galik E, Steele C, Sheppard JM, Warren A, Rosenblatt A, Lyketsos CG (1999) Wandering behaviour in community residing persons with dementia. *International Journal of Geriatric Psychiatry* 14, 272-279.

Margallo-Lana M, Swann A, O'Brien J, Reichelt K, Potkins D, Mynt P, Ballard C (2001) Prevalence and pharmacological management of behavioural and psychological symptoms amongst dementia sufferers living in care environments. *International Journal of Geriatric Psychiatry* 16 39-44.

McGrath AM, Jackson GA (1996) Survey of neuroleptic prescribing in residents of nursing homes in Glasgow. *British Medical Journal* 312(7031) 611-612.

McKeith I, Grace J, Walker Z, Byrne J, Wilkinson D, Stevens T, Perry E (2000) Rivastigmine in the treatment of dementia with Lewy bodies: preliminary findings from an open trial. *International Journal of Geriatric Psychiatry* 15 387-392.

McKeith I, Perry RH, Fairbairn AF, Jabeen S, Perry EK (1992) Operational criteria for senile dementia of Lewy body type (SDLT). *Psychological Medicine* 22 911-922.

An Ordinary Day

I took my mind a walk
Or my mind took me a walk –
Whichever was the truth of it.

The light glittered on the water
Or the water glittered in the light.
Cormorants stood on a tidal rock

With their wings spread out,
Stopping no traffic. Various ducks
Shilly-shallied here and there

On the shilly-shallying water.
An occasional gull yelped. Small flowers
Were doing their level best

To bring to their kerb bees like
Aerial charabancs. Long weeds in the clear
Water did Eastern dances, unregarded

By shoals of darning needles. A cow
Started a moo but thought
Better of it… And my feet took me home

And my mind observed to me,
Or I to it, how ordinary
Extraordinary things are or

How extraordinary ordinary
Things are, like the nature of the mind
And the process of observing.

Norman MacCaig
Surroundings. The Hogarth Press Ltd

3.2 Walking with Beth

by LEE STEPHENSON

When I first met Beth, it looked as if she was trying to walk straight through a wall. I was working as a nurse in a long-term care ward and I saw her leaning forwards against a wall, shifting her weight from one foot to the other. I approached and, placing my hand gently on her forearm, said, "Hello, can I walk with you?". She turned her head towards me. Her face had a vacant expression and her eyes lacked emotion. Then she turned back and continued her treading movements.

I began to copy her and walked with her on the spot for about five minutes. Suddenly she stopped and grabbed my arm – she had a very strong grip. I turned and walked along the ward and Beth followed, still holding on to me, with no apparent emotion in her face. Beth seemed unable to speak or make sounds but her mobility was clearly very good. She needed support at mealtimes and when a member of staff put a spoon to her mouth she would automatically take the food. I never saw her refuse food, but I also never had the feeling she was particularly enjoying it.

I noticed that Beth was prescribed a major tranquilliser. This particular drug is commonly used in older people and helps control agitation and psychotic symptoms. The most striking thing about Beth was her ability to keep walking. Could this be the agitation for which the drug had been prescribed? I felt her mobility was her strength. It was something she could do independently and was a way of interacting with the world. It certainly wasn't causing her or others any apparent harm.

Disorientated

I discovered that Beth had been prescribed this drug when she was first admitted to an assessment unit. At that time her dementia had been making her quite agitated and disorientated which had caused difficulties in meeting her needs. But this was some time ago. There can be a need for drugs at certain stages of dementia but it is important to remember that the disease process is following a path and any treatments should be monitored and adjusted accordingly.

Following a conversation with the manager and consultant, it was agreed she would not be given the drug and would be assessed so see how she coped. I went on holiday at this point; when I returned I could not believe the difference. It was as if Beth's eyes had been re-lit: they had a sparkle I had not seen before. When I looked into her eyes, she was looking back at me. I said, "Hello, Beth. It's good to see you". Beth answered, "Hello". She followed this with a big smile. She didn't say anything more but her face was now full of expression.

Stopping the medication did not change Beth's behaviour. She still needed to walk continuously, but somehow she seemed more emotionally involved with the external world. As soon as she saw another person she would hold on to them and follow them for as long as she could. She was also able to communicate that she valued the presence of another person. This encouraged others to feel comfortable walking with her and, I believe, enabled Beth to have much more control over her life and to enjoy human companionship.

Dementia is different for every person. There are no hard and fast rules about what drugs are necessary and appropriate, or how long they should continue. If you have a friend or family member in a long-term care setting, you must feel comfortable asking questions about the type of medication they are prescribed. The consultant should be happy to discuss this with you. Sometimes it is not possible to describe why you have concerns about a certain drug. You may just have a gut feeling about it. It can be too easy to dismiss changes as being entirely due to the person's dementia.

In certain care settings there is a risk of medication not being reviewed as thoroughly as it could be – perhaps because it seems that the person receiving it appears settled. However, a person with dementia needs to be able to use their remaining abilities and senses to the full. Beth was desperately fighting to keep hold of reality and to interact with others. She taught me how to hear what she was struggling to communicate, and gave me the confidence to ask questions.

'Walking with Beth' by Lee Stephenson is reprinted with permission from the *Alzheimer's Society Newsletter*, August 2000.

Photo: Eileen Richardson

I visited a residential home in Finland a few years ago. As I came through the front door, a group of residents were leaving, well wrapped in winter coats and scarves, for an early evening walk. They came back a little later with hands full of beautiful autumn leaves. The staff explained that it is thought of as every person's right, and good for their health, to go out of doors at least once a day.

Sue Benson, Editor, Journal of Dementia Care

Settings

4.1 Walking in acute hospital settings

by RHONDA KNIGHT

Imagine you are the nurse in charge of a busy acute medical ward. The emergency alarm goes off and when you respond you find that someone has collapsed and is not responding to their name or any physical stimuli. You and the team begin the process of cardiopulmonary resuscitation, and before you know it, the trolley with the emergency equipment and drugs has arrived. However, today there is an extra member in the team – a retired nurse recently admitted with a history of a chest infection and dementia. Unfortunately, because of her memory problems, she does not remember that it is not appropriate for her to be involved in this medical emergency. It sounds like an unbelievable scenario, but it's one that is becoming more and more likely in an acute hospital setting.

As the population ages and increases, the corresponding number of people with dementia is also increasing (Alzheimer's Society 2004), resulting in more people with dementia being admitted to the acute care environment. The number of beds specifically for people with dementia does not match the demand. Consequently, many nurses who make the decision to work in an acute hospital setting feel de-skilled and deceived, as they did not expect to work with so many people with dementia. How can provision be made by health care workers in an acute hospital setting for people with dementia, especially those who walk around?

Admission to hospital is a frightening experience for anyone who is ill or injured. People with dementia experience hospital in exactly the same way as anyone else, but the event may be even more frightening due to their diminishing powers of thinking, reasoning and planning. Norman (2003) suggests that difficulties may arise between staff in an acute care setting, the person with dementia and their relatives because of differences in understanding of the purpose of that environment. The importance of a comprehensive risk assessment is vital (Allan 1994). There also need to be effective lines of communication between the practitioner who is involved in the assessing, planning, implementation and evaluation of care in the acute care setting and the person with dementia, their relatives and carers.

Wandering can appear to be an unrewarding and exasperating activity, and it has been suggested that the actual causes are many and varied (Holden & Chapman 1994; Matteson & Linton 1996; Algase et al 1997; Colombo et al 2001). When working with people with dementia who choose to walk around the care environment, it is important not to link this behaviour to their cognitive impairment alone. There may be other factors contributing to the wandering behaviour that need to be considered.

Why might a person walk about?

For those who work within a person-centred framework, 'wandering' is seen as a form of communication for those people who have difficulty in expressing themselves in a verbal way (Dewing 1999). Rather than seeing this activity as problematic behaviour, the health care worker needs to be alert and observant to the non-verbal message being conveyed. For example, an essential need of anyone is to use the toilet, but a person with dementia may be unable to locate the toilets in strange surroundings, especially if there are no clear signposts.

Cognitive disabilities

As people with dementia may not remember events from the recent past, they may have forgotten why they have been admitted to hospital, or where they are. Enforced separation from the security of home and the support of family and friends, the routine on which everyday life is based, is lost. In the home environment family members often provide cues and clues which enable the person with dementia to adjust to any unexpected events during the day.

In hospital, a person with dementia may be exploring their environment looking for a familiar face and voice to make sense of the situation. Time spent by nurses in getting to know the newly-admitted person, and explaining the routine and any procedures in short, clear steps will lay the foundations for a therapeutic relationship to develop.

Delirium

The toxic effect from an infection, medication, dehydration, metabolic illness or the physical challenges after surgery frequently results in the presentation of signs of delirium in people who have a cognitive impairment (Schuurman et al 2001). Walking around the care environment could be due to the hyperactivity experienced in such a state. Often nurses find it challenging to recognise the signs of acute confusional states in older people, especially in those who already have dementia, and fail to instigate the necessary procedure in order to treat the underlying physical causes (Jordon & Torrence 1995; Schuurman et al 2001). People with dementia who have taken psychotropic medicines over a long period may experience side-effects, which can cause restlessness and consequently result in pacing behaviour (Coltharp et al 1996).

Anxiety

Learning about the life history of the person with dementia facilitates the planning of effective care for that person. Past experiences, especially from wartime, may mean that the person is afraid of being in hospital, being locked in or feeling enclosed, and they may experience symptoms of claustrophobia.

SETTINGS

In the late afternoon, some people with dementia may begin to pace, wanting to get home before darkness falls. This is perhaps a natural feeling, as most people do go home at the end of each day to the place which represents the security and love of the family unit. Dewing (2003) suggests that this activity, known as 'sundowning', could be caused by the individual needs of the person with dementia not being met.

Assessing the person with dementia in a holistic way, considering the implications of their life history, the effects of ill-health, medication and sensory over-stimulation of a busy acute care environment, could aid in planning care which would support and address the needs of the person with dementia during this time of uncertainty.

Pain and discomfort

Pain and discomfort are factors health care workers can influence to improve a person's well-being. Pain is often undiagnosed and untreated in older people, especially those with dementia (Malloy & Hadjistavropoulos 2004). People with dementia who are unable to express their discomfort verbally may pace up and down, as sitting in a chair is too uncomfortable for them. If care workers are aware of this possibility, an assessment of the level of pain experienced can be made using an appropriate pain assessment tool (Davies *et al* 2004a; 2004b).

Offering and administering appropriate analgesia regularly could allow the person with dementia to sit comfortably and relax. Discomfort in the lower limbs arising from impaired circulation, cramp or 'restless legs' syndrome may also result in walking to seek relief from these symptoms.

Mary had been admitted with a recent history of falling. On admission, her son provided some details of her history in order that Mary's care could be planned from a person-centred perspective. For the first 24 hours after admission, Mary walked anxiously up and down the ward and at times wept. Despite reassurance from the staff, Mary still did not appear happy. When care staff spoke to her daughter-in-law, she mentioned that Mary experienced pain due to arthritis, an issue that her son had not mentioned. Mary was then prescribed regular oral analgesia. Within 24 hours she was able to sit engaging in conversation with others, and the signs of pain were disappearing from her face.

Constipation is also common in people with dementia, causing discomfort when sitting down (Jordon & Torrence 1995). Making countless trips to the toilet may appear like aimless activity, especially if the person with dementia has difficulty in locating the toilet. It is important that the health care worker encourages the person to have an adequate fluid intake and where appropriate a diet high in fibre. Resorting to the short-term use of laxatives or suppositories may be a necessary option to resolve the problem of constipation.

Gladys, who had Alzheimer's disease, was admitted from a nursing home with a history of increasing confusion and aggression. When she was assessed after being admitted, it was found that she was dehydrated and constipated. Probably because of the discomfort that she was experiencing, Gladys was continually on the move day and night, unable to sit and eat or drink adequate amounts of food or fluid. She was given finger food and drinks, which she could consume while walking. Her constipation was resolved, but Gladys still spent an inordinate amount of time walking about in a purposeful manner. One day a black Labrador guide dog visited the ward; Gladys showed it a lot of affection and kept repeating the name 'George'. It transpired that she had once owned a black Labrador with that name, and had gone for long daily walks with her canine friend. The dog visited on a regular basis and Gladys always delighted in taking him for a walk up and down the corridors of the ward.

Other factors relating to the comfort of the person with dementia could be that they are looking for their cigarettes or somewhere comfortable to smoke. Another simple and often overlooked reason why a person with dementia might be moving around is that they are hungry or thirsty and hope to find a snack or a drink in their search, or perhaps their favourite alcoholic tipple to help them relax in an unknown and confusing environment (Perrin 1997). Not everyone enjoys the constant company of others that occurs when in hospital and there are people who prefer to be alone, engaged in an occupation that does not necessarily include socialising. It is possible that the person with dementia who is walking around is either looking for company, some gainful employment or conversely a quiet place of solitude away from the noise of a busy care environment (Matteson & Linton 1996).

Life-long habits

In order to understand the reason why a person with dementia might be walking around the acute care environment, it is essential that the care worker becomes acquainted with the person, discovering their likes, dislikes, life-long habits, work and leisure activities, as these may provide clues that will enable the health care worker to create a care environment where the person with dementia will feel more reassured.

Bill had worked as a painter and decorator and had been a workaholic. While in hospital, he continually inspected the ward, noting areas that needed redecorating. One day there was the sound of squirting water from the corridor of the ward. He was spraying the wall with the contents of a fire extinguisher. When asked what he was doing, he replied, "Sand blasting this wall before I paint it". The water was cleared up quickly, with Bill's help.

The need to walk could be due to life-long habits. A person's life story or biography may give vital clues about why a person with dementia might be continually 'on the go' at a particular time of the day. Perhaps they worked night shifts, or their occupation involved a lot of walking or activity – for example the postal, police or armed services, door-to-door collecting of insurance monies, or even nursing.

In order to feel safe within a confusing environment, or due to lack of meaningful activity, people with dementia may wish to engage in familiar routines such as going to work, or picking up the children from school. It is very likely that the person with dementia has a reason, logical to them, for leaving the acute care environment (Greenwood *et al* 2001).

Boredom

Studies have suggested that the time a person with dementia engages in activity within a care setting only amounts to a small percentage of the day (Brooker *et al* 1998). This is also likely to be the experience of the person with dementia in the acute care setting. Lack of an interesting and fulfilling activity may lead to behaviour labelled as 'wandering' (Perrin 1997), where the person with dementia is attempting to relieve boredom, wanting to engage in a familiar pastime, such as rambling, golf or walking the dog.

Sight and hearing

The physical environment of the acute care setting can cause problems for the person with dementia. Reflections from shiny floors, bright lights, and the intensity of background noise can result in the person with dementia finding it difficult to communicate effectively. Ensuring that a person with dementia is not unduly affected by a hearing and/or sight impairment can improve their well-being.

Finding a person wearing the wrong or dirty glasses, or none at all, or finding that a hearing aid is either turned off, 'whistling' or has flat batteries, are common scenarios that only exacerbate the disability experienced by the person with dementia. It is the responsibility of the health care worker to make sure that reading or long-distance spectacles are worn for the appropriate activities and that hearing aids are working correctly. Referral to an optician or a hearing therapist for reassessment may be necessary, so that hearing and sight problems are rectified to enhance the communication process.

Special hazards in the acute setting

The care environment can present external and internal hazards to the person with dementia, causing concern to staff. There are hazards outside the immediate care environment, such as stairs, corridors and busy roads. Within the acute care environment, the emergency trolley, with its assortment of equipment and medication, is readily accessible. Other items of equipment such as fire extinguishers, oxygen cylinders, intravenous infusion stands, vacuum drainage bottles and syringe driver pumps delivering analgesia, can be used by people with dementia in ways other than originally intended.

People with dementia admitted to an acute care environment may require intravenous fluids, urethral catheterisation or oxygen therapy, or need to have their heart rate monitored. Intravenous lines, catheter tubing, surgical dressings and oxygen masks may be frequently removed, requiring careful monitoring from staff who may already feel hard pressed for time.

It can sometimes help to hide catheter tubing under long trousers, and if intravenous access is needed to deliver medication, a capped cannula can be bandaged and concealed under clothing. Recorders for 24-hour heart rate can be kept comfortably in a 'bum bag' belt around the waist and, for some people, oxygen delivered through a soft tube into the nose is more acceptable than wearing a mask. In these situations, health care professionals need to work together as a multidisciplinary team to assess carefully but realistically how much of this equipment is really necessary, and find creative ways of using essential equipment effectively.

Risk and restraint

Health care workers may find that a person with dementia who is continually on the move can raise important issues concerned with risk taking, especially the risk of falling or bumping into furniture and sustaining an injury. The use of chemical and physical restraint is a debatable and emotive issue (Dewing 1999). Research has shown that people with dementia who are restrained physically are likely to experience an even worse injury and can become even more agitated (Rogers & Bocchino 1999; Irving 2002).

Using medication to sedate a person can result in injury from falls or unwanted side-effects from potent tranquillising medication. Every person with dementia is an individual and any decision to use such medication should be made according to local policy, with the full involvement of that person, their relatives and each member of the multidisciplinary team, documented in the appropriate place and reviewed at frequent intervals.

A common fear of health care workers is that people with dementia may leave the care environment unnoticed and not be able to find their way back. Health care workers tend to feel more relaxed when there are baffle locks on the door, as their energy can be directed to engaging with the person with dementia, instead of feeling as though they are gatekeepers. This, however, leads into contentious issues about legal restraint and the implications of holding someone against their will.

Studies looking at different floor patterns and various barriers to disguise exits have been conducted in an attempt to decrease the number of attempts made by the person with dementia to leave the care environment (Hewawasam 1996; Roberts, 1999). However, a review of the literature concluded that there was no evidence to say that disguising exits decreased the number of attempts to leave (Price *et al* 2005).

Understanding and communication

How each person views themself in relation to others is influenced by social psychology which underpins all interpersonal relationships. Positive social interactions serve to affirm that a person is valued as a person. At its worst, negative social interactions can demean a person, thus lowering their self-esteem and undermining their personhood. Kitwood (1997) called this situation 'malignant social psychology', where a person is marginalised and made to feel even less able, thus compounding their disability. 'Putting down' a person is not usually consciously intended, but the emotional consequences can be devastating to the person experiencing it.

Harbourne (1996) suggests that the attitude of nursing staff could influence the behaviour of the person with dementia in such a way that negative regard could increase the level of ill-being experienced by the person with dementia. If health care workers are more aware of the consequences of their actions and words for the person with dementia, the person's level of well-being is likely to increase.

With a history of a chest infection, Hester was admitted to an acute medical ward. She was receiving antibiotics intravenously and responding well to the treatment. She woke early in the morning, got out of bed and walked with the aid of her frame towards the staff who were preparing the intravenous medication that needed to be given at that time of day.

"What are you doing in my house?", Hester demanded angrily. "Get out! Get out!"

The staff nurse gently reminded her that she was in hospital but Hester insisted that the nurses were in her house uninvited. Another member of staff explained that they were preparing medication for the other people in the ward who were ill. The nurse suggested that perhaps Hester herself had not been feeling well, and that was why she was in hospital. Hester readily acknowledged that she was not feeling very well, and appeared to accept the fact that she was in hospital.

Treating a person with kindness and supporting them in an unfamiliar environment can limit some of the difficulties that health care workers perceive to be challenging when working with people with dementia. There may be a necessity to allow time to hold a hand to comfort and reassure. This could challenge the age-old perception within acute care settings that staff are not actively engaged in work if they are seen sitting talking and listening to any person, especially an individual with dementia (Packer 1999).

Enhanced communication skills are vital (Morris 1999; Killick & Allan 2001; Ward 2002). Information overload is minimised when information is delivered to match the person's pace. Bucks and Radford (2004) found that people with dementia maintained the skill to interpret

non-verbal communication despite the cognitive impairment experienced. Therefore it is important to view the communication process in a holistic way, taking into account the verbal and non-verbal content as well as the use of metaphors which can also express meaning.

It is necessary to appreciate the security that a familiar routine offers to a person with dementia. In order to survive the strange and noisy environment of a busy acute care environment, health care workers need to be creative and flexible enough in their approach to understand and accommodate the need of the person who is walking about (McCloskey, 2004). Support and understanding from every member of the multidisciplinary team is required in order that the extra emotional energy is available for effective communication with the person with dementia.

Mavis was an energetic and sociable lady who had had a hard life working in service when she was young. She was admitted to the ward with the symptoms of a urinary tract infection and presented with an increasing level of confusion and agitation. As Mavis walked around the ward, she would stop and look into cupboards and drawers of other people, rearrange the contents and generally have a good 'tidy up'.

Not surprisingly, the other patients and their relatives were intolerant of Mavis' help. As her urinary tract infection resolved with a course of antibiotics, Mavis was asked to help in the household tasks of dusting and rearranging the vases of flowers. Her industry was redirected to a more appropriate activity.

The secret is to step back and begin to understand what the person with dementia might be communicating. What do they need? What are they looking for? What would improve their sense of well-being? Health care workers need to think creatively, remembering that they are working with people who deserve respect and politeness. This also includes the person living with dementia who is receiving care in the acute care environment because of other medical or surgical diagnoses.

The hypothetical emergency may still arise. The retired nurse who has dementia may still want to help in any emergency procedure. There are no magic or easy answers, but how will you as the health care worker deal with situations like this, which are likely to become more and more common in acute care settings?

References

Algase D, Kupferschmid B, Beel-Bates C, Beattie E (1997) Estimates of stability of daily wandering behaviour among cognitively impaired long-term care residents. *Nursing Research* 46(3) 172-178.

Allan K (1994) *Dementia in acute units: wandering.* Nursing Standard 16(9) 32-34.

Alzheimer's Society. (2004) *Policy positions: Demography.* [online] Available on www.alzheimers.org.uk/News_and_campaigns/Policy_Watch/demography.htm and accessed 14.08.05

Brooker D, Foster N, Banner A, Payne M, Jackson L (1998) The efficacy of Dementia Care Mapping as an audit tool: Report of a 3-year British NHS evaluation. *Aging & Mental Health* 2(1) 60-70.

Bucks R, Radford S (2004) Emotion processing in Alzheimer's disease. *Aging & Mental Health* 8(3) 222-232.

Colombo M, Vitali S, Cairati M, Perelli-Cippo R, Bessi O, Gioia P, Guaita A (2001) Wanderers: Features, findings, issues. *Archives of Gerontology and Geriatrics* 33 (Supplement 1) 99-106.

Coltharp W, Ritchie M, Kaas M (1996) Wandering. *Journal of Gerontological Nursing* 22(11) 5-10.

Davies E, Male M, Reimer V, Turner M, Wylie K (2004a) Pain assessment and cognitive impairment: part 1. *Nursing Standard* 19(12) 39-42.

Davies E, Male M, Reimer V, Turner M (2004b) Pain assessment and cognitive impairment: part 2. *Nursing Standard* 19(13) 33-40.

Dewing J (1999) Dementia, part 4: risk management. *Professional Nurse* 14 (11) 803-805.

Dewing J (2003) Sundowning in older people with dementia: evidence base, nursing assessment and interventions. *Nursing Older People* 15(8) 24-31.

Greenwood D, Loewenthal D, Rose T (2001) A relational approach to providing care for a person suffering from dementia. *Journal of Advanced Nursing* 36(4) 583-590.

Harbourne A (1996) Challenging behaviour in older people: nurses' attitudes. *Nursing Standard* 11(12) 39-43.

Hewawasam L (1996) Floor patterns limit wandering of people with Alzheimer's. *Nursing Times* 92(23) 41-44.

Holden U, Chapman A (1994) *"Wait a minute!" A practical guide on challenging behaviour and aggression for staff working with individuals who have dementia.* Stirling: Dementia Services Development Centre.

Irving K (2002) Governing the conduct of conduct: are restraints inevitable? *Journal of Advanced Nursing* 40(4) 405-412.

Jordon S, Torrence C (1995) Bionursing: Confusion in elderly people. *Nursing Standard* 10(6) 30-32.

Killick J, Allan K (2001) *Communication and the care of people with dementia.* Buckingham: Open University Press.

Kitwood T (1997) *Dementia reconsidered: the person comes first.* Buckingham: Open University Press.

Malloy D, Hadjistavropoulos T (2004) The problem of pain management among persons with dementia, personhood, and the ontology of relationships. *Nursing Philosophy* 5(2) 147-159.

Matteson M, Linton A (1996) Wandering behaviours in institutionalised persons with dementia. *Journal of Gerontological Nursing* 22(9) 39-46.

McCloskey R (2004) Caring for patients with dementia in an acute care environment. *Geriatric Nursing* 25(3) 139-144.

Morris C (1999) Building up a toolbox of strategies for communication. *Journal of Dementia Care* 7(4) 28-30.

Norman R (2003) Acute nursing care for people with dementia. Developing practice guidance. Dementia care in acute hospital settings. [on-line] Available on http://changeagentteam.org.uk/_library/RACHEL%20Guidance developmentreport.PDF and accessed 20.08.05

Packer T (1999) Dementia Part 3: communication. *Professional Nurse* 14(10) 727-731.

Perrin T (1997) Occupational need in severe dementia: a descriptive study. *Journal of Advance Nursing* 25(5) 934-941.

Price JD, Hermans DG, Grimley Evans J (2005) Subjective barriers to prevent wandering of cognitively impaired people (Review) *The Cochrane Database of Systematic Reviews Issue 3.* Available on http://www.mrw.interscience.wiley.com/cochrane/clsysrev/articles/CD001932/pdf_fs.html and accessed 30.08.05

Roberts C (1999) The management of wandering in older people with dementia. *Journal of Clinical Nursing* 8 (3) 322-323.

Rogers P, Bocchino N (1999) Restraint-free care: Is it possible? *American Journal of Nursing* 99(10) 26-34.

Schuurman M, Sijmen S, Shortridge-Baggett L (2001) Early recognition of delirium: a review of the literature. *Journal of Clinical Nursing* 10(6) 721-729.

Ward, R. (2002) Dementia, communication and care. *Journal of Dementia Care* 10(5) 33-36.

 4.2 # 'Walking the walk' in the day unit

by PAM WILSON

West Port Day Unit is situated in the heart of the Scottish Borders surrounded by beautiful countryside – a walker's paradise at our doorstep. This paradise is still much appreciated today as it was when our clients were children. Fond memories are often shared: walking miles to school, walking to church, walking to the store for groceries, the way play activities involved more walking and running compared with the pastimes of children today.

Walking was part and parcel of every adult's life – they wouldn't think twice about walking to work, or five miles to Robertson Village Hall for a dance. Walking was a social event in those days. Groups of young ladies would go out walking and would regularly meet up with a group of young men; friendships and even marriages might evolve. One lady recalls how she met her husband of 60 years while walking up Ruberslaw Hill. Even today in the town's public park, you see small groups of elderly men enjoying the exercise and socialising that walking can provide. Once you acknowledge how important walking was and still is for this generation of people, it is not surprising that the day unit is often faced with issues surrounding walking both in and outside day care hours.

The biggest challenge for the day unit is convincing a person that attendance will not disrupt too much of their usual routine: the walk down the street for the pension on Thursday, the walk to the shops on Tuesday, the walk every day for bread and milk and the paper, not forgetting the dog's daily walk. The planning of days, pick-up times and offering meaningful activities is paramount to aid successful transition into day care life. We try to decrease anxieties to pave the way for a clearer assessment of short-term memory and cognitive ability while aiming, ultimately, to produce an increased sense of well-being. Research has demonstrated that greater duration of customary physical activity increases survival in the older person; examples of activities were walking, shopping, gardening and housework (Morgan & Clarke 1998).

Bearing all this in mind, liaison with the client, relatives and carer is necessary to get started on the right footing, which is to maintain a person's independence for as long as possible, not to take the feet of independence from them. To achieve this aim staff have to be resourceful, open-minded, tactful and of course professional. At times this can prove difficult, when clients display little insight into their illness or deny that they were at risk walking their dog in the middle of the road.

Patient transport is used to ferry clients to and from the unit. There are regular complaints of how ridiculous it is to get the bus: "I only live up the Loan", (approximately 200-300 yards away), "I've walked all my life, why can't I walk now?" Yes, they are right, why can't they? It comes down to responsibilities. The nurse in charge is responsible for ensuring that all clients are transported safely. If the issue is creating a lot of anxiety with the client, it will be discussed with them along with the carers and members of the multi-disciplinary team. Clients' wishes will be documented and, if it is not posing any harm to them or us, they can walk to and from day care. The situation will then be continually monitored. We must not forget the reason for the client attending and the benefits envisaged from attendance, nevertheless we cannot penalise them by being over-protective.

Lifting the spirits

Unfortunately, we have no enclosed garden space for clients to walk freely. I feel this is a real disadvantage; it can make some clients feel imprisoned within the unit. We overcome this with frequent visits to the park and gardens (weather permitting) or having a walk down the street. It always surprises me how many people we stop and chat to. The clients always feel uplifted. People have acknowledged or recognised them; saying "Hello" always brings a smile to their faces. Clients will comment frequently how the fresh air and exercise does them the world of good both physically and in lifting their spirits; perhaps we should take more heed of what they are saying. Coghlan (1994) reinforces this comment, quoting studies which have shown that exercising reduced depression, with the most marked effect in elderly people.

Most people with dementia who attend the unit are at the mild to moderate stage of their illness and can be quite aware they are losing some of their functional abilities. Walking can regenerate a feeling of self-control and independence. "Look, everyone can see I'm okay, I'm out walking, I can walk to the shops, I can walk to the post office..." Yes, on the outside Mrs Smith appears fine. She is walking in a spirited way around the town, she does not look as if she is suffering from a degenerative illness. Some, I believe, rate the degree of their illness by what they can achieve in physical terms and how well they feel physically. The perception of what being ill means was probably founded in a lack of knowledge of mental illness as well as the stigma surrounding it. If walking creates a coping mechanism in this ever-increasing world of confusion, then it merits support.

Lack of staff and demands of workload do not make it easy to support walking outings at the drop of a hat. When it seems it will be impossible for staff to take people out, we offer alternative meaningful activities or perhaps change the programme for that day to involve some gentle physical exercise, for example, armchair hockey or netball. In essence, the staff are trying to fulfil clients' desire for exercise. However, I admit I have sometimes had to prioritise workload/activities to enable someone to go out for a walk accompanied by a nurse. On these occasions I have witnessed clients' burning desire to go out walking; if not supported, this can generate more anxiety which in turn creates increased confusion and resentment at being at the day unit.

I empathise with clients at these times and feel that perhaps they want to escape from the constraints of the service. They want to have the opportunity to do what they want and when they want. Getting outside, taking in the fresh air, putting one foot in front of the other, is something they can do without being afraid of doing it wrongly. Walking off the anxiety, attempting to decrease the confusion and going down familiar streets means memories of happier times flood back, anxiety starts to decrease and they begin to feel more secure and more composed. Spirits are uplifted so returning to day care doesn't seem such a bad idea.

Constant risk assessment

I mentioned earlier the responsibilities for clients' safety. As a nurse I am constantly assessing risks, making decisions and implementing care, but to do this effectively you must gain as much knowledge and understanding of the person as possible. In possession of this knowledge I can feel I have acted responsibly, for example when coming to a compromise with Mr Brown that he can go out for a walk while at day care as long as he is back for coffee. Off he goes armed with a large note in his pocket reminding him of just that. The compromise works. He feels satisfied that he can still pursue his favourite pastime, and I am happy because he continues to attend day care and I have attempted to decrease the chance of him going for that daily walk afterwards when it is winter weather and darkness falls early.

We receive phone calls from carers and neighbours also very concerned because, for example, Jessie is out walking very early in the morning or late at night or has been walking the same street for hours. Reports like these are alarming. The reason for going out for the walk has disappeared, the comprehension of the usual routine gone; Jessie's life is becoming fragmented. As cognitive decline increases, the purposeful walk now appears to an observer to have little direction; even for Jessie the meaning has become clouded. It may be considered that Jessie has begun to 'wander'. The loss of self-concern may cast doubts on road safety and weather conditions; loss of ability or motivation to react or comprehend puts Jessie at risk from muggers and exploitation.

These difficulties resulting from Jessie's cognitive decline are the commonest reason for breakdown of care packages and admission to residential care. In an attempt to delay admission to care, the day unit refers people to social services to provide Extended Home Carers (specialised in dementia care) and/or Outreach Workers to attempt to support Jessie. Again, having sound knowledge of the person helps to bridge the gaps; for example, knowing Jessie has always walked to the paper shop every morning at 8am the carer will accompany her, attempting to re-establish her usual routines.

Decorating the environment

Within the day unit, clients are not confined to their chairs but are encouraged to walk when they wish. Although it is a small unit, we try to make the walk more interesting by decorating the environment, for example with articles of interest about our town such as the Hawick town map, old pictures of Hawick, and cuttings from newspapers.

Finally, some evidence suggests that walking may be as effective in promoting general health and well-being as higher intensity exercise such as aerobics (Wimbush 1994). Bearing this in mind and the love for walking our clients have, the day unit has proposed a new venture, the Tuesday Walking Group, which consists of four keen members, three of whom have kept themselves very fit by walking regularly over the last 70 years, and other members who want to improve their posture (all have undergone physical assessment). Clients have been eager to support favourite walks. The walks will be accompanied by a trained nurse with, of course, a mobile phone!

References
Coghlan A (1994) Life getting you down? Go and work up a sweat. *New Scientist* September 9.
Morgan K, Clarke D (1997) Customary physical activity and survival in later life: a study in Nottingham UK. *Journal of Epidemiology and Community Health* 51 490-493.
Ashenden R, Silagy C, Weller D (1997) A systematic review of the effectiveness of promoting lifestyle change in general practice. *Family Practice* 14(2) 160-175.
Dishman RK, Buckworth J (1996) Increasing activity: a quantitative synthesis Medicine and Science in Sports and Exercise 28(6) 706-719.
Hillsdon M, Thorogood M, Anstisis T, Morris J (1995) Randomised controlled trials of physical activity promotion in free living populations: a review. *Journal of Epidemiology and Community Health* 49 448-453.
Wimbush E (1994) A moderate approach to promoting physical activity: the evidence and implications. *Health and Education Journal* 53 322-336.

4.3 Seating and wandering

by BRENDA DUNN

When we enter a room where we know we are going to sit for some time, we tend to look at the chairs and pick the one which looks about the right height and size to be comfortable. This is because we know what suits us and makes us comfortable. We build up our knowledge over many years of trial and error. Even if the chair isn't completely comfortable we know we can make small adjustments to our position whenever we feel uncomfortable. In most circumstances we also know roughly how long we are going to have to sit there. Even a hard chair can be tolerated with this information.

We tend to have comfortable chairs at home, because when we buy them, we make sure they suit us by sitting in them. Chairs at work and in other public places tend to be less comfortable because somebody else bought the chairs, probably as part of a contract when the building was fitted out. The function the chairs have to fulfil tends to be a secondary consideration (Jones 1999).

Residents in care homes are a group of people who may be disadvantaged by chairs bought in this way. They often have to make do with a restricted choice in seating. Unlike most people, they tend to spend periods of several hours at a time sitting (DOH 2000). Even an easy chair which does not give the person the support they need can be the cause of discomfort and, eventually, pain. If the person also has dementia, there may be the added complication of communication difficulties, as a result of which they cannot express their discomfort to staff caring for them. If a person finds themselves in this situation, they will do what would be natural to us: they get up and move to ease their discomfort and stretch stiff joints. Because they do not appear to have a reason for moving about, however, this tends to be thought of as 'wandering'. Often, if this is the case, the person will be taken back to their chair and remain sitting for a short time – then 'wandering' due to discomfort is repeated.

This happened to Mary. She was a little lady, about five feet high. As well as having dementia, she had had arthritis in her back for many years. All the chairs in the home she lived in were the same standard size, about 18 inches from seat to floor. When Mary sat down, her legs dangled a few inches from the ground. This made her feel unsteady and she felt pressure on the back of her thighs after sitting just for a few minutes. If she sat forward to put her feet on the floor her back began to ache because it did not get any support. Whenever these aches got too much for her, she went to try to find another more comfortable chair, but they were all the same. She went from one to another, sitting for a time, then moving on again in a never-ending search for comfort. The care staff were concerned that she wandered about so much, but Mary could not tell them how she felt when she was sitting. When the (taller) staff sat down with her, the chairs felt comfortable to them, so the underlying problem was never addressed and Mary continued to 'wander'.

There is a happy ending to Mary's story. A new carer who knew about seating needs came to work in the home and solved her problems by giving her a footstool to support her feet. The pressure was taken off her thighs and her back was supported, so she did not get sore. Her wandering reduced because she was comfortable, but she still enjoyed a little walk every now and again.

References
Jones L (1999) An overview of seating for use by people with a disability *Nursing & Residential Care* 1(4) 218-221.
Department of Health (2000) *The health survey for England 2000 – The health of older people.* London: The Stationery Office.

Confinement

5

5.1 Rights, risk and restraint: guidance for good practice

by DONALD LYONS & ALISON THOMSON

Those who care for people with dementia are often faced with the difficult dilemma of how to keep the person safe without placing restrictive limits on their liberty or freedom of choice. Staff in care homes and hospitals will often express how difficult it is for them to strike a balance between respecting the autonomy of the individual and the duty of care owed to the individual by the care home or hospital.

Although the term wandering has negative connotations, it is usually a positive experience for the person, providing physical and psychological benefits.

Many different types of behaviour can be classified as wandering; these are discussed fully in other chapters.

This chapter will focus on the decision-making process to be considered if carers or staff believe they need to interfere with a wandering behaviour in order to maintain a person's physical and mental well-being.

What is restraint?

In 2002, the Mental Welfare Commission in Scotland published its document *Risks, rights and limits to freedom*, which sets out principles and guidance on good practice in caring for residents in care homes and hospitals where consideration is being given to the use of physical restraint and other limits to freedom.

The definition of restraint used in that document was as follows:

> "In its broadest sense, restraint is taking place when the planned or unplanned, conscious or unconscious actions of care staff prevent a resident or patient from doing what he or she wishes to do and as a result is placing limits on his or her freedom."

If we accept this definition of restraint then many of the ways in which carers interfere with wandering behaviour can be viewed as a type of restraint.

The primary justification given for the use of restraint is to reduce risk to the individual concerned. However, as a general rule, we all have the right to take risks in our lives, and risk-taking is a part of normal activity. Unfortunately it is the case that dementia can impair a person's ability to identify risk and take appropriate actions to reduce that risk.

Carers have the unenviable task of having to decide if they should interfere, how they should interfere and for how long. Because a person has been given a diagnosis of dementia, this does not mean that they are automatically to be considered incapable of making decisions and choices about their life and how they wish to live it.

The use of any type of restraint without the consent of the individual concerned should only be considered where that person has a diminished capacity to understand the risk that they are putting themself in.

Physical or mechanical restraint

Preventing the individual from doing what they wish to do is restraint, but restraint can take many forms.

Direct mechanical restraint involves, for example, the use of restraining chairs, limb restrictors, bed rails, secure sleeping bags and other means. These mechanical restraints are designed to prevent people who are mobile, or think they are mobile, from walking or attempting to walk. In the past, restraining chairs were used on a routine basis in care homes and hospitals caring for people with dementia. Their use was long-term and indiscriminate rather than as a result of an individualised assessment and care plan. Use of these chairs often caused extreme physical injuries due to inadequate assessment and supervision.

Direct physical restraint is by definition the actual or threatened laying of hands on persons to stop them from embarking on some movement or activity. The grounds for intervention would be that the individual's action is likely to lead to hurt or harm and that immediate intervention is necessary.

Direct physical restraint may be necessary in an emergency situation, to prevent injury, but any intervention should be the minimum necessary and done only in the interests of the individual at risk. Any planned direct physical restraint must only be applied under clear guidelines with careful monitoring and review. If planned direct physical restraint is being considered, attention must be given to ensuring that this happens within a clear legal framework to ensure maximum protection for the individual and the carers.

Locked doors

Locking the doors in care homes, hospitals and people's own homes must also be considered a form of restraint. Any restriction on freedom of movement by others is a serious matter and should only be considered when an individual is at risk if out and about unsupervised, and when their judgement of when and where it is safe to go is impaired. A reason often cited by care homes and hospitals for locking front doors is that the security of the building and the residents must be maintained by barring entry to unsolicited visitors.

While this is of course extremely important, what we are concerned about here is residents within the care home or hospital or their own home not being able to leave when they choose to do so because they meet a barrier such as a locked door or a door with a keypad exit system.

Medication

Medication is occasionally used for the symptomatic treatment of restlessness or other disturbed behaviour. If prescribed, sedative and tranquillising drugs must be regularly reviewed by the medical practitioner and carers must be aware of possible side-effects.

A full and clear multidisciplinary assessment of the disturbed behaviour and its possible causes is essential before drug treatment is initiated. In most cases drug treatment can be avoided unless there is a clear underlying cause such as a medical condition, depression, fixed delusions, severe anxiety or emotional lability.

Sometimes people with dementia will not be capable of giving a legally valid consent to medical treatment; the law on this varies from country to country. In general, if a person is incapable of consenting or refuses to consent to drug treatment but the treatment is considered necessary, then legal advice should be sought.

Occasionally medication is given in a disguised form (eg in food or drink). Disguised medication should never be given to a person who retains the capacity to consent to or refuse that treatment. Furthermore, this should be done only in exceptional individual cases for people who lack capacity. Nursing and medical staff considering giving medication in this way to an individual must seek legal advice and refer to the professional guidance issued by their relevant registration bodies.

Restraint by default

It should also be remembered that it is possible to restrain somebody by default, for example by deliberately not giving a resident a walking aid or wheelchair which would enable them to move about independently.

Use of technology

There are many examples of the creative use of assistive technology in care homes, hospitals and in individuals' own homes. These technologies include the use of sensor pads (beds, chair, floor), call systems, community care alarms, panic buttons, fall and movement sensors, temperature and gas sensors, flood alarms and controls, intruder alerts and epilepsy seizure monitors.

There is no doubt that these technologies can enable people to live longer and more confidently in their own homes and can also increase independence for some within care homes and hospitals.

There is also an increased interest in the use of 'wandering technology' in care homes, hospitals and in an individual's own home. This is also often referred to as 'tagging'. It involves the use of boundary-crossing alarms, which are worn on the person and activated when an individual crosses a pre-designated boundary.

The alarm alerts care staff that an individual is possibly at risk of leaving a certain area, though the system does not actually prevent them from doing so. The term tagging is often associated with criminal activity and surveillance, and although the system used there is different, tagging remains an emotive term when used in care settings; there is an implication that the tagged person is

being restricted or treated as a commodity in some way.

Wandering technology or tagging devices can also now include the use of tracking devices which can locate the wearer if they become lost or fail to return using satellite global positioning system technology.

This type of system is becoming increasingly available and affordable; it could perhaps be considered for individuals identified as being at risk if they leave a care environment unescorted. A survey reported by McShane (1994) suggested that up to 40 per cent of individuals with dementia become lost at some point in their illness, five per cent get lost repeatedly over many months and 70 per cent of those who repeatedly get lost are admitted to institutional care.

Bearing this in mind, assistive technology may be considered in order to help people remain in their own home or to prevent residents from an open residential setting being transferred to a more restrictive environment. However it is important that this technology should never stigmatise the individual, and should never replace direct human contact or be used as a substitute for effective and compassionate care.

The key to best management of wandering behaviour is to allow the person to walk freely and to destinations of interest without subjecting them to unnecessary risk or causing unnecessary distress. Any intervention to restrict the movement of a person with dementia must be consistent with this basic principle. The use of physical barriers or technology may help to minimise risk or distress, but only in conjunction with good design of the living environment, stimulation and activity appropriate to the individual and appropriately trained caregivers.

Legal principles covering this issue vary from country to country. We believe that Scottish incapacity legislation (Scottish Executive 2000) provides a useful legal framework for decisions about control of wandering behaviour and a guide to good ethical practice in this difficult area. What follows is a description of how the Scottish principles can be applied to the use of wandering technology in particular and other interventions designed to interfere with a wandering behaviour.

Benefit

Scottish law demands that any intervention must be of benefit to the person. What will be the benefit of using a particular technology? It may ensure the safety of the person. It may allow caregivers to assess the person's movements and make decisions about appropriate freedom. When used appropriately, it may increase the person's dignity, independence and sense of freedom. It may reduce the need for sedative medication (although it must be emphasised that medication often has little effect on wandering behaviour).

There may be drawbacks to the use of technology. Apart from unnecessary restriction of freedom (see below) it may provide a false sense of security. The person may travel within an apparently safe area, but may not be alert to significant risks within that area. Also, the person may leave the safe area and suffer harm before caregivers can respond to an alert. The use of technology may reduce personal contact with caregivers and this is unlikely to benefit the person. On no account should such technology be used merely to save on the cost of appropriate staffing.

Least restrictive intervention

It is essential that the person's freedom is restricted as little as possible in order to achieve the desired benefit. Will the intervention result in the least restriction consistent with the person's dignity, safety and independence? There will be a tension between protection and safety versus privacy and dignity. Technology may allow the person more freedom than locking doors or having a member of staff watch the person at all times. However, if the person often has to be retrieved and returned to the place of residence, it may result in increased distress and possibly public ridicule.

Past and present wishes

We also must consider the person's wishes and feelings. In assessing the need to use technology to monitor or restrict the person's movements, it is important to assess, as much as possible, where the person is trying to go and why. The person may be searching for familiar people or objects. They may be trying to find a familiar place, for example an old address or place of work. By paying attention to these wishes, caregivers can understand the meaning of the person's behaviour and adopt the most appropriate strategy to manage it.

In many cases, this will result in a discussion of the risk of wandering with the person. Caregivers should make every effort possible to discuss such risks and to help person to understand the benefits of technology solutions, even where the person appears to lack capacity in relation to the decision.

The views of others

It is vital to consult widely if intervention is considered necessary to restrict the person's movements. A wide range of people will have valuable roles to play in the decision on whether to use particular techniques. This includes close relatives and friends who know the person best and will provide valuable information about their life. This may be crucial in understanding the person's behaviour. They will also have their views about risks and dignity and these should be taken into account.

A relative or friend may have legal powers over the person's welfare; this will need to be determined in each individual case. Those powers may include, for example, the authority to consent to the use of wandering technology. Professional carers will have experience in management of wandering behaviour. In particular, advice on environmental design and modifications and on assessment of risk will aid the decision-making process.

The introduction of the European Convention of Human Rights into UK law has implications for the use of technology and restraint in general in care homes and hospitals. Articles 3, 5 and 8 have particular relevance.

Article 3 concerns the prohibition on torture and inhuman and degrading treatment. This Article would require that steps be taken to ensure that the risk of the use of technology being potentially degrading to the individual is minimised. Article 5 concerns the right to liberty and security of the person. The restriction of liberty in certain circumstances is sometimes necessary but this must be justifiable and appropriate. Any interference with the liberty of a person may be justifiable when the individual is in danger of harming himself or others. Article 8 concerns the right to respect for private and family life and there may be implications here for the use of wandering technology. Any inappropriate restrictions placed on a person's liberty could be challenged under Articles 5 and 8; care staff need to satisfy themselves that the use of wandering technology is the least restrictive intervention available and does not reduce standards of privacy for the individual.

Key points

- When considering the use of any type of restraint and the implications of the European Convention on Human Rights, care staff must be able to demonstrate how they attempted to limit possible restrictions of liberty, privacy or potential degrading use. As these rights are compatible with the principles of the Adults with Incapacity Act, it is likely that attention to the principles of the latter will result in actions that are compatible with human rights law.

- There may be occasions when carers feel it is necessary to interfere with the personal freedom of someone with dementia in order to maintain their safety and well-being. To say that this must never happen is unrealistic and a possible failure of a duty to care. However, carers in all settings need to be aware that their actions, including use of technology, can constitute restraint.

- When consideration is being given to the use of restraint in whatever form, there must be careful examination of the pattern and causes of a person's behaviour.

- Restraint should only be considered as a last resort following careful assessment. Carers must be able to justify its use and it must be a proportionate response to the behaviour displayed.

- People with dementia have a right to liberty and a diagnosis of dementia does not automatically negate this. It should also be remembered that this extends to a right to liberty and security of the person.

- The person with dementia should be reassured that on occasions other people may take steps to protect their physical safety if they are not able to do this on their own behalf, but that this will only ever be done in a legal, compassionate and ethical manner.

References

McShane R, Hope T, Wilkinson J (1994) Tracking patients who wander, ethics and technology. *The Lancet* 343 1274.

Mental Welfare Commission for Scotland (2002) *Rights, risks and limits to freedom*. Edinburgh: Mental Welfare Commission for Scotland.

Scottish Executive (2000) *Adults with Incapacity (Scotland) Act 2000*. HMSO.

5.2 A walk with Jean

by TRISHA KOTAI-EWERS

Jean loved to walk. At the dementia-specific day care centre she seldom stayed seated for any length of time. In her walking she acknowledged no obstacle. Doors must open for her or she would rattle them aggressively. Even people seemed in danger of being mown down by her determined progress.

When I first met her I felt quite frightened by the sense of invasion as she marched up to me, almost nose to nose. Frightened and frustrated. Because Jean also loved to talk. She accompanied her steps with a constant stream of words. Or rather, of sounds. In what I later learned was possibly a reaction to medication, her tongue had become so swollen that her speech was almost totally incomprehensible. The more she spoke, the less I felt I could understand.

As I came to know her I learned to see the sweetness of her nature. And to understand some of her words. Most of the time she spoke in incomplete sentences, which tended to be negative: "I couldn't...","She shouldn't...", "I don't want to...".

Then one day I joined Jean in her walking. Arm in arm we bore down on the wire gate separating us from the outer world. Jean rattled the heavy chain that locked it, then clutched the gate with both hands and gazed down the path.

I was overwhelmed by the desolation of being locked in, a prisoner longing to be in the real world. Without a sound we resumed our walk, Jean leading me by the hand. Along the fence that enclosed the yard to another gate. This time we just looked out for a moment with the same sense of loss.

On to a third gate, where again Jean grasped the wire, rattled the gate on its supports and gazed soulfully down the driveway. Once more I was swamped by the desolation of imprisonment. I had mental pictures of concentration camps, of figures progressing around an exercise yard. Again I felt miserable. I seemed to have become part of a ritualistic 'beating of the bounds' in a futile hunt for escape. It was only two years later that I heard of Patrick Casement's term 'projective identification' (Casement 1985; discussed in Killick 1999).

In his book *On learning from the patient*, Casement had described the way in which people with an intense need to communicate their feelings can project their emotions on to the listener without any word of explanation or even facial expression. I realised then that Jean had communicated effectively with me in spite of her fractured sentences and her abnormal tongue.

As I learnt more of her home life, the sensations of that walk made more and more sense. Jean lived with her daughter on a semi-rural property. She passed her days with the horses and dogs in open spaces.

Several times a week she and her daughter would spend time on one of Perth's wilder northern beaches surrounded by sea, sand and open sky. To be shut in a suburban backyard was anathema to her.

And is it fanciful to imagine that Jean was also metaphorically rattling the chains that bound her to a no-longer useful physical form? In her 80s, she could not move as freely or energetically as she once had.

Her speech, impeded by that swollen tongue, was also shattered by the language losses of advanced dementia. And from the reactions of many other visitors to the centre, it was clear that they felt repulsed by the physical image she presented.

She certainly had many reasons to feel that her present physical form had her real self captive, as surely as her physical body was incarcerated by those gates that she rattled on our walk together.

References

Casement P (1985) *On learning from the patient*. London: Routledge.
Killick J (1999) Pathways through pain: a cautionary tale. *Journal of Dementia Care* 7(1) 22-24.

5.3 At risk of abuse

by ANN FERGUSON

The abuse of vulnerable adults is only now being recognised as an important social issue in the UK although it has grown in importance in some other countries over the last two decades. With this increased awareness, a greater understanding is developing that abuse is not just about physical violence but can also involve psychological, emotional, sexual, and financial abuse or intentional or unintentional neglect and that abuse can cause significant harm or distress to the person being abused.

There are a number of definitions of what adult abuse is and who a vulnerable adult is likely to be. While the definition of a vulnerable adult used by the Department of Health (2000) has been challenged by some as being too restrictive it does suggest that "abuse is a violation of an individual's human and civil rights by another person or persons".

Physical abuse is most easily identified as this usually involves bruising, burn marks, fractures, bite marks, cuts or other visual indicators. The more subtle forms of abuse are much harder to identify. Psychological abuse can involve withholding affection, treating the adult as a child, demeaning or humiliating the individual. Neglect can include not meeting a person's essential and basic needs.

Criminal charges

Much abuse is criminal and could lead to criminal charges and prosecution although this is less likely to happen than in reported instances of child abuse. Family members are often reluctant to involve the police, even if this means the abuse continues.

The alcoholic adult son of an 82-year-old man stole his father's money, food and firewood leaving him with no heat or light or anything to eat. The elderly man still refused to make a complaint to the police, as he didn't want his son to get into any more trouble.

Even when abuse is not considered to be within the definition of criminal assault, theft and so on, it can still be an infringement of an individual's human rights. Article 5 of the Human Rights Act 1998 establishes an individual's right to liberty and security of person while Article 3 prohibits torture, inhuman or degrading treatment or punishment.

However, if an individual is unable to express his or her distress or tell anyone about the harm they have suffered, does this make the action or inaction any less abusive? What may be distressing or harmful to one individual may be less so for another. Is it necessary to know what an individual would consider to be abusive in order to know whether they have suffered abuse?

Whose definition of abuse is relevant when making a judgement about a potentially abusive situation? McCallum *et al* (1990) observed an unwillingness to label abusive behaviours directed at older people as abuse. Service providers were wary of inflicting their values and opinions on families whose caring motivations, care-giving styles and socio-economic status were different from their own.

This could however open the door to not recognising or responding to incidents of abuse simply because the person being abused is unable to express his or her distress or hurt in a way which others understand.

If people who have dementia walk for a purpose, and it is not just an aimless activity, is it abusive to stop or limit them, that is, remove their right to liberty? Or on the other hand if a person who has dementia is at risk of harm if they go wandering on their own, does that affect their security of person? Balancing the individual's rights against the risks is a huge challenge.

The role of design

Abusive behaviour is generally attributed to the actions of family members or formal carers, but when considering the range of risk factors relating to abuse, environment can also play a significant role. Inappropriate building design can restrict movement in and around the building, thereby limiting activity and enjoyment. Design which does not take account of a range of individual needs and wishes may create an environment which is inaccessible, hostile and which does not support recreation or physical activity. Poor design can also be the cause of significant psychological abuse for a person who is searching for the past or who feels they have a job to perform.

Very soon after admission to a small domus unit an elderly man who had dementia became anxious and distressed about the same time every afternoon, when he would march angrily up and down the short corridor banging against the walls as he turned around. The staff only found out by accident of his previous employment as a cattleman when he went out to the fields at the same time every afternoon to bring the cows in for milking.

Physically restraining an individual by holding them, grabbing them, blocking their exit, pushing a table up against their chair or other means to restrict movement and stop them walking is assault (physical abuse) even if the intent is to safeguard.

A visitor in a nursing home observed a man striding out into the garden on a nice sunny day. He had only walked about a hundred yards when she witnessed a nurse rush out and grab the man by the arm and take him back inside. This happened three more times before it was explained to the visitor – "we don't like them wandering too far away from the house."

Locking a person in his or her room or house is another means sometimes used to safeguard an individual who wanders during the night or during the day when carers are otherwise engaged. Other than the possible psychological harm caused by imprisoning an individual in this way there is the very real risk of physical harm if there was to be a fire or if they tried to escape.

Reasonable expectations

Enjoying social contact, taking part in pleasurable activity, leisure interests and physical exercise are all reasonable expectations for anyone to have.

When walking is intrinsic to meeting these needs or is a continuation of lifelong habits but is denied, this could be defined as neglect and psychological abuse. Neglect involves denying an individual the necessities of life which must include opportunities for social interaction and physical activity.

Mrs T was a keen hill walker for most of her life, often taking her small dog with her. When Mrs T developed dementia she continued to live at home for a number of years with support from a carer. Her carer was also fond of walking and the two of them enjoyed many a happy day out in the countryside. After Mrs T was admitted to a nursing home she was unable to go walking despite being physically fit, as there was no one to go with her.

Where the underlying reason for wandering is an expression of boredom, agitation, being uncertain about a new environment, discomfort or pain simply limiting the ability to wander does nothing to address the root cause. If measured against the widely used definition of elder abuse this lack of appropriate action to meet the individual's basic needs could be construed as abuse.

The risk of abusing a person who has dementia and who wanders is obviously very real and requires an individual response to every situation.

Looking to the future and the use of new technology as an aid there may be even more ethical issues to address. Hughes and Louw (2002) argue that ethical considerations are possibly more important than practical benefits when considering tagging of people who have dementia who wander.

They question seeing the argument as simply two-sided – one side stressing the need to ensure safety and the other waving the banners of civil liberties and human rights.

They also suggest that decisions about limiting a person's liberty should remain a matter of ethical concern even when technology finally makes the practical management of wandering easier.

Risk factor

Coyne (2001) suggests further research is needed to refine our understanding of dementia as a risk factor for abuse and to determine how best to help family members cope with the demands of caring for a cognitively impaired relative without resorting to abusive behaviour.

He puts forward the view that one way we can help to make adults less vulnerable is by providing them with concrete services necessary to improve the quality of their lives and by providing their caregivers with support and services required to extend their ability to cope with what can be difficult burdens.

Concluding an article in the *British Medical Journal* in 2002, Julian Hughes reminds us that people who have dementia might still have the capacity to make some decisions, and if so their views should be respected.

In the absence of this capacity he suggests a decision will have to be made about a person's best interests, but not just a person's best medical interests:

"Rather, the determination of what is best will require careful inquiry, negotiation and judgement. It is especially at this point that understanding the wandering behaviour and looking for the least restrictive way of dealing with it will become imperative."

Obviously, the issue of walking, wandering and abuse is extremely complex and will require further research and discussion in order to develop a better understanding and more appropriate responses. Not having all of the answers at this point should not, however, be seen as failure but instead as recognition of the seriousness with which we regard the rights of a person to liberty, privacy and security especially when he or she has dementia.

References

Coyne AC (2001) The relationship between dementia and elder abuse. *Geriatric Times* II(4) 15-18

Department of Health (2000) *No secrets: Guidance on developing and implementing multi-agency policies and procedures to protect vulnerable adults from abuse.* London: Department of Health and Home Office.

Hughes JC, Louw SJ (2002) Electronic tagging of people with dementia who wander. *British Medical Journal* 325 847-848.

McCallum J, Matiasz S, Graycar A (1990) *Abuse of the elderly at home.* Office of the Commissioner for the Ageing, South Australia and the National Centre for Epidemiology and Population Health, Adelaide.

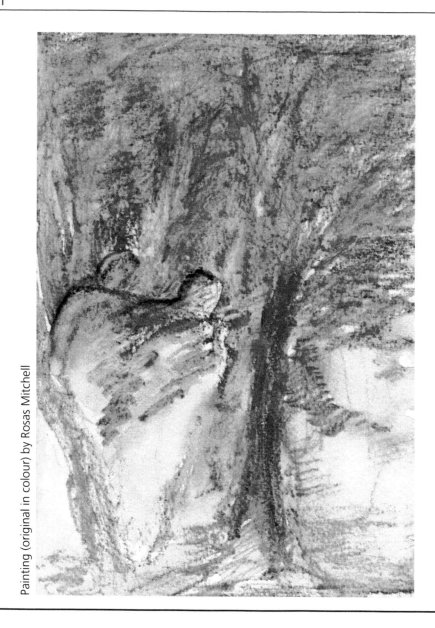

Painting (original in colour) by Rosas Mitchell

In theory, at least, the whole of Australia could be read as a musical score. There was hardly a rock or creek in the country that could not or had not been sung. One should perhaps visualise the Songlines as a spaghetti of Iliads and Odysseys, writhing this way and that, in which every 'episode' was readable in terms of geology.

'By episode', I asked, 'you mean "sacred site"?'

'I do.'

'The kind of site you're surveying for the railway?'

'Put it this way,' he said. 'Anywhere in the bush you can point to some feature of the landscape and ask the Aboriginal with you, "What's the story there?" or "Who's that?" The chances are he'll answer "Kangaroo" or "Budgerigar" or "Jew Lizard", depending on which Ancestor walked that way.

'And the distance between two such sites can be measured as a stretch of song?'

'That', said Arkady, 'is the cause of all my troubles with the railway people.'

It is one thing to persuade a surveyor that a heap of boulders were the eggs of the Rainbow Snake, or a lump of reddish sandstone was the liver of a speared kangaroo. It was something else to convince him that a featureless stretch of gravel was the musical equivalent of Beethoven's Opus III.

By singing the world into existence, he said, the Ancestors had been poets in the original sense of poesis, meaning 'creation'. No Aboriginal could conceive that the created world was in any way imperfect. His religious life had a single aim: to keep the land the way it was and should be. The man who went 'Walkabout' was making a ritual journey. He trod in the footprints of his Ancestor. He sang the Ancestor's stanzas without changing a word or note – or so recreated the Creation.

Bruce Chatwin (1987) The Songlines. London: Picador

Focus on
the past

6.1 Walking to see the cattle

by ROSEMARY TAYLOR

My father was a farmer, and farmers never retire. Even after he moved out of the farm to the 'retirement bungalow', he was always still down at the farm, trying to keep up with my brother, even though there was a 35 year difference in age!

After he had his first 'black out' while driving the cattle lorry, and therefore lost his driving licence for one year, he walked from the bungalow to the farm, and could still walk to see the animals in the fields surrounding the bungalow. At the end of the year he regained his driving licence, and although he no longer drove the cattle lorry he continued to drive the car, or more often his favourite old, battered, Ford van. He was happy again.

We were later to realise that the accident was the beginning of vascular dementia, and over the next few years the disease progressed. He still had his driving licence, but although he did not recognise it, he was no longer safe on the roads. Fortunately, any decision about removing his licence as a result of the dementia was avoided, as he also had glaucoma and his eyesight was deteriorating; the doctors would not sign the medical certificate to renew his driving licence.

Daddy was devastated – his whole life was taken away from him, and this time it was not temporary. What we did not understand at the time was that, because of dementia, he would not have been able to comprehend this fully. It must have been extremely confusing, and it is no wonder that he was angry. Unfortunately we, his family, did not have any insight into this, and therefore can have been little help to him. Looking back, I am sure that the distress of this caused the dementia to progress more rapidly; and indeed the next years were very difficult.

Now that he could no longer drive, daddy took to walking. He would walk down the road to the farm and down the fields from the farm. He would walk up the road to another set of fields. The reason was always the same: he had to see the cattle. It did not matter if there were no cattle in the fields – daddy was still going to see the cattle. Irrespective of the weather daddy would go to see the cattle – rain, hail, snow or shine. He would come back into the house, maybe take off his coat and boots, maybe not, and would turn round and go back out again. He did not remember that he had just come back from 'seeing the cattle'. And we did not understand.

At first he would tap the window with his stick (he always had a stick with him – having always used it for driving the animals etc), to wave a cheery "goodbye", but gradually he stopped this, and went on his way with his head down.

As the dementia progressed, he continued to walk. But now there were more complications. Firstly he might not want to put on his coat and boots, even if it was raining. We would argue that he could not go out without these, and he would get cross. Eventually he would be appropriately dressed, but we would all be frustrated and annoyed. We bought a fluorescent waistcoat (the type worn by cyclists or workmen) so that he would be seen on the road. The road was quite busy, with a lot of large sand lorries, and although the regulars knew him walking up and down, there was always the worry that he might not be seen, and would be knocked down. We told him how well he looked in his 'waistcoat' and he was happy to wear it.

As the dementia deteriorated, we became more concerned about his safety. Many times we would go out and look for him, as he was away for so long. Sometimes we found him just slowly walking back, sometimes in a neighbour's house, and on several occasions he was found stuck on a gate that he had tried to climb. It was becoming more and more worrying and stressful for my mother.

Eventually it came to the point where she would lock the door to stop him going out, as we were worried that he would cause an accident, injuring himself or someone else. This made daddy cross, however, and he became increasingly grumpy. I can understand now; none of us did at the time. After this he deteriorated rapidly. He got a place twice a week in a local day centre (entirely unsuitable for a farmer, but fortunately I think he was beyond understanding this, or remembering from one day to the next). Within two months, assistance was required to get him up in the morning and put him to bed at night. In another month and a half we needed two care workers in the morning and evening. By the new year (four or five months after the 'door was locked') daddy was in hospital for assessment, never to return home. Before he was discharged from hospital to the nursing home he fell; he does not walk now, and has not done so for approximately a year.

Looking back, I feel guilty. If only I had walked with him, and enabled him to keep 'going to see the cattle' for longer, would his deterioration have been slower, and would he have remained at home longer? If we had been offered assistance in the form of someone to walk up and down the road or over the fields with daddy rather than a day centre place or other traditional support, would it have helped to slow the progress of the dementia, and enable him to remain in his own home for longer? It was never suggested. One thing I am sure of, if he had had this opportunity his quality of life would have been much, much better.

6.2 Lifestyle factors influencing present behaviour

by FAITH GIBSON

The New Oxford Dictionary (1998) defines wandering as "to walk or move in a leisurely, casual or aimless way". It gives synonyms of meander – "a circuitous journey, especially an aimless one"; amble – "to walk or move at a slow relaxed pace, especially for pleasure"; ramble – "to walk for pleasure, usually in the countryside without a definite route".

Ideas about the place, purpose and acceptability of walking and wandering have changed over time. Wandering was once more socially acceptable than it is now, as illustrated by Taylor (1649) who described how he "travelled neere 600 miles" in *Wandering to see the wonders of the west*. Even in those distant days, however, the term wandering had other less acceptable, more moral or judgmental associations, as in Allan's *Antidote against heresy* (1648) intended "to stay the wandering and stablish the weak", an idea that still lingers on in the phrase "to wander from the straight and narrow". A lighter, less earnest touch combining work with pleasure, perhaps more generally typical of the Antipodes, is reflected in Finch-Hatton's *Advance Australia: an account of eight years work, wandering and amusement* (1886).

Throughout Victorian times and well into the twentieth century, walking related both to employment and to recreation was commonplace, as many novelists like Hardy, Trollope, the Brontes and others show. It was central to pre-industrialised agricultural labour:

> Only a man harrowing clods
> In a slow silent walk
> With an old horse that stumbles and nods
> Half asleep as they stalk.

> *In time of 'The breaking of nations',*
> *Thomas Hardy (1840-1928)*

Much twentieth century nostalgic literature, like Blythe's (1979) *View in winter*, Taylor's (1988) *To school through the fields*, McDowell's *Other days around me* or Thompson's (1939) *Lark Rise to Candleford*, all illustrate the importance of walking in the lives of adults and children. Young people may not appreciate how walking and associated memories remain so significant for today's older people who grew up in times when family walks on Sunday afternoons were the major highlight of the week.

On the other hand, some people have always avoided walking, and not just in contemporary culture. A character in *The way of the world* by William Congreve (1670-1729) declares vehemently "I nauseate walking: 'tis a country diversion, I loathe the country".

In England, probably as much as anywhere in the western world, walking is encouraged by history, landscape and public provision. Here 1.3 million acres of common land, 120,000 miles of footpaths and public rights of way invite walking. Add to this incentives galore, if an earnest reason for walking is required, with 445,000 listed buildings, 12,000 medieval churches and 6,000,000 known sites of archaeological interest to explore (Bryson 1995). The number and size of walking clubs is not known but walking is frequently quoted as a major informal recreation and comes highly recommended by the health promotion lobby.

Our ideas are formed and influenced by the cultural and historical contexts in which we live. In many parts of the developing world, walking remains a major form, and often the only form, of locomotion. Perhaps dementia and any associated wandering when seen in these contexts, especially in rural communities, attracts far less attention and censure than in western urbanised societies. Here walking is downgraded to wandering and usually regarded very negatively.

This chapter explores how lifelong attitudes and experience influence present behaviour. It deliberately uses the terms walking and wandering interchangeably. This is contrary to common usage by health and social care professionals who tend to use walking in reference to able-minded and able-bodied people (like themselves) and wandering in reference to people thought not to be fully in charge of themselves (like people with dementia). Such negative linguistic labelling limits our understanding and influences our behaviour.

Understanding walking or wandering behaviour

Our attitudes to walking generally, and our tolerance of walking by people with dementia, are both significantly influenced by our own personal past histories and life experience, and those of other people around us. In dementia care there seems to be an implicit hierarchy of acceptable/unacceptable behaviour.

Most acceptable of all is behaviour that is understood to be purposeful or intentional and appropriate to the present circumstances, as understood by people who do not have dementia. Next in acceptability is behaviour that while being inappropriate to the present time and living context may be thought appropriate to an earlier time in a person's life. Behaviour that is viewed as random, aimless and incomprehensible, or is considered to be excessive or inappropriate in its timing, frequency, intensity and duration, or in which others are persuaded to join, arouses deep anxiety. The most unacceptable of all is behaviour judged to be dangerous, risky or that causes distress, harm or upset to the person themself or to others around them. Such behaviour is readily labelled 'challenging' and prompts strenuous efforts to ensure that it is 'managed' – meaning extinguished, controlled or contained.

In dementia care, when faced with wandering the reason for which is not readily understood or which is considered excessive, inappropriate, a nuisance or a potential danger, carers have several options open to them. They may try practical remedies like hiding keys, fitting special locks, electronic alarms and identification bracelets. This approach can be useful but it promises false security if not accompanied by a careful review of the present care environment and an attempt made to unravel possible reasons for the wandering of each person causing concern, viewed within the perspective of their life history.

As caregivers we need to extend our self-understanding and assess our own attitudes towards walking and associated behaviour. Greater self-awareness may modify our immediate response. This in turn may extend our threshold of tolerance towards people whose physical capacity for walking and desire to walk may outstrip our own. In essence, we shift our definition of what we regard as 'challenging' because we better understand why we, rather than the person with dementia, feel challenged.

When people with dementia wander, either from their own homes or a care setting, their caregivers and others around them often become fearful. Whereas the person themself may not appear unduly agitated, others may become exceedingly anxious. This anxiety arises from appropriate concern and fear of the consequences if the person gets lost or harmed (perhaps by traffic or inclement weather), is exploited or their nutrition, health and well-being are compromised. Often there is also fear of litigation if negligence should be proved on the part of professional carers who legally have a duty of care.

So at least a part of the problem is in the mind of the carer who needs to unravel what belongs to the person with dementia and what belongs to others, especially ourselves. Together with this understanding we need to take responsibility for that part of the problem that belongs to us, whether we are a family or a professional carer. Such self-understanding can grow out of solitary self-examination or a supervisory relationship. It may come more easily if discussion and reflection take place within a carers' support group or a staff team, especially one which is accustomed to group supervision. In this way group norms are developed and personal and professional understanding and confidence grow.

Next we need to try to understand the underlying purpose or purposes that might be served by the walking. To do this we should carefully observe the behaviour over a number of days and systematically record these observations. Some of the questions to be asked include:

- Is there any regular pattern to the walking?
- At what times of the day and/or night does it occur?
- How long does each episode tend to last?
- Are regular or casual companions recruited or does the person walk alone?
- Does the walker have a regular beat?
- Does he or she rest along the way or continue without

deviation, distraction or disruption?
- Is anything regularly carried by the walker?
- Does any person, event or place appear to trigger the walking or terminate it?
- Does the walker convey a wish to be outside?
- What emotions are associated with the walking?
- Does it appear to bring pleasure/comfort/satisfaction?
- What are the associated risks, disruptions, inconvenience and implications, if any, and for whom?
- Does the person cause concern in other ways?

Observation may suggest possible explanations. Stokes and Goudie (2000) identify the following:

- separation anxiety
- confusion
- habits of a lifetime
- living life
- physical discomfort
- coping with stress
- failure of navigation
- boredom
- loneliness
- curiosity
- fear
- avoidance
- perseveration
- agnosia
- sundowning
- fragmentation of experience.

A study of Australian nursing home and residential hostel residents, undertaken by the Commonwealth Department of Health and Family Services (1997), reported that 'excessive wandering' was the type of behaviour most frequently classified as challenging. Possible explanations are listed:

- confusion after moving (into care)
- setting off for the shop, friends, home etc
- may enjoy walks
- looking for people and places from the past
- physical discomfort
- physical changes in the brain
- bored, restless or upset.

Influence of the past on the present

While walking beside any distressed person at his or her own pace must be the immediate caring response (where it is indicated that companionship is welcome), more may need to be discovered about what walking means to any individual person.

Several interacting factors rather than a single factor are likely to be involved. Just as it is important to consider the interaction between personal or intrinsic factors and environmental or external factors, so it is important to consider how the past may influence present behaviour.

Stressing the lifetime or lifelong dimension does not mean the present context, including present relationships are unimportant. They too may be highly relevant. Past history, of course, may not contain the clues, or may not contain all the clues necessary to explain present behaviour. It is only one complex dimension in understanding dementia and related behaviour whose causes are multiple and result from a complex dynamic interaction between biological, psychological, social and environmental factors (Kitwood 1997; Cheston & Bender 1999).

Intentional or random behaviour?

Some writers distinguish between behaviour which is intentional, even if the underlying intention may be forgotten, and behaviour which appears to be unintentional or random and to have no discernible motive or purpose. Intentional behaviour consists of a cognitive element described as a purpose, and an affective or emotional executive element resulting in action – in this case, walking.

The executive function may be impaired because of physical frailty but with people with dementia who are persistent walkers the executive function may still be very much intact. In dementia either or both of the cognitive and the executive functions may be impaired to varying degrees so that a person may begin walking intentionally, then forgetting the reason still carry on. Those who wish to walk but who are incapable of doing so or are restrained from walking may experience extreme frustration that may be expressed in other ways.

It is wise to suspend judgement about whether behaviour is intentional or random, an inevitable consequence of neural degeneration. It is better to assume behaviour is intentional, even if the intention is forgotten, distorted in its execution or eludes explanation (Gibson 2004). We need to try to understand the individual whose behaviour is thought to be an observable outcome of interactions between the person with a long life history reacting and acting within a web of relationships in a present context. Any solutions or amelioration must equally attend to both the person and their situation. One without the other will lead to invalid explanations and flawed interventions.

The central principle must be to know the person and this is not possible without knowing the fine-grained detail of their life history. You cannot understand a person with dementia if you do not take the trouble to understand their past. Because people with dementia experience overwhelming threats to their sense of identity, self-esteem and security (Cheston & Bender 1999) we need to use a detailed knowledge of a person's past, gathered in many different ways, to guide our responses (Gibson 1998).

Anxieties and threats to well-being

Reassurance and present security come not from facile assurances that all will be well, but from a carer's capacity to empathise with the anxieties that arise from multiple losses and present ill-health. To be able to offer some security in the present the carer needs to be finely tuned to loss of many kinds, unresolved grief and threats to past and present well-being. Equipped with this background knowledge they can offer themselves as present comforting substitute companions on a journey full of threat and encroaching isolation. Just as the person and their present context require examination when searching for explanations of troubled and troubling behaviour, so too must the person's past be studied in order to understand and respond effectively.

Perhaps wandering could be viewed as a metaphor translated into action for the mind that wanders when contending with dementia. Perhaps wandering is an indication of the person's efforts to live in two worlds and to cope with the confusions and discontinuities of moving between them. One is the well-known, familiar lifetime experience of certainties embedded in familiarity. The other is forever shifting, changing, uncertain, unfamiliar and threatening; and the manifold sources of threat may arise as much from an unfamiliar present as from hints, intrusions and memories of other times and other places.

Helpful responses

Attachment theory offers both explanations for some wandering behaviour and ideas about how to structure staff and family carers' responses. Carers, as they seek to allay fear, minimise uncertainty and increase a sense of security, need to know sufficient about significant others in the past life of the person with dementia to be able to identify references to them and to talk comfortably about them. Using this detailed knowledge can increase trust, offer reassurance and increase the possibility of being accepted as a travelling companion and guide in the unfamiliar terrain of the present.

Cheston and Bender (1999) suggest that identity is closely linked to social roles and that people to whom fewer social roles are available are more vulnerable to neurological deterioration, which in turn makes them less able to sustain residual social roles. Thus the quality of a person's social environment and relationships, and the richness or paucity of the social roles it makes possible are crucial in counteracting the advance of dementia. They suggest that a sense of personal continuity between the past and the present helps to maintain a sense of identity.

Therefore, viewing present behaviour as aberrant and undesirable (characteristics commonly attributed to wandering) is unhelpful, indeed undermining. If the person is using non-verbal behaviour to make heroic efforts to maintain personal identity embedded in previous social roles, they need to be encouraged, not discouraged. If they are using behaviour patterns laid down in long-term procedural memory, perhaps associated with earlier occupational or recreational roles, it is reasonable to suggest that such behaviour should be reinforced rather than efforts made to extinguish it.

It is never possible to reconstruct the past but the past informs our understanding of the present. Talk about the past is not fixed or unchanging. Each time a person tells their story it is influenced and modified according to the social context of the present and the interaction between the teller and the hearer who influences the story as it unfolds. Past relationships are usually central to recall; they are mostly remembered, however, within a broader context of culture, community, neighbourhood and home. Significant life events, personal milestones, achievements, cherished possessions and personal values are also common themes of recall and reminiscence. All memories are bound together by emotional cement so that emotion is usually an important part of the memories recalled. So when encouraging people to recall their past it is imperative to be willing and able to hear their story and work with the accompanying emotions that may be aroused (Gibson 2000).

The search for past certainties

Whether or not we have dementia, most people (but not all) are impelled to search for lost familiarity and past certainties. We all struggle to make connections between our past and our present. While we realise the future is unknowable and unavoidable we gain some reassurance from evidence of past survival, of difficulties overcome and lessons learned.

These memories provide a basis for future hope. People with dementia frequently have impaired capacity to distinguish the past and the present. Some of their wandering may be seeking and searching for a lost past that offers, if fondly remembered, more security than a present perhaps perceived as bleak, barren, lacking human reassurance and devoid of fulfilling roles and relationships.

Sundowning, a tendency to walk in the late afternoon or early evening, has been explained in various ways (Dewing 2000). Explanations include attachment behaviour, visual/perceptual disturbances associated with changing light and shadows, habitual rituals linked to a particular time of day or a misplaced conviction that certain family tasks or duties are necessary as evening approaches.

Effects of the environment

Too many contemporary care environments fail in both design and human terms to offer emotional and physical security. Some, especially those built, equipped, furnished and managed as hospitals or their counterparts, may achieve the opposite.

Even if hospital has been part of a person's past experience, it will usually be associated in memory with feelings of threat, pain, and discomfort. It will arouse feelings of anxiety, uncertainty and dependence and may rekindle feelings associated with separation from others who embodied security and love. Little wonder then that dementia care environments can arouse in some people deep unease, suspicion, and a determination to escape. Staff have to work tremendously hard to overcome, or at least ameliorate, such spontaneous, if scarcely conscious, feelings. They must offer themselves as consistent emotional substitutes for lost key figures if attachment anxiety is to be avoided or contained (Bruce 1998).

Past trauma and dislocation

For some at least, the antecedents of any present wandering or other troubled behaviour associated with dementia may well lie in much earlier trauma or abuse whose consequences surface or re-surface in late life (Hunt et al 1997). People who grew up in one country and culture, yet for many different reasons find themselves relocated in another, describe feelings of dislocation and estrangement.

They experience a sense of simultaneously belonging and not belonging. People who voluntarily choose migration or resettlement describe the insecurity associated with being an 'insider' and an 'outsider'. Even more threatening must imposed or forcible relocation be for refugees, asylum seekers and victims of war or famine. Increasing numbers of people experience extreme dislocation, internationally, nationally, communally and within broken and re-constituted families. So we must anticipate potentially disturbed behaviour in people who in late life are faced with the double jeopardy of growing old in a second homeland and having dementia.

Clues from past occupation and activities

For some people with dementia who walk excessively or at particular times of the day or night, their earlier occupations may provide a possible explanation. We need to establish whether or not walking was a past occupational or recreational interest. 'Occupational remnant' is a phrase used to describe behaviour appropriate to an earlier life stage that intrudes into the present where it is no longer relevant.

The habits of a lifetime may spill over although the present context may make such behaviour inappropriate or redundant. For example a retired farmer who all his working life walked to check his stock may be unable to shed this habit even though other aspects of his life have changed. Postmen and policemen also come to mind – although it is important not to leap to facile, hasty conclusions, and it is imperative to bear in mind that single explanations are seldom sufficient.

Life history may impact in other ways as well. For example, sometimes behaviour will be exaggerated in one context out of willingness to please or not to risk offence but present quite differently in another context with other people. Sabat (1994) described a case history of Mrs R who, at home with her husband, wandered aimlessly, doing nothing. At the day centre she only wandered if there was nothing else to occupy her and she was extremely helpful to others. Sabat interpreted Mrs R's behaviour as being largely influenced by the two different care environments where one context was undermining and the other supportive. This, however, may be too simple an explanation and more would need to be known about the pre-dementia marital relationship and the possible restriction of domestic roles undertaken by this woman throughout her marriage.

For some people, walking has had ritual, tribal or recreational significance. For example, in Lancashire towns annual Whit walks provided a celebratory community outing, and for members of the Orange Order, the Apprentice Boys or the Hibernians, parades on fixed days of the year are invested with religious, political and tribal significance. For these people, 'to walk' means combating threats to group identity, claiming access to territory, and an annual reassertion of historic rituals.

Where livelihood and leisure combine, we might speculate that such influences would be even more significant and long-lasting. For example, a BBC broadcast in the

Open Country series (16 February 2002) provided a rich example of a man whose whole life, economically and recreationally, is bound up in walking. He is an upland Northumbrian shepherd and a researcher, writer and publisher of guides to recreational walks. Would it come as any surprise if in the future such a man might want to continue his lifelong love of walking, no matter what his cognitive capacity might be?

For some, walking is pilgrimage or walking towards a goal, freedom, adventure, personal achievement or a rite of passage (Slader 1990). For others walking may be escape – an attempt to leave behind the unpleasantness or pain of the past.

> I have been one acquainted with the night
> I have walked out in rain – and back in rain.
> I have outwalked the furthest city light.
> I have looked down the saddest city lane.
> I have passed by the watchman on his beat
> And dropped my eyes, unwilling to explain.

Acquainted with the night
Robert Frost (1874-1963)

Yearning for the world outside

Life history and life experience may intrude in still other ways. People accustomed to the outdoors who develop dementia may crave real life experience of the outside world, and for many it is imperative that this, rather than simulated substitutes, be provided (Pollock 2001; MacDonald 2002).

In the northern hemisphere where the climate dictates that more of life is lived indoors we often pay scant attention to providing continuing opportunities for fresh air and outdoor activities. The outdoor sensory world can provide freedom, stimulation, endless varied interest, comfort and pleasure, scarcely realised until denied.

This overwhelming sense of imprisonment, this urge to escape, to be outside, to experience life as it has been lived, is brilliantly caught in the poem 'Grass', which relates to a woman with dementia who is confined inside:

> A young fella carried me
> in here, it were a long way
> and a long time ago.
> I were lying on grass …
>
> I don't want to stay, no
> there's nothing for me
> they're all very kind
> but I don't want to be
>
> inside anywhere at all
> it's much too hot and bright
> it just don't feel right
> I've not been used
>
> I need the fresh air
> I keep calling out:

> nurse, nurse, carry me
> outside to where
> I were lying on grass …

Grass
John Killick (Killick 1997)

The impoverishment of present life, with its diminished opportunities and its social and sensory deprivations, may account for at least some of the seemingly bored behaviour observed in some older people who have dementia.

Loneliness too may be a powerful incentive for wandering. The family home or residential care may not always provide companionship. Help may be needed if people are to retain friends or make new friends. Influenced by dementia, some may be unable to initiate reaching out to others but be able to respond if assisted and encouraged.

Sometimes walking behaviour viewed from the sidelines seems born of apathy, yet is used as an active defence against despair. Daniels (1991) captures this feeling in the introduction to her film *Exiles*:

> *Mary, Gertie and Eve live in a Jewish home for old people in north London. Born in Europe, they came to England to escape oppression, tragedy or poverty… Their community is Rubens House, where sixty people live intimately, side by side… They measure their days by mealtimes… They wander the halls and corridors, aware of the world outside but no longer part of it. They murmur, they sleep, they dream of people and times gone by…*

These people are twice exiled – first from their countries of origin because of world events and then again in old age, exiled from community and family life to become uneasy, restless dwellers in a residential home.

People as well as buildings may be experienced as confining and oppressive. The outdoors may be unreachable. Gardens and surroundings attached to dementia care facilities can provide many varied opportunities for enrichment yet many fail to do so. Gardens designed and planted to provide a natural or naturalised environment can play an important part in any activity programme. They need to provide shelter from sun and rain, give wheelchair access and discreet security. Raised beds, socialising areas with comfortable furniture, plants reminiscent of domestic gardens including shrubs, trees, flowers and vegetables with varied fragrances and textures, are desirable. Paths should actively invite wandering and encourage exploration with cues for recognition and orientation as well as special features and structures to attract interest and encourage conversation and occupation.

An attractive garden needs to provide both stimulation and relaxation, to invite work and offer rest. Too many gardens attached to care facilities are grand, prestigious horticultural spectacles. They are largely passive environments where exploration and genuine activity is positively discouraged. Maybe a council allotment would provide a more relevant model to emulate?

Finland and other Nordic countries provide many examples of aesthetically pleasing, safe environments where the outside world merges easily with the inside care environment in ways that make spontaneous movement from one to the other easy and safe. Imaginative examples abound of growing lifelong familiar plants indoors, even the ubiquitous potato. In Australia, at the other extreme of geography and climate, culturally appropriate design, occupation and a community-based ethos sympathetic to the habits and beliefs of Aboriginal residents are used in Booroongen, Djugun Aged Care Home. In this example, present care is based upon the habits of a lifetime and the culture of a people (Fleming 2001).

Care planning and managing risk

While a well-designed environment and an ethos sensitive to the impact of lifelong experience are important in dementia care, individualised care plans (prepared and delivered within a person-centred framework) are crucial to informing an adequate response to wandering or any other behaviour that indicates diminished well-being. Plans must identify problems but they should focus on people's remaining assets and preserved abilities and be informed by detailed knowledge of the person's life history as well as their sense of present reality.

Care plans need to demonstrate respect for each individual and be aimed at preserving identity, enhancing self-esteem and providing emotional as well as physical security. All care plans need to be dynamic, experimental and hence subject to regular review and input from all those who have regular contact with the person, including family carers.

They should incorporate the views and skills of all disciplines and have a clear commitment to implementation by management. Plans should be culturally sensitive and comprehensive. They should cover physical, social and psychological aspects, including issues of pain control, medication, nutrition, sensory impairment and risk assessment.

In order to provide social and intellectual stimulation, occupation and recreation, care plans also need to include arrangements for interests and activities. These should aim at preserving and exploiting the 'ordinary' in ways that are appropriate to the person's present level of functioning. As far as possible, everyday domestic tasks and previous interests as well as lifetime pleasures should be encouraged.

This approach is also relevant to people living in their own homes where familiarity and neighbourliness may protect against risks and possible dangers, as Gilmour's (2003, p413) study of people with dementia living alone in a rural area suggests:

> Suppose he went out as he can go out and some neighbours saw him they would take him back. It's a close knit thing. He was in... for respite and got out. Somebody must have left the door open. He was walking on the main road.

> He goes across the road. All the locals know him and they slow down but I am afraid of some stranger in a car. He goes for a drink with a neighbour ... I'll find him on the floor in the morning but sure that's how it always was.

Situations like these, however, require a careful balancing of rights and risks and an explicit acceptance by family and professional carers that the individual person's choices will be respected and responsibility for the consequences shared.

Depending on the understanding reached as to the possible purposes being served by any persistent wandering behaviour, the care plan will need to identify specific interventions. If there is a more or less regular pattern to the wandering, then for some people it will be appropriate to plan diversional activities, perhaps at a particular time of day. Having regular walks, being able to go outside or to take some other form of exercise may well help. Recruiting suitably trained and supported sympathetic volunteers with an interest in walking can provide for the physical and social needs of both people with dementia and their volunteers.

Despite the emphasis in this chapter on knowing about and using previous life history to inform present practice, there can be enormous merit in trying something new. Physical exercise, exploration and adventure, not necessarily only walking, may bring immense satisfaction to people with dementia, their families and professional carers.

We have scarcely yet begun to explore the possibilities inherent in vigorous outdoor activity holidays (Brooker 2001) or in very active indoor pursuits like ten-pin bowling (Redfern 2000) for people with dementia whose life chances, especially for having fun, are too readily constrained by our lack of imagination.

Conclusions

Walking is observable; there is no denying it is taking place. The meanings attached to it, however, or the purposes it serves are open to many interpretations. Whether or not it is experienced as a problem, and for whom, depends upon who the walker is, the other people affected and the context in which it is occurring.

What might be experienced as a problem within a small house may attract no adverse comment if it occurs within a larger building, especially one with direct access to a safe, secure garden where risks are minimal and personal freedom is relatively unrestricted. Like beauty, the problems and opportunities associated with walking are very much in the eye of the beholder. Strain arises when there is a mismatch between what is acceptable to the person with dementia and what is acceptable to others on whom the behaviour impacts.

Wandering is a pejorative label whose meaning is imprecise and whose interpretation is enormously varied. The norms we use to consign other people's behaviour to the categories of acceptable or unacceptable are very largely determined by our own and our peer group's lifetime experience.

Nevertheless, anyone who has lived with a person disabled by dementia or worked in a dementia care setting will know someone whose walking is, by any standards, excessive, habitual, and disturbing to others. We may describe it as meaningless because we do not know its meaning.

If we call it rambling, ambling or wandering we have decided it lacks purpose. We need to reconceptualise the observed behaviour and challenge ourselves by asking: How can we restructure the walking so that others around the person will discern a purpose and hence become less critical and more accepting of the person and their behaviour?

To respond in this way demands careful observation, willingness to explore life history details, rigour in preparing care plans, and creative imagination in implementing them. Walking a dog is never seen as pointless. Walking to undertake a message, post a letter or deliver something to another part of the building is not pointless.

Walking companionably is seen as socially desirable. Walking to obtain physical exercise is highly laudable or indeed walking because an earlier occupation, location, lifestyle or recreation required it, is considered both understandable and acceptable. The possibilities are limitless if we begin to get behind the label to discover the person. Labels may be economical to use; they rarely lead us to respond creatively.

Part of the satisfaction derived from walking comes from its cessation, of effort ended. The pleasure of walking may be as nothing compared to the pleasure of it being over, of sinking into a comfortable chair or relaxing on a bench or a bar stool, as we survey the way we went and the journey taken. Our pleasure comes as much from the walk being over as from the walking itself. Might it be the same for people with dementia? Person-centred care then, according to this argument, should provide opportunities for walking, if these are desired, and opportunities too for rest, relief and relaxation at its end.

Curiosity, or the need to explore, to discover, is a central facet of behaviour for most, if not all, human beings. So walking can be regarded as a vital aspect of this drive towards exploration. It can be made the more urgent, and endlessly repeated, under the influence of the havoc wrought by failing short-term memory, surroundings repeatedly perceived as novel (or boring), loss of significant roles, growing anxiety and threats to identity and security that usually accompany dementing conditions. With disturbed perception of time, place and space, constant exploration, even if apparently serving no constructive purpose and bringing little or no reassurance or comfort, is hardly surprising.

If, as Davis (1989) wrote, people with dementia inhabit a smaller and smaller playpen with permissible actions curtailed and personal freedom increasingly restricted, is it any wonder that some seek to break out, to get away, to wander off? Few avenues of freedom and personal comfort are left to people with dementia, and walking may be one of the last.

Shakespeare wrote: "Give sorrow words. The grief that does not speak knits up the heart and bids it break" (Macbeth Act 4 Scene 3). Perhaps it is not too fanciful to suggest that for some people with dementia, walking is a substitute for grief – mourning translated into motion. When words fail, the body speaks.

References

Allan R (1648) *An antidote against heresy*. London: Macock.
Blythe R (1979) *The view in winter: Reflection on old age*. London: Allen Lane.
Brooker D (2001) Enriching lives: evaluation of the ExtraCare activity challenge. *Journal of Dementia Care* 9(3) 33-37.
Bruce E (1998) Holding on to the story: older people, narrative and dementia. In Roberts G, Holmes J (eds) *Healing stories*. Oxford: Oxford University Press.
Bryson W (1995) *Notes from a small island*. London: Doubleday.
Cheston R, Bender M (1999) *Understanding dementia*. London: Jessica Kingsley.
Commonwealth Department of Health and Family Services (1997) *Residential dementia care environments, care practices, staffing and philosophy*. No 28. Canberra: Commonwealth Department of Health and Family Services.
Daniels J (1991) *Exiles*. London: High Ground Films.
Davis R (1989) *My journey into Alzheimer's*. Amersham: Scripture Press.
Dewing J (2000) Sundowning: is it a syndrome? *Journal of Dementia Care* 8(6) 33-36.
Finch-Hatton, H (1886) *Advance Australia: an account of eight years work, wandering and amusement*. London: Allen.
Fleming R (ed) (2001) *Challenge depression*. Canberra: Commonwealth Department of Health and Ageing.
Gibson F (1998) *Reminiscence and recall*. London: Age Concern Books.
Gibson F (2000) *The reminiscence trainer's pack*. London: Age Concern Books.
Gilmour H, Gibson F, Campbell J (2003) Living alone with dementia: A case study approach to understanding risk. *Dementia* 2(3) 403-420.
Gibson F (2004) *The past in the present: Reminiscence in health and social care*. Baltimore MD: Health Professions Press.
Hunt L, Marshall M, Rowlings C (1997) *Past trauma in late life: European perspectives on therapeutic work*. London: Kingsley.
Killick J (1997) *You are words*. London: Hawker Publications.
Kitwood T (1997) *Dementia reconsidered: The person comes first*. Buckingham: Open University Press.
MacDonald C (2002) Back to the real sensory world. *Journal of Dementia Care*. 10(1) 33-35.
McDowell F (1960) *Other days around me*. Belfast: Blackstaff.
Pearsall J (ed) (1998) *New Oxford Dictionary of English*. Oxford: Oxford University Press.
Pollock A (2001) *Designing gardens for people with dementia*. Stirling: Dementia Services Development Centre.
Redfern C (2000) A double strike for dementia care. *Journal of Dementia Care*. 8(1) 24-25.
Sabat SR (1994) Excess disability and malignant social psychology: A case study of Alzheimer's disease. *Journal of Community and Applied Psychology*. 4 157-166
Slader B (1990) *Beyond the Black Mountain*. Belfast: Quest Books.
Stokes G, Goudie F (2000) *Challenging behaviour*. Bicester: Winslow
Taylor A (1988) *To school through the fields: An Irish country childhood*. Dingle: Brandon Books.
Taylor J (1649) *Wandering to see the wonders of the west*. Thomason Tracts. 88. London: Thomason.
Thompson F (1939) *Lark Rise to Candleford*. Oxford: Oxford University Press.

6.3 Always a walker

by JANET PRICE

All walking is discovery. On foot we take the time to see things whole.
Hal Borland, US naturalist (1900-1978)

I walk for the sheer pleasure of putting one foot in front of the other. I walk everywhere and anywhere. "But you're a hill walker", people say. "Why do you want to walk down the road, along the canal, under the railway bridges, past graffiti-covered walls and through the back-streets of the city?" Because I can explore, discover new pathways and enjoy the city from a simple pavement. On my walks I can see things I did not expect to see and meet people I did not plan to meet. I get ideas from gardens I pass or from a glimpse through a curtained window of a colour on a wall. Walking enables me to sort things out in my head to my own rhythm while getting some gentle regular exercise at the same time.

Yes, I am a hillwalker. The hills are great and it is a privilege to be able to walk in wonderful landscapes away from towns and crowds. That sort of walking brings its own rewards of the joy of hard exercise and the views from the summits. But most importantly, it is the freedom of putting one foot in front of the other that stimulates me, wherever I walk and for however long.

It's hardly surprising we like walking. It gives us our first taste of freedom. Watch the expression on the face of the child who first learns to walk. It's wonderful to be independent, not to be carried or picked up or pushed in the pram. We're good at it and it doesn't cost anything. It's easy!

While walking we can saunter and enjoy looking around us. We can dream or work out solutions to problems without having to concentrate on where we are going, because putting one foot in front of the other is natural and automatic. We can race along if we choose, trying to beat yesterday's record or pick our pace to suit ourselves, our mood and our physique.

Many of us have lost the habit of walking because we make the excuse that we're too busy or that it's not economic to take time to walk to the corner shop to get a pint of milk or the paper. We get our exercise in other ways. Anyway we have to justify the purchase of the car.

The chances are we will return to walking again, even those of us who have lost the habit and spurned the activity in a busy life. When we cease to drive or can no longer stay upright on a bike or after we lose the inclination to travel far from the house even to take a coach trip where everything is organised for us, we will go back to putting one foot in front of the other. Our physical horizons will reduce. We will be content to stay around the house more. But that doesn't mean that we won't want to move. So we return to the option that is left to us:

walking for 10 minutes round the block, or 15 minutes to the park bench, or five minutes to the pub or half an hour with the dog.

Human beings have been walking from the beginning of our history. Some will say that walking should remain in the history books. Even though we have moved on and have other means of transport, looking back at history we understand our walking inheritance and why there may be something fundamental in our need to walk. We should give walking its rightful status, not see it as a poor alternative to other means.

History

So history tells us that cave men would walk a hundred miles on a hunt and bring back enough meat for their families to live on for the whole frozen winter. The Bible tells us that the Israelites walked for forty years in the wilderness before they found their land of 'milk and honey'. All the great migrations were on foot.

Even though, for example, Tatars, Mongols and Huns all conquered on horseback, the ones who came and stayed were those who travelled on foot, bringing their gods, tools and household arts and their families. The men on horseback may have been the conquerors but the men on foot have been the thinkers, the dreamers, the organisers and founders of civilizations. The conquerors could not manage without their men on foot. The Roman legionary walked comfortably more than twenty miles per day, a heavy pack on his back, across Britain and elsewhere.

In the Middle Ages, people walked their way to adventure. On pilgrimages and on the Crusades the bosses rode but ordinary people walked in their thousands to the seaports, travelled across the waters and then walked at the other end.

There are numerous tales of the walking feats of our great writers and poets too. John Ruskin, for example, walked six miles a day; Coleridge walked 10 and worked out his epic poem 'The ancient mariner' in his head on a walking tour with his friend Wordsworth. Wordsworth himself walked 14 miles a day and in the course of his life must have walked about 185,000 miles in the Lake District, no doubt composing as he went. Shelley eloped to France with Mary Wollstonecraft and because they could not afford a coach they planned to walk all the way to Switzerland. They managed 100 miles in six days before a sprained ankle forced them to hitch a lift.

With all this good historical and literary stuff, what a great tradition we walkers are upholding!

Closer to home, our grandparents or great grandparents may have told us of their walking feats of many miles across the hills to market or into town on their evening off to go to a dance. They were part of the great walking tradition. Were we impressed at their achievements or did we feel sorry for them, glad that life is no longer like that?

Even today we read of places in the world where walking for miles is still part of the present way of life whether it be walking miles to school or taking beasts to market or visiting relatives in distant villages are part of the great tradition. Are we impressed at their achievements or do we feel sorry for them, glad that our life is not like theirs? Such histories are an integral part of our cultures and our civilisations.

When I have stopped wanting to travel far from home, stopped using the car, can no longer balance safely on my bike, don't want to climb to the top of every peak in sight, I will still walk – simply moving, free and independent. I will be doing what our forebears have done for thousands of years, and it will not be second-rate. It will be essential to my physical and mental well-being. Do not offer me a lift, or have pity on me and take me somewhere in your car that you think may be more interesting. Please just leave me be.

When I become forgetful I will still want to walk. I will then wander off and may not know where I am going, but leave me be. Just recognise how important it is to me and find ways of allowing me to carry on walking.

References:

Borland H (1967) To own the streets and fields. In Sussman A, Goode R (1967) *The magic of walking* New York: Simon & Schuster.

Sussman A, Goode R (1967) *The magic of walking.* New York: Simon & Schuster.

Photo: Northern Ireland Tourist Board

6.4 Mary's story

by JAMES MCKILLOP

You see me 'wandering' but unless you can read my mind, how can you be certain what I am actually doing? I get up in the night. This was the norm for my generation. Husbands started work early and had long walks to work. There was no question of fares which were better spent on ravenous children and bus networks were in the future. It was unforgivable if a man went to work cold and hungry while his wife idled in bed. I would be affronted if I had done that to your father.

Though I dimly realise that you have flown the nest and have children of your own, I still hear you crying in the night. I get up to walk the floor and comfort you through teething, upset tummies and bad dreams. Having to look after the house without the aid of washing machines, vacuum cleaners, dishwashers and other gadgets, I was physically tired and paced the linoleum on automatic pilot. You were never left to sob alone. In addition, I was always on the alert for sirens wailing their blood chilling warnings – you had to be sprinted to the Anderson shelter. I got so used to being 'on call' that I could never switch off. And today I am still on alert. Perhaps the cry of a nocturnal animal or the twang of a bed spring triggers a mother's love and I rush into action without pausing for thought. When I find you're not there, I'm bewildered.

There were no fridges in my day. For you to eat fresh products I had to go shopping early, daily. And many a time money and coupons were not enough. You had to be ready to dash off at speed and queue patiently when you heard that a certain item was available in the shops. Coupons were useless if the product was not available.

Beseeching eyes were the norm. During the winter this meant leaving in the dark and walking or scurrying. No one had a car or could afford taxis. No matter how bad the weather or how ill I felt, I simply had to propel myself and go out – I was a mother! I had to ignore a protesting body and just get on with it. That sheer determination got me through then and it is still there when I imagine you need me.

Things were slightly better by the time I had another infant. The pram could share the load and I could tread easier behind it. However, later on with more mouths to feed I had to stagger along with arms wrecked with heavy shopping and my face getting more and more ruddy. You don't see my like, these car-owning days. Don't you understand that I had to subjugate my inner voice telling me to let up? I had to keep going. I couldn't afford to take it easy. I needed a strong will or I wouldn't have lasted the pace.

I can't shake off this compulsion; it was ingrained over the years. So when you see me walking, I am not 'wandering'. I am still, in my own way, setting out to take care of those I love.

The wheel has turned full circle. Please don't look stupefied at what I do – I may get confused when I transpose and blend today with yesteryear.

I am not going about blindly. I have a clear purpose in mind and I find it distressing enough when things are not as I expect to find them. Please don't lecture me; just gently guide me back to the present which is your past.

Photo: James McKillop

6.5 Reflections on walking

When I was a locum inspector for Buckinghamshire County Council I had the pleasure to visit a Methodist home for people with dementia many times. This was a marvellous home with a calm and serene atmosphere. On one occasion, having popped into the office to let them know I was in the building, I headed upstairs to sit in one of the lounges with the residents and have a cup of tea.

The lounge I was in overlooked a circular path within the garden, and as I sat I noticed that one of the residents was walking in a determined fashion around the path. I couldn't help but think that there was something rather familiar about her and then it struck me that she was wearing my jacket and and carrying the briefcase that I had left in the home's office.

This at first left me surprised, and I said to the member of staff on duty in the lounge that the lady had both my jacket and my briefcase. The staff member told me that this particular resident had been a doctor at the local hospital. She was always on the go and would often come into the office and pick up whatever she fancied. Briefcases were a particular favourite of hers!

We went down together and the member of staff found a clipboard and the resident's own coat. We met the resident just as she was about to undertake another circuit of the garden and offered the coat and the clipboard in exchange for my things. The resident seemed pleased with the items on offer and was soon on her way around the garden once more. During my visits to this home this lady would often take my jacket and briefcase, and on subsequent visits I did not bother to retrieve them until I had to leave. She always accepted the swap quite happily though, when it was time for me to go. I also used to watch her as she walked purposefully around the home, asking how residents were, pausing in the office, where she was a frequent visitor, to collect a clipboard, briefcase or jacket, whichever took her fancy. She remained the busy individual that she had always been, striding out purposefully, taking an interest in all around her.

Fiona Fowler

Granny might have lost her memory but she hasn't lost her wit – my 16-year-old daughter remarked. I was telling her of the latest 'granny' incident. Someone had called the ambulance for my mother, after finding her lying on the footpath. The paramedic explained that she refused to get into the ambulance and appeared confused. "What day is it?" he asked. "I know but I am not telling you", she replied. She did accept a lift home from the two women who found her on the pavement. On several occasions recently, people have reported their concerns: "I had to swerve to avoid your mother, she was walking out on the road." Someone had contacted the police because they found her leaning over a bridge staring at a river. A nurse had picked her up in the car a few days before this latest incident as she found her "confused and breathless".

My mother has always been a 'walker'. Like many of her generation, she never learned to drive a car because a bicycle was the main method of transport. She reared six children who were provided with a licence as soon as possible, but she never aspired to drive. After they left home, she thought nothing of walking the five-mile round trip to get her shopping. Over the past year she walked more frequently to visit my father's grave, and it appears to be on this journey that she has encountered concerned members of the public. Neighbours willingly give her lifts in the car, and some have told us how they now slow down when near to her house.

Rights and responsibilities jostle with each other. She has the right to walk but people around her have a right to be safe. We are concerned about her safety too, particularly as her hearing has become increasingly poor. She lives alone so supervision is difficult. "She seems to be a very independent woman," the paramedic said. How long can she remain so, I wonder?

Anon

Paradise in walking

I have found in my psychological work with people that during periods of acute psychological turmoil, walking is an activity to which one naturally turns.

Walking claims turmoil. Prisoners circumambulate the yard, animals exercise back and forth in their cages, the anxious pace the floor – waiting for the baby to be born or to hear news from the boardroom.

Heidegger recommended the path through the woods for philosophizing; Aristotle's school was called 'Peripatetic' – thinking and discoursing while walking up and down; monks walk round their closed gardens. Nietzsche said that only thoughts while walking, *laufenden* thoughts, were of value – thoughts that ran, not sitting thoughts.

One goes for a walk to get the stuck, depressed state of mind or its whirling agitations into an organic rhythm, and this organic rhythm of walking takes on symbolic significance as we place one foot after the other, left-right, left-right, in a balanced pace. Pace. Measure. Taking steps.

With the soul-calming language of walking, the dartings of the mind begin to form into a direction. As we walk, we are in the world, finding ourselves in a particular space and turning that space by walking within it into a place, a dwelling or territory, a local habitation with a name.

The mind becomes contained in its rhythm. If we cannot walk, where will the mind go? Will it not run wild, or stay stuck, only to be moved by the rhythms of pharmaceuticals: uppers and downers, slowers and speeders, calmers and peppers.

There is probably an archetypal cure going on in walking, something profoundly affecting the mythical substrata of our lives. When we are most in the grip of anxiety, as in nightmares, we are often unable to move our legs.

There is a long association between fright and motion of the feet – the word for fright in German, for instance, means to leap or jump up. Could it be that the less we move our legs, the more subject we are to anxiety; that by not moving, we are already living an unconscious nightmare?

In ancient Egypt, one of the main hieroglyphic conventions for *Ba*, the soul, was the calves and feet, the lower limbs extended as if striding forward. The soul walked. When we no longer walk, what happens to the soul?

Walking also brings me in contact with my animal nature. I am as I move: cat-like, nimble and stealthy, bullish, stiff as a stork, waddling like a duck, strutting and prancing like a young buck. There is an animal display in our motion by which we are known.

In the temples once we were blessed for our 'coming in and going forth'. The blessing took into account the human as a moving being, a soul with feet, a physical being in the midst of a physical world made to walk in, as Adam and Eve walking in Eden. That garden is the imagination's primordial place of the nostalgia which recurs unconsciously in all utopian dreams. And that garden was created, you will remember, by a walking God. That image says, there is walking in Paradise; it also says, there is Paradise in walking.

Paradise in walking, James Hillman
Reprinted with permission from Resurgence
magazine, www.resurgence.org

Photo: Mary Marshall

Movement

7.1 Physical activity and exercise

by ROSEMARY ODDY

This chapter looks at how walking can form part of an exercise programme for people with dementia. It also suggests how, when walking becomes increasingly difficult, we can create a programme that produces a reasonable level of physical activity in other ways, or that helps to prevent some complications.

Those of us who are fit and active are able to choose whether to walk outside for pleasure, or to do so specifically in order to enjoy the health benefits that such exercise can provide (see p78). Alternatively, we can settle for walking only when it is absolutely necessary, with some of us seemingly making a conscious effort to avoid any that is unnecessary! It is obvious that walking means different things to different people, depending upon circumstances and individual wishes and abilities. It is, however, an ability that tends to be taken for granted until some injury or accident makes it impossible or difficult in the short or long term. Only then do we realise the consequences of its loss on our lives.

The loss is not always sudden and dramatic; some older people may gradually become less able on their feet, especially those who are unfortunate enough to be affected by multiple pathology (one or more of the many physical conditions that can be associated with older age, such as arthritis, osteoporosis, heart and lung conditions, stroke etc) and who also develop dementia. It is easy to see that these people do not have the same choices about walking that most of us have. In fact, it is true to say that unless steps are taken to prevent this, many of them might not move out of their chairs even though they are physically able to do so.

A change of culture

In the past, a diagnosis of dementia was usually not made until the condition was well advanced and affecting many aspects of the person's abilities. Some people with dementia – restless and constantly on the move – did maintain full mobility (their ability to move and walk) until they died, but the majority were expected, sooner or later, to become chair- or bed-bound.

Over more recent years there has been a change of thinking, with the old negative approach being replaced by the new positive 'person-centred' one (Kitwood & Benson 1995). Also, pioneering work over many years has shown that with imaginative 'problem-solving' approaches (Oddy 1998), immobility must no longer be regarded as the expected and inevitable outcome of dementia.

Research is now showing that physical activity has what is called "a positive association with cognition" (Simonsick 1997; Etnier *et al* 1997). In other words, exercise may have a beneficial effect on the mental processes (eg reasoning, decision making, judgement) which are affected by dementia. So, physical activity should benefit mental processes as well as muscle strength, joint flexibility and balance. Earlier diagnosis of dementia is now paving the way for the early introduction of a physical activity programme into the care package of every person diagnosed with dementia. Some of the mobility problems associated with dementia may in this way be avoided, delayed or lessened.

Individualised programmes

The content of a physical activity programme must match the needs of the person involved. A fit older person with early dementia and a relatively healthy body is likely to be able to follow a programme that is active and varied. On the other hand, a person with severe dementia may only be able to manage a very few exercises. I shall describe the programmes at three different 'levels'. In practice, however, it is not always easy to allocate people with dementia neatly to a particular 'level'. We also have to bear in mind that the person's physical ability can vary from hour to hour, or from day to day. It is, therefore, obvious that each programme, however well thought out, should also be flexible.

Caregivers should, ideally, be given early access to a dementia service where they can obtain guidance and support. Physiotherapists, or occupational therapists with experience in working with people with dementia, are able to give advice about physical activity and mobility, and how to give help safely and effectively. This early involvement enables some problems associated with mobility to be avoided. This is a change from the past, when help from a therapist was not sought until a problem had developed.

Level one: Programmes using walking as a source of exercise for active older people with early signs of dementia

Walking is one of the obvious choices to include in a programme because it provides a readily accessible source of excellent exercise. Another advantage is that it is a sociable activity when carried out with another person, or in a group.

Research evidence

Research shows that it is never too late to start walking. For example, a project in Sweden (Frändin 1995) involved a group of people, aged 70 years, who carried out a daily walk of 30 minutes over six years. At the end of this period, it found that they performed better in functional performance tests and remained fitter than a similar group who did not walk. This project also showed that people who had been fit and physically active during their younger years were also fitter and more able to continue being physically active when they grew older – a valuable message for all of us.

A 'walking' programme

Most active people with dementia need an escort while walking, unless they are very familiar with the route and do not lose their way. The distance covered, or the time devoted to the walk, needs to be gradually increased until the desired length or time is achieved. It is helpful to set goals, but it is wise to ensure that these are achievable, so that a sense of satisfaction accompanies their successful completion. A purposeful walk to the post office to collect the newspaper provides a more satisfactory goal than a 10-minute walk around the block. Carers, however, may not always feel able to provide a daily walk for their loved one. In this case, they must decide what they can manage – two or three times a week might be a good compromise. Alternatively, they can consider providing the opportunity for several short walks during the day, rather than one longer one – the beneficial effects are thought to be the same.

In urban areas walking is likely to take place on pavements; in the countryside, footpaths across rougher and more uneven land offer interesting and enjoyable alternatives. Strenuous walking and steep hill climbs may, however, not be suitable choices for older people with heart problems or breathing difficulties.

Additions to a 'walking' programme

Physically fit and active older people with early signs of dementia may need much more exercise than can be provided by a walking programme alone. Daily household chores, simple maintenance tasks, decorating, and playing with grandchildren, for example, also provide an opportunity to be physically active and are encouraged. In addition, any previously enjoyed sporting activities and active interests should be continued as long as practicable: bowls, swimming, cycling, dancing, Keep Fit, T'ai Chi and gardening come to mind.

Combining walking with aerobic exercise

A local gymnasium or fitness centre may offer suitable programmes for older people with dementia. For example, an interesting and structured programme was created in an American gymnasium by combining walking and vigorous exercise (Arkin 1999). The goal was to achieve 20 minutes of continuous aerobic exercise on equipment twice a week, plus 20 minutes or more of walking per week. Students or carers provided support for each participant who took part in a warm-up, an aerobic session (treadmill and stationary bicycle), weight-lifting (leg press, seated rowing machine, torso weights and overhead press), and a final warm-down.

A walking programme for people who are restlessly active

Regular, supervised daily walks may also be beneficial for people with dementia who are restlessly active and constantly 'on their feet'. It is important, however, that the reason for the restlessness is investigated before any such programme is introduced. A walking programme would not be appropriate for the person who is thought to be trying to 'walk away' from a pain or a discomfort – here the underlying problem needs our attention. It might, on the other hand, be helpful for a person who is bored and frustrated as a result of a lack of physical exercise, or to improve the sleep pattern of a person who is restless at night (Holmberg 1997). In countries where the weather makes outdoor living more possible, walking circuits are often incorporated into the garden. This makes it possible for restless people to enjoy the exercise, or to relieve their boredom.

Restless people who are free to walk when they wish to, often fall. Any fall is distressing and can result in a fracture, especially of the hip. Carers and relatives are understandably anxious that this should not happen. As a result, they may be tempted to stop the person from walking. This can be very frustrating for the restless person who is unlikely to understand why he or she is being restrained.

Hip protectors (hip pads)

Nowadays, we are able to prevent the hip from fracturing when people fall. Hip protectors can be worn. These specially reinforced pants are proving to be completely reliable and are preventing an untold number of fractures (Gross *et al* 2000). They cannot stop people who wear them from falling. However, carers are now able to let restless people walk freely, knowing that a fall will not result in a painful and expensive hip fracture.

An assessment process aimed at identifying a wide range of risk factors is required before hip protectors are prescribed. At present, three pairs of these special pants are supplied to each person 'at risk'. An increasing number of hospitals are providing them free of charge to their in-patients who are judged to be 'at risk', but otherwise the person is likely to have to pay for them. General practitioners are able to recommend their use.

The pants fit snugly, but need to be correctly applied. The carer of a person with dementia oversees this process and ensures that the protectors are worn at night as well as by day. The design of the pants is under constant review and improvements can be expected.

When walking becomes more difficult

Dementia is a progressive condition which gradually worsens over a period of time. The combined effects of the environment, multiple pathology and increasingly severe changes in the brain usually lead to some difficulties with mobility, including walking. When this happens, walking outside can no longer be used as the main source of exercise. This does not mean that walking should be completely abandoned; its loss can often be as upsetting for people with dementia as it would be for anyone else. The ability to walk short distances, with or without help, even a few steps, is well worth maintaining. But how can this be achieved?

Identifying problems

Certain problems will make walking unnecessarily difficult:

1. Is medication for any pain effective and administered regularly?
2. Do any corns, callouses or in-growing toe-nails need attention?

3. Is the person wearing supportive footwear, in good condition?
4. Would a walking aid be helpful?
5. Are the carers able to give assistance that is effective and risk-free? (Backcare 1999)
6. Is the person unable to walk because their chair is making it impossible, or difficult, for them to rise from it? (Wagland & Peachment 1997; Harris & Mayfield 1983)
7. Can any highly polished flooring that looks 'wet' be dulled down?

A thorough assessment by either an occupational therapist or a physiotherapist can help to provide answers to questions three to six and identify any other problems.

A note about footwear
Slippers should not be worn as a matter of routine by people with dementia – they offer no support to their feet and contribute to trips, slips and falls. Shoes for indoor or outdoor use must be comfortable and fit snugly with the aid of laces or Velcro fastenings. A broad heel of a moderate height is essential for both men and women, and the soles should be flexible and relatively thin. Trainers are not suitable.

Level two: A walking programme for people with dementia who are mainly housebound but able to walk short distances

When a walking programme outside is not feasible, as much walking as possible needs to take place inside the home. This situation may arise when the weather is particularly bad, or when the person with dementia no longer has the 'staying power' to manage any distance walking.

Walking at home
The space inside a private house is likely to be limited, so carers must make the best use of it. Frequent movement from one room to another is one way of achieving this. For example, by using meals, drinks or other activities as the 'attraction', movement of the person between two rooms provides a regular source of short walks. In a confined space, the person may choose to use the furniture for support and this is perfectly acceptable – but they may still need their carer to show them the way, even in their own home. If personal help is needed, the carer provides this from the side of the person and walks 'in step' with them (Oddy 1998). It is NOT safe to give support by facing the person, taking both their hands and then walking backwards.

If the person is having difficulty in managing the distance between the two rooms, it is best to break it up into stages. The carer marks these with a series of dining chairs, making sure that they are placed so that the person will always be able to see one. In this way they are helped to walk from chair to chair, sitting down if need be, until they reach their destination.

Additional exercise
Frequent standing up from a chair in order to walk also provides additional valuable exercise. And climbing up and down the stairs is another source of effective exercise for the hip and thigh muscles; it is also an ability and a convenience that should be maintained so long as it is safe and practicable.

A simple chart, ticked to show the number of walks carried out, is a valuable way of recording the level of daily activity.

Level three: A walking programme for people with dementia who are mainly housebound and unable to walk

The ability to walk even a few steps may eventually become impossible. The mounting effects of dementia, plus increasing physical problems, gradually take their toll. Even carpets with a particularly deep pile and loose rugs can add to the person's struggle to move their feet.

Movement from one chair to another is now achieved by using 'transfers'. These can be carried out in a variety of different ways. Various special pieces of transfer equipment are also available. Carers and staff should seek advice from an occupational therapist or a physiotherapist on the best method to use for an individual.

A wheelchair now becomes essential. It is not, however, a good idea to allow a person with dementia who is no longer able to walk to sit in it all day. They should sit in an armchair that suits their needs, and move in and out of it frequently. The wheelchair provides their daily means of transport from room to room. So, for each little journey, the person transfers into the wheel-chair and on arriving at the 'destination' (eg the dining table) transfers out of it onto a dining chair, preferably one with arm-rests. These transfers provide a very basic but essential level of physical activity. Each pair of transfers should have a meaningful purpose; for example, the purpose of the transfers just mentioned was to eat a meal at the dining table.

The activity chart, previously mentioned, is now changed to show the number of transfers carried out. The level of daily activity should be carefully monitored.

Additional physical activity at home for housebound people, and those with limited mobility who live in care homes

Extra physical activity needs to be added to these basic walking or transfer programmes. Those who care for people on either a walking or a transfer programme should:
  • use the first of the two exercises outlined below, and
  • consider using the second one.

The carers of people on a transfer programme, or of those people who are only able to walk a few steps, are advised in addition to follow the three special routines described towards the end of this chapter.

Exercise one:
Moving sideways along the side of a bed.

This should be incorporated into the person's daily routine, so that it is carried out every time they are assisted out of or into bed. It provides some extra weight-bearing, with valuable exercise for the hip and thigh muscles.

Briefly, it consists of 'shuffling' along the edge of the bed using a series of little sideways movements. The person uses their hands so that they can raise their bottom a few centimetres off the bed each time. The height of the bed must allow them to place their feet flat on the floor throughout this exercise.

Exercise two:
'Cycling' on a set of floor pedals.

A model with footplates makes it easier for the person's feet to stay on the pedals. The number of turns of the pedals or the time spent cycling can be recorded on the activity chart, mentioned earlier. The carer might even choose to join in on a second set.

Additional physical activity at a day centre

Some people with dementia have access to a special day centre. Good centres provide a mix of therapeutic and social activities, planned so that people have to move from one area to another in order to reach each activity. This is achieved when there are different areas for different activities, for example, for meals, rest and relaxation, group work and exercises. Such planning ensures that the people who attend are kept active and, depending upon their ability, walk or transfer regularly.

Special routines

The three special routines described below are carried out daily with the aid of a carer. They are designed for use by people who do not walk at all, or very little, but who are able to transfer.

Routine one: Standing to a support

Sitting for long periods can cause some muscles to shorten, especially those of the hips and the knees. If this happens, the person becomes increasingly 'chair shaped' and standing becomes impossible. Steps should be taken to reduce the chances of this happening. 'Standing to a support' provides one way of achieving this.

The routine: The person is helped to stand up several times a day. They stand upright with their knees as straight as possible, using the back of a chair for support. While they are standing, the carer can encourage them to look from side to side around the room so that some movement of their body, but not of their feet, takes place.

The ability to stand to the support for three minutes is of practical use to carers; they can adjust the person's clothing, or carry out other care, while he or she is standing and holding onto the support.

Routine two: Sitting on a stool

For most of the time that a person with dementia is seated, their chair is giving support to the back. This can easily cause them to become unable to sit upright when there is no back support. As a result, carers find that the person falls backwards as soon as they sit on the edge of the bed, making handling very difficult. This 'loss of sitting balance' can often be avoided with the very simple daily activity described below.

The routine: The person walks a few steps, or transfers from a wheelchair, to sit on a low stool. The stool should be about 40 centimetres high, so that the person's feet are flat on the floor. The surface of the stool must be padded – sitting on a wooden surface could lead to the development of pressure sores – and the carer must stay at their side. They sit together for about 15 minutes, during which time the carer keeps the person actively occupied. For example, this might involve: talking, singing or reading together, helping with a jig-saw, or playing a well-loved game. The activity should involve some movement by the person, such as leaning forwards, reaching sideways or turning to look from side to side.

Routine three: Lying flat on a bed in the middle of the day

There are several reasons for using this daily routine. First, it enables the person to stretch out fully, helping to prevent muscles from becoming shortened; second, it provides a change of position from sitting, relieving pressure from the 'sitting areas' of the buttocks and the bottom of the spine; and third, it gives the person's neck muscles a well-needed rest, resulting in an improved posture of the head afterwards. The most convenient time for this routine to be carried out is probably after lunch when the person is feeling sleepy.

The routine: The person is helped to lie on his or her back on their bed (the mattress should have a pressure relieving surface). They are made comfortable, using pillows to support their head and legs. A blanket keeps them warm. They may need three pillows for their head to begin with, but once they have relaxed and are 'nodding off', it is often possible to remove one or more of them. The person is only allowed to sleep for about 30 minutes, otherwise they may not sleep at night. During this simple but effective routine the carer must stay nearby.

Conclusion

I have outlined the contents of a series of different physical activity programmes for people with dementia. My main theme has been walking as a source of exercise. I have, however, also suggested alternative physical activities that might be used when people with dementia become less active. I have taken a realistic approach, based on long experience, presenting simple exercises and physical activities that should be easy to follow. Carers and staff should have access to members of the dementia or medical team for support and advice. Training provides them with essential communication, handling and other skills (Oddy 1996).

The importance of physical activity should be stressed from the moment of diagnosis: every person with dementia should be given a personal physical activity programme. The content of each programme is chosen to meet the person's needs and abilities – much of it is designed to fit into the normal daily routine. Goals are set so that they are achievable, and regularly reviewed and changed as necessary so that they remain so. In this way a positive attitude is maintained. Success is important: it gives satisfaction to carers and keeps people with dementia 'on the move'.

References

Arkin SM (1995) Elder rehabilitation: a student-supervised exercise programme for Alzheimer's patients. *The Gerontologist* 39(6) 729-735.
Etnier J, Salazar W, Landers D, Petruzzello S (1997) The influence of physical fitness and exercise upon cognitive functioning: A meta-analysis. *Journal of Sport & Exercise Psychology* 19 249-277.
Frändin K (1995) Physical activity and functional performance in a population studied longitudinally from 70-76 years of age. PhD Thesis, Goteborg University, Sweden.
Harris C, Mayfield W (1983) *Selecting chairs: For elderly and disabled people.* Institute of Consumer Ergonomics, University of Technology, 75 Swingbridge Road, Loughborough LE11 0JB.
Holmberg SK (1997) Evaluation of a clinical intervention for wanderers on a geriatric nursing unit. *Archives of Psychiatric Nursing* 11(1) 21-28.
Kitwood T, Benson S (eds) (1995) *The new culture of dementia care.* London: Hawker Publications.
Oddy R (1996) Strategies to help keep people moving. *Journal of Dementia Care* 4(4) 22-24.
Oddy R (1998) *Promoting mobility for people with dementia: A problem-solving approach.* London: Age Concern England.
Safer handling of people in the community (1999). Backcare, 16 Elmtree Road, Teddington, Middlesex TW11 8ST.
Simonsick EM (1997) Physical activity and cognitive function in old age. In Fillit HM, Butler RN (eds) *Cognitive decline: Strategies for prevention.* London: Greenwich Medical Media.
Wagland J, Peachment G (1997) *Chairs: Guidelines for purchase of lounge, dining and occasional chairs for elderly long-term residents.* Stirling: Dementia Services Development Centre.

Health benefits of walking: Benefits to older people

- **Mortality is halved in retired men who walk more than two miles every day**
(Hakin AA, Petrovich H, Burchfield CM, (1998) Effects of walking on mortality among non-smoking retired men. *New England Journal of Medicine* 338 94-99)

- **Regular walking can help to strengthen the bones and therefore reduce the risk of osteoporosis and associated fractures**
(Brooke Wavell K, Jones PRM, Hardman AE, (1997) Brisk walking reduces bone loss in postmenopausal women. *Clinical Science* 92 75-80) and (Cummings SR, Nevitt MC, Browner WS *et al* (1995) Risk factors for hip fracture in white women, *New England Journal of Medicine* 332 767-773)

- **Hip fractures in over 45-year-olds could be reduced by up to 50 per cent with regular walking**
(Health Education Authority, (1995a) *Health Update 5 – Physical Activity*, HEA, London)

- **Physical activity can improve balance, co-ordination and joint flexibility in older people which can help to prevent falls**
(Buchner DM, Cress ME, de Lateur BJ *et al* (1997) A comparison of the effects of three types of endurance training on balance and other fall risk factors in older adults. *Ageing* 9 112-119).

- **Walking can help reduce the pain associated with osteoarthritis of the knee**
(Ettinger WH, Burns R, Messier SP, (1997) A randomised trial comparing aerobic exercise and resistance exercise with a health education programme in older adults with knee osteoarthritis. JAMA 277 25-31).

- **Lifelong exercise has been shown to lessen the chances of developing Alzheimer's disease**
(Smith A, et al (1998) The protective effects of physical exercise on the development of Alzheimer's disease. Study released at the American Academy of Neurology's Annual Meeting in Minneapolis, 25 April – 2 May 1998).

- **People who exercise into late adulthood show less than the expected level of deterioration in aerobic fitness with ageing**
(Health Education Authority, (1995a) *Health Update 5 – Physical Activity*, HEA, London).

7.2 A dance therapy perspective

by HEATHER HILL

Walking about, or wandering, is often seen as a symptom of dementia – a result of certain parts of the brain being damaged. As a dance therapist, however, I would want to know who's doing the walking (What is this person like? What might he/she need?) and I'd also be interested in the quality of the walking – not all walking is the same. What I see missing from the symptomatic approach to walking is that of individuality – the individuality of the person and the individuality of his/her walk (and impulses to move).

I would therefore like to look from a dance therapist's perspective at some of these aspects, not only because I believe it is important to come to an understanding of the individuality of this activity, but also because the discussion will hopefully give some clues as to the ways in which a dance programme might be beneficial.

Why walk?

There are many reasons why a person with dementia might walk. Here are some of them.

Physical discomfort

Sitting is one of the most stressful positions for our bodies. Gore, an Australian physiotherapist, has pointed out that it is better even to stand than sit, since sitting exerts tremendous pressure on the discs: "When you lie down there is about 25mm mercury pressure on the discs in your lower back; when you stand up there is about 100mm mercury pressure on the discs; when you sit down there is 400mm mercury pressure. So apart from bending and twisting, sitting is the worst thing you can do for a healthy or an unhealthy back" (Gore 1993). In other words, sitting is bad for you.

Remaining still for any length of time is unnatural and most uncomfortable. Try sitting without moving for a mere ten minutes and you will very soon understand why it can become intolerable to stay in one place. Add to this bad, frozen postures and usually inappropriate chairs and you have a recipe for physical discomfort.

Another aspect which perhaps receives insufficient attention is the pain people might be experiencing for various reasons – certainly some due to posture. I remember during childbirth how much I moved around. I was very glad to be giving birth in an era when women no longer had to endure labour in stillness and flat on their backs.

Finally, we should remember that for many older people walking has been a regular part of their life. Therefore it is only natural they might feel the need to walk, especially if they are coping with the many changes dementia and possibly institutionalisation may bring.

Boredom

So often we tend to usher people back to their seats. But to do what? Usually, nothing. Is it any wonder that people want to get up and go somewhere else?

Psychological discomfort

Dementia is not a comfortable state to be in. It is a state of dis-ease, feeling incomplete, fragmented. Unable (because of expressive difficulties) to talk it out, what more natural thing is there to do than to walk, to walk your way out of this psychological discomfort? Haven't we all done this when troubled with life's events? It simply helps to move at times when troublesome feelings and thoughts surround us. Sometimes walking helps to clarify our thoughts; at the very least the act of moving eases some of the discomfort.

It seems also to be a way to get back in touch with oneself. The feet are highly sensitive, with multiple nerve endings, and perhaps this serves to stimulate and to reinforce our being. Possibly too the regular rhythm of our feet making contact with the floor gives us a reassuring rhythmic structure and a feeling of being held, contained by the ongoing, regular flow of movement. Walking can help us think, but walking can also provide us with stimulation and a reminder that we exist.

One is also uncomfortably reminded of the pacing walk of prisoners or caged animals – the strong impulse to move, but without spatial direction or purpose. This is the walk of someone or something who has lost meaning and purpose in life.

Individuals who walk

Here are two definitions:
Walk: Move along on foot at a moderate pace by placing one foot on the ground before lifting the other.
Wander: Move or go about aimlessly; go to a place in a casual or indirect way.

As I have reflected on the use of the word 'wandering' to describe the kind of walking people do, I feel more and more that it is not an accurate description. The word 'wander' to me implies moving in a directionless way, both in spatial terms and in intent or impulse to move. In terms of space, when I wander, I do not move directly towards a place, I meander, I go here and there. I may wander in the woods, but would not think of wandering to work in the morning. In terms of intent, there is no strong will to go, to reach a place, or even simply to move. It's all rather laid back. To describe people as wanderers seems to miss the differing character of individual walks and walkers.

The definition of walking itself seems to miss out the multiplicity of ways in which people do that simple action of placing one foot on the ground and then the other. There are a million or more different ways of walking – as many as there are walkers. A person's walk tells a lot about the person, how they function, their current state of mind.

Let us look at some of the walkers I have encountered and reflect on the nature of their walking.

Can you tell me the way out?
Mr C is a big man, an ex-cricketer, who seems to dwarf every chair he sits in. I can't help wondering how he feels being enclosed in a small unit of a nursing home – he seems to need space. When I see him walking, he is often looking to find the way out and will ask staff if they can help him. He is still very spatially aware and knows where the exit buttons are – knows that he needs to find someone to tell him the combination. Eventually, he seems to give up, sits down and dozes in a chair.

I have loved and lost
Ms L is a gentle, loving woman with a warm smile, but often she is seen walking in between the various units of the nursing home. Her attention is inwards and she seems totally involved with her thoughts. She gives off an air of sadness and seems to be aware of what she has lost. Whenever I cross her path, I give her a hug, which she reciprocates smiling almost gratefully, but then, almost regretfully, she must keep going. It seems that her sad thoughts push her on.

It must be here somewhere...
Mr G walks with a sense of mission, but with no particular external purpose. He can get very involved in picking up my audiotapes, but at the same time, one senses this is more to do with his inner world than attention to and awareness of the external.

I have to get home
Mrs B walks because she needs to get home to her children. The food's on the stove and she's worried that it will burn over.

I'll come along with you
Sometimes two residents will walk together. Indeed walking can be 'catching'. If one person starts to walk, others may follow. It may also be that they mistake the other person for their own spouse and cling on to them for security.

The free spirit
Mrs S is regularly seen walking all over the nursing home. She stops for a while to sit, possibly chat, then is off again. Sometimes she loses her bag, but is content to ask staff to help her find it. Once it's found, she goes off walking again. She likes to dip into activities and sometimes will stay for a whole session, but at other times merely passes through

with a friendly wave. S's walking is a much less driven affair than some of the other people I've seen walking. She has, so her son said, never engaged in intense involvement with people outside the family, though because of her lovely nature, she has always been well liked. Her family and the staff see that the way she now lives in the nursing home is really a continuation of her life outside, flowing here and there as she fancies. And she is content.

There are clearly many different types of walkers. We need to spend more time trying to understand their walk since it may tell us something about each person and in what ways we might better meet their needs. I sense in many of the people I have worked with a strong inner motivation/intent and determination – a walking flow which is hard to deflect. While they walk through space, in only some do I see actual interaction with the space. Rather they seem lost in space, very much impelled by and involved with their own inner space. It seems that perhaps there is a correlation between their withdrawal from 'outer' space and the degree of dementia. With increasing dementia comes more involvement in inner space, although, as with Ms L, it is not a comfortable place to be.

There seem to be common themes: finding a way out, looking for something or someone lost. Early on, they are literally like Mr C attempting to find a way out; later it seems to be more a symbolic losing and searching for, but is just as strong an impulse. Some seem more reflective, others are pushed on relentlessly by their inner workings. Given that dementia entails multiple losses, it is not surprising that themes of loss seem to pervade so much of the symbolism of the words and actions of people with dementia.

Walking, like all other movement, is particular to each individual and we would do well to try and get inside and understand something of what motivates each person. I think the worst we can do is to stop them walking. We can try and meet some of their needs in ways which will be more effective than their own strategy of walking, but at times we will need to accept that walking is what they need to do. If there are difficulties, risks of falling and so forth, then some way to still allow walking needs to be found.

The role of dance
It is always hard for me to explain to people exactly what a dance session with people with dementia involves. Immediately they tend to think of formal dance, like 'old-time dancing' but this is not what we do. My work as a dance therapist is about working with the whole person – mind, feeling and body, the medium being the body in all its expressiveness. I will use anything which touches and has meaning for the people I work with. Typically therefore dance sessions might include:
- exploring movements – different body parts, different qualities of movement (fast, gentle, etc)
- music
- touch

- voice
- props – such as scarves, elastics etc – which allow for movement exploration.

Underlying the work are certain important principles:
- Every activity is done with sensitivity to and respect for its quality. Nothing should be done mechanically.
- We affirm and reinforce the individuality of each person. This individuality is of course very much expressed through the body.
- We draw on the contributions of each individual.
- We create an atmosphere of total involvement in what is happening, focusing the group energy.
- Most important is relationship – building relationship between you and the residents and among residents. This relationship is very much one of equals, who relate to each other as fellow human beings.

This then is a very brief description of the character of dance sessions. I believe that there is much about dance which can meet many of the needs of the walking person, and of course it relates to some of the reasons for walking, listed earlier, in such aspects as:
- attention to the physical
- occupation – having something to be involved in
- holding/containment of restlessness
- relationship.

Physical activity

In the dance sessions, people stretch, shake, wriggle. They MOVE. They touch and are touched, tickled, kneaded. They FEEL. They do conscious breathing, they straighten their bodies as they breathe, giving themselves a different perspective on their world. They become more aware of the world in this position. They yawn, yell, make sounds of all descriptions. As the sounds reverberate round the room and in their bodies, they announce their existence to the world and themselves.

All of this relieves physical discomfort, the stress of stillness one might call it, and offers an outlet for pent-up energy and emotion. The physiological benefits of exercise are accompanied by psychological benefits: feeling at ease, feeling positive. Last but not least, it reminds people that they are alive and that it's good to be so.

Occupation

By this I mean not just something to keep people occupied, but rather something which involves them, something to which they give a bit of themselves, something which draws them out of their internal preoccupations. One of the aspects which is particularly potent is the energy generated within dance sessions. This really has the power to draw people towards it, giving them incentive to leave their worrying thoughts. People are drawn out of themselves and into positive social interaction with others.

Holding or containment

This has partly to do with the energy, but also the form/structure and rhythms inherent in dance sessions.

The ongoing impulse of walking which propels people ever onwards can sometimes be caught up in a different rhythm (eg the steady beat of clapping), or may be contained within a different structure – walking forwards and backwards in a 'bush dance' formation.

Relationship

This is the cornerstone, by which all the above succeed or fail. Relationship is the medium through which all aspects of the dance are brought to the person with dementia. Through relationship, the person can be affirmed as a worthwhile human being, can be made aware of their very existence and can be called out to life.

None of this can be delivered like a pill to work every time and with all people. And of course it is preferable that such activities are in a philosophical context which is person-centred rather than symptom-centred.

The impulse to walk is a very strong internalised impulse in some people with dementia, and cannot be met head on. One needs first to meet the person where they are, then hopefully move them into a different internal space. The physical activity and the mental/emotional energy of dance sessions may well lure them out of their walking mode even if just for a while. However, if not, then let the person go with good grace. Never let the person feel he or she has let you down by not changing to do what you want.

Some difficulties

I have described the benefits dance may offer people who are restless and need to walk. However, having them in the session can create its own difficulties. They may often walk right across the circle, or stand in front of others – all of which breaks the focus I am trying to create within the group. At such times one may well need to weigh up the needs of the individual versus the other members of the group in deciding whether a person who is restless should stay. Furthermore, their walking can also infect others to do the same. Once my whole group walked out on me, following one of the other residents. Nothing makes a group leader feel quite so foolish – not an experience I recommend!

If there is someone who is restless, I tend to bring him/her into the group last so that we start immediately to do things, to stimulate and to interest. Where the person walks during the session, one can sometimes incorporate this into a walking dance of the Scottish country dancing or Australian bush dancing style. But again the motivation to go in a certain direction can be so strong that the person may not be willing to follow.

It may be that the person can be engaged for a while. However beyond a certain point, it becomes counter-productive to persist. In the first place it becomes too stressful for the person who wants to move around, but it can also be stressful to other participants and the group leader as she tries to hold the group together. At this point, it is best to say, thank you for being with us, we hope we'll see you next time and let the person go. The most important thing is that he/she is recognised and affirmed, and leaves the room feeling good.

For some people it works well, if they have the possibility of coming in and going out as they please. I have found that the energy of the group can be most appealing and will attract people to it, although they may only be able to maintain their concentration for a short time.

For some, it may simply be too stressful for them (and the group), to participate in a group experience and one just has to accept that.

People who are restless often find it quite impossible to stay during quieter sessions focusing on touch. However, we found that Ms L (the resident mentioned above) was able to stay for the whole session when her husband came in and did some of the touch/massage we were doing. Of course, since it was husband and wife, it gave the experience a whole different meaning and was quite poignant to see. Ms L seemed at ease and very happy, glowing in the love she received from her husband.

The desire to walk can be seen not just in people who can walk. One resident was in a bucket chair, unable to maintain balance in standing. However, she was often very restless in her chair, and at times staff would let her crawl on the floor. In one session we got her on to the floor and she showed the same need to move as people walking. I then rolled her on to a piece of stretchy lycra material and we rocked her in it. Within a minute she had fallen asleep. There are, of course, practical difficulties, with lifting for example, but this made me wonder about the possibility of giving some of the basic movements such as rocking to the more disabled people who cannot actually walk but who, I sense, need to.

Some further thoughts

Other chapters in this book look at the environment and other factors which might help meet people's needs. Here are some ideas from my perspective and based on my experience as a researcher in the arts and dementia.

Walk with the person
By doing this you may get more of an idea of what's happening for them internally, and also what they are experiencing as they walk. I walked with one resident, who proceeded to sit down outside the nursing home office and make very perceptive comments on the people passing by! If you take a step further and try to get into the person's walk (not mimicking, but rather absorbing the quality of the walk so that it is done with respect), it can be a powerful way to feel the other person's reality.

Make contact
Make sure you make some contact – a smile, a hand touch, a hug, a hello – as you pass the walking person. Acknowledge their existence and make them aware of yours.

Make the environment interesting
Have plenty of pictures, objects to touch or wall hangings. While people do seem to be very caught up in their internal workings, one cannot underestimate the impact and attraction of eye-catching objects, or objects that make sounds (such as chimes).

Have volunteer 'listeners'
Perhaps volunteers can be brought in to be 'listeners'. I found it interesting one day when I stayed sitting in the dance room after our session with one of the nurses, and some people walked by, stopped for a while to talk and then moved on. Having a person there and receptive attracted people, gave a point of focus. Again, whenever a walker comes by, make contact.

Don't worry if people don't stay
We may worry too much about people staying for an activity. I think one should focus on the activity, making it as interesting and involving as possible. The energy of the activity will very likely draw people towards it. Have a revolving door policy where walkers can move in and out as they please. The motivation to walk is much too strong and you are literally hitting your head against a brick wall if you put all your energy into keeping a person in the group.

I cannot pretend to totally understand walking, and writing this piece has made me determined to return to my workplaces with renewed awareness and a desire to learn more. However, to conclude, let me summarise some of the issues I think we need to look into further, and to which we should take a creative approach:

• Why is walking in dementia a problem, and for whom?
• There are different individuals who walk – and we need to look at who they are (which is basic to a person-centred approach). This might include their habits of the past but also an understanding of their life now. Are they bored? Sitting too long? Anxious?
• There are different ways of walking in terms of rhythm, spatial intent, transfer of weight, inner impulse to move. Let us not dismiss it simply as 'wandering'. Anyone who has tried to stop a person with dementia walking will know of the strong impulse to keep going – and that's not wandering. Getting into their walk may help us understand something of their experience.
• A creative arts programme like dance has much to offer physically, psychologically and emotionally. It will be a most effective part of an overall program of person-centred care.
• Given the symbolism of loss and searching, we may need to seek many and creative ways to meet people at this level, to help them create a life which retains some meaning.
• Most of us have known times of stress when we simply need to walk. Why should it be different for people with dementia? We need to be realistic about whether walking is a problem, and creative in providing a meaningful way of life which may or may not involve walking.

References
Gore A (1993) *The office athlete*. Cremorne, Australia: Lifestyle Press.

Staying
safe
and
healthy

8.1 Walking for comfort

by MARY DIXON

Mrs Watts is a 76-year-old woman who was placed in nursing home care some 10 months ago. She has dementia which was diagnosed over seven years previously. Mrs Watts lives within a 30-bed specialist dementia unit in a 60-bed nursing home. The home is well laid-out with lots of spaces in the long corridors, although there is no outside space that can be securely used.

Mrs Watts walks the corridors for roughly 10 hours a day. Sometimes she walks alone, other times she is joined by another female resident, with the two walking hand in hand for periods of up to an hour. When not accompanied, Mrs Watts normally walks holding on to the rail, sliding her hand along. When she reaches the end of the rail and the corridor, she turns round and comes back again.

Mrs Watts does not give any appearance of 'searching' for any particular person or place. She sometimes stops near the front door, but often does not look out; staff feel she merely stops because the rail has run out. Mrs Watts will sometimes vary the corridors she chooses to walk in, but staff have not noticed any particular pattern to this.

Mrs Watts does have family who visit regularly, but she will often walk away from them to continue her corridor walking. Her concentration span appears to be very short. There have been difficulties in getting Mrs Watts to stop long enough to have something to eat. However this seems to have eased of late and she will accept being guided into the dining room. If staff are concerned about her not settling to eat, they will give her sandwiches which she is happy to eat as she walks along.

There have been concerns about Mrs Watts's feet and about the need for her to have the right calorific intake given the amount of exercise she takes. Both problems are monitored closely by staff. Mrs Watts has a degree of dysphasia and has word-finding difficulties; it has not been possible to find out how she is feeling with any confidence.

Mrs Watts enjoyed hill walking in her younger days, but there is nothing in particular from her past life that would explain her tendency to walk.

There seems to be some comfort for Mrs Watts in walking. She always looks quite cheerful, she seems to have a rhythm to her walk, and she seems to like the feel of the rail.

Photo: Laura Benson

8.2 Food, eating and walking

by HELEN CRAWLEY

For most of us, the drive to eat calories in the form of food is stimulated by the energy we burn up doing everyday tasks. In an increasingly sedentary world, nutritionists are urging everyone to be more active – to burn up more fuel so that we can eat more food without gaining weight. The reason we need people to eat more food is to ensure that they get all the nutrients they need – small food intakes may allow people to remain thin, but are unlikely to provide all the vitamins and minerals we need for good health.

There has been much research on the importance of remaining physically active into old age – with many studies showing considerable benefits to health and well-being when exercise programmes are introduced even among those of very advanced years. For most of us, the very best activity we can do to increase our energy expenditure is walking – and it is the decline in walking in particular and dependence on the car which many nutritionists believe is the key to the current obesity epidemic. The reason walking is so important is that it is habitual energy expenditure which contributes most to increased calorie needs – walking for just 30 minutes every day gives a weekly total of three and a half hours exercise – an amount few people will manage to make up in other activities.

The walking associated with dementia can therefore be suggested to have both positive and negative implications for health and well-being in food terms. On the one hand the increased activity is likely to result in a greater drive to eat, increased appetite, increased food consumption and therefore, it is hoped, adequate nutrient intake. On the other hand, if people with dementia walk a lot and do not increase their food intake, they may well lose weight (because they burn up more energy than they consume).

Estimates have been made of what the energy cost of walking in dementia might be. It will vary a great deal depending on the size of the individual and the time spent walking (and moving their body in other ways) each day. Estimates for the increased energy requirement range from 600-1600kcals a day – and this is of course on top of the approximately 1800-2100kcals/day older people require for the everyday energy cost of living. If this extra energy isn't consumed, the body will start to burn up energy stored as fat and other tissues – and the person will lose weight.

Weight loss remains one of the key indicators of nutritional risk among people with dementia and unintentional weight loss should always be monitored and acted upon. Some people have suggested that weekly weighing is important among those who walk continuously, and monthly weight checks are recommended for everyone. An unintentional weight loss of 7lb or more should always be referred to a doctor or dietitian. More information about monitoring weight loss among people with dementia can be found in *Eating well for older people with dementia* (VOICES 1998).

How to eat?

Increasing walking means an increase in energy intake is needed – but this may be at a time when food intake actually starts to decline, as the time spent sitting down for meals may be restricted.

Food on the move may be one solution to increasing energy intakes. Relying on sit-down meals to provide all the food someone needs when they find sitting at table difficult to achieve is unrealistic – so carers and staff will need to think of ways of getting food energy in throughout the day. This may be by offering five smaller meals made up of easy-to-eat foods which are energy- and nutrient-dense (ie they provide lots of energy and nutrients in a small package).

Such foods include cheeses and other dairy foods (such as yoghurts and milk-based desserts), meats, poultry and fish, eggs and egg-based dishes, fruits and vegetables including dried fruits, fruit-based puddings and vegetable snacks, breads, biscuits and cakes and foods such as chocolate and ice cream. All these can be included to provide a varied menu.

For people who have difficulty in using cutlery, finger food diets are often appropriate – and these fit in well with the 'little and often' approach to eating that many people who walk may require. Finger food diets aim to provide all the food in an easy-to-eat format throughout the day. Finger foods can be served at room temperature so that people can eat at their own pace and spills and waste are often minimised. It has been suggested that the use of finger foods focuses attention more on eating and food – and increases involvement in the eating process. In their excellent book *Finger foods for independence* (Newton & Stewart 1997) the authors give this story of a re-awakening when finger foods were introduced:

> People who for years had shown no inclination to feed themselves at a 'normal' meal setting, put out their hands, grasped the food in their fingers (fingers which may not have held anything but bedcovers for years), conveyed the food to their mouths, chewed it and swallowed it.

Another possible solution for someone who is unable to sit still during meals is to give them a 'brown bag' meal – suitable finger foods in a bag that can be carried around, attached to their waist for example. It might be more practical, however, to ensure that snacks are available around the person's usual route, and that people are encouraged to stop and eat. Positive benefits on communication skills have been shown if carers or staff talk to people with dementia as they walk – taking a break for food with them during a walk may also help encourage eating.

So how much food is an extra 600kcals a day? This would be provided by:

- a Mars bar and a large glass of milk
- two eggs, a matchbox-size piece of cheese and two slices of toast and butter
- a mug of malted milk drink and four digestive biscuits
- a portion of chips and three sausages
- a medium slice of quiche and 10 boiled new potatoes
- a slice of flapjack and 15 dried apricots
- a tin of sardines on two slices of toast and butter.

Snacks become increasingly important during the day when energy needs are high. Menu planners need to take the particular needs of some individuals into account and supplement their food with extra calories as necessary. While many people with dementia require the same healthy balanced diet as is recommended for the population as a whole, those with increased energy needs are likely to need more fat in their diet, as this is the most concentrated source of energy. Adding extra cream, butter or cheese to soups and sauces adds calories, as does adding extra sweetening to food using honey or sauces.

Using purchased 'supplements' can be helpful in some cases – but people often tire of the tastes of these quite quickly and wastage (of what are very expensive food products) is often high. Supplements can be useful in the short term to help reverse trends in weight loss, but it is not difficult to achieve an increase in the energy content of foods, drinks and snacks served from the main menu.

Other ideas that have been found to be helpful in increasing energy intakes among those who need extra energy include:

- making afternoon tea an opportunity for tasty and nutritious sandwiches as well as cakes and scones
- having a 'cocktail trolley' which does its rounds in the early evening, offering fortified milk drinks or milkshakes
- offering meals which are colourful and offer a good combination of textures and flavours
- stimulating the taste buds with well-flavoured food – mild curry flavour for example.

Nutrition needs

Those nutrients we know are often in short supply for people with dementia include vitamin D, vitamin C, the B vitamin folate and iron. It may be difficult for people who walk a lot to obtain enough of these nutrients if their food choice is limited, and it is important to find ways of including these important nutrients regularly in the diet.

Vitamin D is unusual as a vitamin, in that the body can make its own if the skin is exposed to summer sunlight. Most adults make enough during the summer to last all year round – but we know that many people with dementia do not get enough access to sunlight and often have very low vitamin D status.

Walking outside in the summer should be seen as important for everyone with dementia. Lack of vitamin D makes the bones more likely to fracture; walking increases muscle strength and tone and improves joint flexibility making falls less likely, and the added benefit of improved vitamin D status can be seen as an extremely positive health benefit to walking. For those who do not go outside, vitamin D supplements (which can be prescribed) are essential.

Vitamin C is often found to be consumed in smaller amounts by people with dementia, but it is essential for the immune system and preventing infection, for wound healing, and for helping the body absorb iron. Vitamin C is found in fruit and vegetables and in fruit juices such as orange or cranberry juice and in drinks fortified with vitamin C. Ensure that people who walk have access to drinks throughout the day and that fruit and vegetables (cut up and ready to eat) are provided as snacks. Giving a drink rich in vitamin C with a meal will help with iron absorption.

The B vitamin folate is essential for preventing a type of anaemia in which the blood cannot carry oxygen efficiently, leading to tiredness, apathy and depression. Folate is now known to be essential in many vital body processes, and may contribute to maintaining good memory and be associated with prevention of heart disease. Folate status is typically low among people with dementia. Good sources in the diet include green leafy vegetables, oranges and other citrus fruits, fortified breakfast cereals, liver and yeast extract. Some other foods are fortified with folate (eg some breads) and diets which contain lots of fruits, vegetables, meat and cereal products usually provide enough.

Iron is also essential for preventing anaemia, as well as for preventing infection and helping the body to regulate its temperature. Many older people have low iron status for a number of reasons, and diets which provide lots of folate (ie with plenty of fruit, vegetables, meat and cereals) will also provide iron. Other good sources of iron include oily fish, pulses and nuts, dried fruit and egg yolk.

Walking and drinking

Walking may mean extra water losses through the skin (particularly if the ambient temperature is warm) as well as a reduction in the number of drinks consumed. Dehydration remains a major cause of ill health among people with dementia – and so all those caring for people who are spending time walking need to think creatively about how they can ensure food and fluid needs are met. People with dementia need to be encouraged to drink as the thirst mechanism declines and people may not realise they are thirsty. The consequences of dehydration can be

Photo: Tony Price

There is much evidence that a flexible and relaxed approach to mealtimes helps people with dementia to eat well.

weather. Milk-based drinks can be a useful source of nutrients in the diets of people with dementia. Whole milk provides more energy than skimmed milk, and extra milk powder can be added to milk to increase the protein and energy content. Hot milk-based drinks such as hot chocolate or malted milk drinks can be comforting at night or in colder weather. Cold milkshakes in a variety of flavours and colours can add variety during the day.

Relaxing mealtimes

There is much evidence to show that what works in helping people with dementia to eat well is a flexible approach to meals. The importance of eating to overall health and well-being is fundamental. Many staff and carers embrace the need to focus on eating and actively take part in the process themselves. For those who walk or who find it difficult to sit still at mealtimes, staff and carers still need to be engaged in helping with the eating process: gently encouraging periods of rest with snacks and drinks and being alert to times when someone may want to eat.

Mr C was always on the move, always in motion and hungry. Often he would eat his own meals at the table, and would then spot something he fancied on someone else's tray – usually something he could take off with him. We found that placing plates of easy-to-eat foods such as sausages, strips of spicy chicken, small boiled potatoes or green beans in the middle of the table meant he could help himself to extras if he wanted them, and in fact he now sits for longer at meal times as the urge to go 'hunter-gathering' may not be so immediate!

severe: constipation, headaches, falls, confusion and urinary tract infections are all associated with insufficient fluid intake.

It is recommended that people have at least 1500mls of fluid every day – equivalent to eight teacups. This can be in the form of drinks of water or tea, coffee or other beverages, or in foods such as soup, jelly or ice lollies. For people who may spend time walking, drinking cups of tea may be an ineffective way of encouraging fluid intake as it means a pause, and concentration on the drinking activity. It might be useful to encourage drinks to be taken along for the walk too – cartons with straws might be useful for some people – and nutritious drinks such as orange juice or cranberry juice are available in small cartons. You can also buy special containers for drinks on the move, used by sports people or in packed lunch boxes. These 'carry along' drink containers may appeal to some people with dementia if they are simple to use.

Ice lollies can be taken along when walking as well – homemade ice lollies can use fresh fruit juices or even milk-based drinks to provide a variety of tastes and flavours as well as other nutrients and are ideal in warmer

The relationship between hunger, appetite and exercise is not one we are all tuned into any more, as food is constantly available and our energy expenditure is often low. It is likely however that people with dementia who are active are also hungry, and finding ways to replace those lost calories is a challenge to creativity and caring skills.

To end on a personal note, I remember so well the time when I was nursing my first baby: the endless nights of pacing around the bedroom, stroking and patting to find wind and soothe the wakeful soul. I think of how hungry I would then be by morning, ravenous, but able to eat fast and satisfy my craving for energy. I think of that now when I look at my grandmother who restlessly paces the room and yet finds it hard to eat with gusto.

References
Newton L, Stewart A (1997) *Finger foods for independence.* Creative State, Australia.
VOICES (1998) *Eating well for older people with dementia: a good practice guide for residential and nursing homes and others involved in caring for older people with dementia.* Potters Bar: VOICES. Available from VOICES on 01707 651777 or cwt.org.uk

8.3 Designing for walking: creating rich environments

by KIRSTY BENNETT

Walking plays an important role in many of our lives. Sometimes we walk for a specific purpose, and at other times we just walk. The difference may be found in the words we use to describe what we do (such as stroll, potter, amble, meander, wander, or mosey about), but often the activity is outwardly the same and we are the only ones who could make such a distinction.

As architects we are told of the tendency people with dementia have to wander. In this context the word is often given a negative connotation (perhaps because the reason or meaning behind a person's actions is not clear), and movement is raised as a problem to be addressed. Instead, we need to recognise the broader role that walking plays in many of our lives, and approach this area of design with renewed enthusiasm and inspiration.

An environment can be designed to provide opportunities for us to move about, and to encounter a range of experiences as we do this. Designing for walking is important for people with dementia, and the environment plays a significant role in their lives and those of their caregivers. A setting can influence how people feel and what they do. It can encourage them and provide opportunities for them to participate, or it can restrict and inhibit them.

When designing for walking, it is important to focus on how opportunities for movement can be created, and how these can be achieved. It is appropriate to start, however, by considering some of the key principles of designing for people with dementia. Any response to people's desire to move about should be considered in this broader context. After all, walking is just one part of a person's life.

Design principles

There are a number of key principles which are important when designing for people with dementia. As Judd *et al* noted in *Design for dementia* (1998), there is considerable agreement on areas such as maximising independence; compensating for disability; enhancing self-esteem and confidence; assisting orientation; controlling stimuli; reinforcing personal identity; welcoming relatives and community, and caring for staff. Other areas of agreement include small size; familiar; domestic style; scope for everyday activities; unobtrusive safety; use of cues; enhancement of visual access; and controlling of stimuli, especially noise.

Photographs by Kirsty Bennett

A view into another room can help a person with dementia know where they are in the building.

A number of these areas will now be described in more detail. While different aspects of design will be discussed under distinct headings, it is important to recognise that these design principles are interrelated and many design approaches could be described under a number of headings. It is also important to remember that these are design principles and not rules. They give an indication of issues which are important to consider. The built response to these will of course vary enormously as a result of people's priorities, expectations, lifestyles, cultural background, and the climate where they live.

Top and middle: Lounges at Aldersgate (Adelaide, Australia) show the potential to create strikingly different settings.
Above: The Meadows (New South Wales) successfully explored the idea of total visual access.

Scale
The scale of a facility is one of the first things to consider because it influences how a person feels and behaves. An environment of an appropriate scale helps a person to have a sense of place and well-being. A small-scale setting reduces the number of decisions a person has to make, and the number of people they need to interact with. The scale of a facility is determined not only by its overall size, but by the scale of its many components.

Domestic environment
A domestic environment is residential in scale, character and detail. It will evoke memories of home, and allow older people to continue to undertake tasks of daily living and use their skills. Typically it will allow for choice and independence. It can take many forms, as it will be influenced by a person's expectations and past life experiences.

Close to community
Interaction with the local community is important both for older people and the wider community. It can be achieved in a number of ways, for example by locating a facility close to housing and shops, by promoting visits to local activities and settings such as a garden, or by encouraging visits to the facility by people from the wider community.

Way finding and orientation
It is essential that people are able to negotiate their environment as easily as possible. *Way-finding and orientation*

Residents at Flynn Lodge (Alice Springs) can see clearly and choose between different destinations - for example, the lounge (top) or outdoors.

An external path can be an integral part of a circulation route, providing an alternative way back to where other people are.

devices and *cues* are a key aspect of any environment, but are particularly relevant in environments for people with dementia. Important stimuli should be highlighted and others minimised. *Visual access* is also desirable, as is providing clear choice and decision-making within a setting.

Way-finding and orientation devices are important as they form landmarks which can help people with dementia orientate themselves within a building. Natural light, for example, can be introduced to highlight decision-making points, and make a break in what would otherwise be a continuous space. A view into a lounge room (see illustration on p88) can help someone to know where they are.

Audible and olfactory cues can also be integrated successfully, so that a person associates a place with a certain smell (such as lavender or mint), or the sound of wind chimes. This not only has the benefit of creating a point of recognition, but adding to the experience of the space.

There is an enormous range of cues and wayfinding and orientation devices, which play an important role in enhancing a person's experience. Colour contrast can be used to differentiate between doors. Landmarks can designate and separate certain parts of a building from others. Colour contrast and texture add a richness that cream and beige decor cannot give to a room.

Lounges designed by Brian Kidd at Aldersgate (Adelaide, Australia) in the 1980s were among the first to show the potential to create strikingly different settings (illustrated on p89). The use of richly-coloured wallpaper, distinctive fabrics and different ceiling forms all combine to create rooms which have the same lounge room function but are easily recognisable and distinguishable.

The selection of appropriate cues will be strongly influenced by a person's previous life experiences and cultural background. For some people the built environment will not be the most appropriate cue at all, and instead a rock or a certain view will be meaningful.

Visual access is desirable, so that people with dementia are able to see where they have come from and where they are going. Circulation within a building can be designed so that people can be visible from a central point. This needs to be carefully and sensitively done, as the intent is not to create a prison environment. The idea of providing total visual access has been explored very successfully by Hammond Care at The Meadows , New South Wales (photo on p89; described in Judd *et al* 1998).

A domestic-style kitchen is the hub of the unit where meals are prepared and staff are often present. The kitchen opens on to dining/lounge spaces and has two passages leading from it. There is also a clear view to the back yard of the facility. Staff working in the kitchen can therefore see everyone at a glance in an unobtrusive way. Conversely, anyone moving through the building can always see the kitchen and see where other people are likely to be.

A key aspect of walking is being able to determine where one is, where one has been, and where one can go.

While this may be achieved by simply creating clear lines of sight to and from destinations, this is not always possible or desirable. At times a richer and more varied experience is preferable.

In such situations, it is vital that people are given simple choices and clear information about what they can expect to find at their destination. At Flynn Lodge in Alice Springs, for example, residents can consider, "Shall I go to the lounge or outside?" (see photos on p89.) In this instance an internal passage leads directly from bedrooms to social spaces, whereas an external path leads residents outside (and then towards the same social spaces but in a more circuitous way which offers quite a different experience).

An example of a 'rest spot' which should be provided at regular intervals along a walking route.

Familiarity

The use of familiar elements will be important to assist a person with dementia to move about with a minimum of difficulty. This is relevant not only to furnishings and furniture within a facility, but to all aspects of a setting such as building layout, room size, view and external appearance.

This may mean choosing the width of a passage so that a person feels secure, or selecting a ceiling height which is recognisable. A familiar space can induce a sense of well-being as a person moves about, rather than a sense of being lost and exposed. Familiar items such as a favourite photo, a special armchair or dresser can also form important cues for people with dementia.

It is important to remember that the design of a familiar environment will be affected by a person's cultural background. What feels familiar and comfortable for one person is not necessarily the same for another. Our attitude to scale, for example, can vary enormously, as can our relationship with possessions.

Privacy and community

Creating a balance between privacy and community is important. A setting should provide opportunities for older people to spend time with others or be on their own. For some people it will be vital to retain and express their individuality, for others it will be more important to be part of a community.

Safety and security

Safety and security are key aspects of a setting. An environment should provide opportunities for older people to participate in life and pursue their interests without taking unnecessary risks. An environment should be secure, while allowing for unrestricted movement.

Accessibility

An environment must be accessible. People with dementia will have a range of abilities that are likely to alter over time. An environment needs to be accessible so that people can use their remaining abilities to the full. The facility should be enabling. It should provide necessary support in an unobtrusive manner while allowing opportunities for independence.

Creating opportunities for movement

The principles outlined above give an idea of the range of issues that need to be addressed when designing for people with dementia. Designing for visual access, way finding, orientation, and familiarity will be particularly relevant, as are designing for safety, security and accessibility.

An important starting point when creating opportunities for movement is to try to understand why people move. Only then can we respond to the need to move in the most appropriate way. What are people looking for? Is

Boundaries can be obscured, not highlighted, for example by planting shrubs to hide fencing.

Another approach is to design the fence so that it 'disappears' into an open view of the landscape.

it something that the environment can respond to?

One of the most important aspects when designing for movement within a building is to design for purposeful wandering. It is essential when designing environments that we do not start with the aim of simply filling up a person's day or giving people something to do. Instead, we should aim to enrich people's lives. Our task is not to design environments that waste people's time. Time is precious to us all.

Planned movement

Where do people go? There are many ways in which the environment can facilitate movement and offer people with dementia a range of experiences that they can enjoy. It is important to consider both the internal and the external setting, and how the two can interrelate. We also need to spend time designing the places that people walk to.

An important part of designing for movement is creating opportunities to be still, and do something else. While focusing on circulation, we also need to design areas where people can take a break from walking. These can be internal or external spaces which are designed with a particular character (such as a lounge room), or simply an area where there is something to look at, such as a view.

Opportunities for movement should be planned, without encouraging movement as a goal in itself. We need to think about designing the circulation within the building and the outdoor environment in a way which recognises people's need to move and directs this appropriately.

Internal circulation routes need to be clearly marked and designed to take people to key places. Outdoor areas also need to be clearly defined to assist people to find their way and head to an intended goal, such as the back door. External paths can form an integral part of a circulation route, and provide an alternative way of returning to a place where other people are (see illustration on p90). Internal and external paths need to be integrated and designed as part of the total circulation system within the building. Passages and paths need to lead somewhere and not just finish with a dead end. The travel route needs to be clearly defined, so that people are encouraged to head in a certain direction and reach a destination.

The experience of walking itself is something which should be considered. How do people feel as they move about? What do they experience? How are their senses stimulated? What do they see, smell and hear? What events take place on their journey? What have they gained by taking this path?

Redundant cueing

It is usually most appropriate to provide a range of cues and way-finding and orientation devices in a building. This is in accordance with the principle of providing redundant cueing. Redundant cueing means providing more than one cue in a location, recognising that what is significant for one person may not be for another. Whereas one person may notice a certain smell, another may be drawn to a plant or a painting on the wall. Colour contrast and view are also important cues which can be used to great effect.

The use of cues must, however, be carefully managed to ensure that they assist a person to find their way and do not add another layer of confusion and complication. The introduction of too many cues can add to the complexity of a space and make it more difficult for a person with dementia to negotiate. In this instance it has the opposite effect to the one which is intended. Cues must therefore be used only with great sensitivity and care.

Managing stimulation

Managing stimulation is also important when designing for movement. There are many areas in residential care settings, for example, where a person with dementia does not need to go.

Staff areas, service areas and storage areas are generally necessary, but are not used by residents. When designing for movement it is essential to highlight where a person is to go and hide areas that are not directly relevant. This can reduce the number of decisions a person with dementia has to make, and help them to focus on areas that are relevant and important to them.

Designing for movement

We also need to address the question, 'How do people move?' Do they walk, use mobility aids, crawl, hobble, shuffle or slide along the ground? How wide does the passage or path need to be to allow for movement?

Gradients and widths

A person who uses a mobility aid is likely to need an area which has a clear width of 1000mm, while a person who uses a wheelchair, or crutches, or a cane for mobility will need a clear width of 1200mm. A clear width of 1500mm will allow a wheelchair and a pram to pass, but 1800mm is required for two wheelchairs to pass comfortably.

Changes in levels also need to be carefully managed. Ramps should be introduced only as necessary, and any gradient should be gradual and continuous. Clear guidelines exist for gradients of ramps. The Australian Standard AS1428.1, for example, sets the maximum gradient of a ramp that is longer than 1520mm as 1 in 14.

Finishes, surfaces and widths

The finishes and surfaces used on circulation routes will be important to assist people to move about easily and with a minimum of risk. Loose pebble paths, for example, are a hazard, particularly for people who may shuffle rather than take clear steps.

Ideally external surfaces should be non-slip and homogenous so that changes in levels over time can be minimised and maintenance reduced. Path surfaces need to be fixed and firm, and surfaces such as asphalt and concrete are generally ideal. Colour additives can be used in both of these to introduce variety and distinguish between different paths and path edges. Brick pavers and tiles should be selected carefully as they can become slippery over time. Where used they should be laid on a firm base with all joints and surfaces flush to avoid tripping hazards. Irregular surfaces such as cobblestones,

flagstones, and timber decking should be avoided.

Internally, surfaces should be selected for ease of walking. Timber floors, for example, are easier on the legs than slate. Where carpets are used they should be dense low pile to facilitate the use of mobility aids. Non-slip tiles can be used, but the abrasive nature of the surface needs to be carefully examined.

Many people with dementia will have difficulty negotiating changes in contrast and patterns in floor and path surfaces. People will often see a pattern or change in colour as an obstacle that needs to be stepped over, or even removed.

The use of patterns and contrasting finishes should be managed carefully so that people do not encounter a path which looks like a minefield full of hazards to be negotiated.

This can, however, be used to advantage to direct people to certain areas and away from others, for example by continuing a carpet border past a door to a service area. Irregular surfaces such as cobblestones, flagstones, and timber decking should not, however, be used as a means of discouraging movement.

Hazards

Hazards which could lead to an accident or injury should be removed from paths and corridors. Externally this may mean cutting back trees so that branches do not overhang, avoiding planting deciduous trees over paths where leaves can fall and get wet, and avoiding the use of grates in paths.

People with dementia will not necessarily look up as they walk, and so may not be able to take evasive action to avoid a hazard. The camber of paths needs to be managed too. While it is good for the path slope to allow rain water to run off and avoid ponding, the cross gradient should not be more than 1:40 so that this does not form another hazard.

Rest spaces

It is important to recognise that some people with dementia may feel the need to move about although they are relatively frail and have limited stamina. Rest spots (see illustration on p91) should be provided at regular intervals so that they are able to rest in appropriate locations, rather than try to perch on a handrail and gain their breath. These can take the form of either internal sitting alcoves (perhaps with a view to outside), or a spot under a verandah, or a seat under a tree. External rest spots should be shaded.

Creating secure environments

Creating a safe and secure environment where people with dementia can walk about is an integral part of designing for movement.

Physical barriers

Fencing is probably one of the first things that people think of when trying to create a secure environment for people with dementia. There is, however, a range of approaches that can be considered, even for this relatively simple design element.

The most obvious approach to fencing is to hide it, for example by planting the fence out with shrubs and plants. This can be seen at Parkside in Elsternwick (Victoria), where the fence has been almost obscured by bushes (see illustraion on p91). This approach creates a contained garden where boundaries are somewhat obscured and not highlighted.

At The Meadows in suburban New South Wales, the service corridor which runs between the different units has been used to delineate the back yards and create a walled garden with clear boundaries.

Another approach has been taken at Flynn Lodge in Alice Springs where the fence has been designed to disappear into the landscape. In this instance residents see through the fence to the Todd River beyond. Most residents in this hostel are used to uninterrupted views to the surrounding country, and so here it was appropriate to make the fence 'disappear' so that people could look through to the landscape (see illustration on p92).

Fences obviously need to be of a height that does not allow residents to climb over them easily. Fences also need to be continuous to the ground so that people cannot go under them. Cross rails need to be minimised and placed externally so that people are not given easy footholds to use to scale the fence. The design of the top of the fence needs to discourage a person from climbing over it, but take into account that people may indeed try to climb it. It must not contain sharp edges that could potentially hurt someone. It is also important to remember that a fence gives a very visible message to people who are both inside and outside it, and so needs to be designed to convey a positive and valued image.

We also need to recognise that our attitude to fencing can be influenced by our cultural background. While for some of us a fence may represent a barrier or an obstacle to be overcome, for others it is an important statement of ownership and possession. It can therefore be seen as a very positive element that marks out territory and defines space. At Flynn Lodge, for example, where there is a secure and non-secure section of the hostel, residents of the non-secure area complained when they moved in that they didn't have a fence!

It is also important to remember that what may be a negative image for one person can be a positive one for another. As we drove past a fence on Arrente (Aboriginal) Lands in Alice Springs, an architect colleague exclaimed: 'Isn't that a terrific fence?' While I saw a large, high, imposing steel fence, she saw something which the people had worked together to build, something which defined their land and identified it from the street.

Use of technology

Another key aspect of creating a secure environment is to monitor and control movement within the site. The use of technology can allow us to create many opportunities for movement in a non-restrictive way.

Technology allows significant freedom and flexibility in design. The use of electronic locks to external doors can allow doors to be located at numerous points in a facility,

yet be controlled in a simple manner. This approach was taken at Flynn Lodge in Alice Springs.

Many of the residents at Flynn Lodge are used to living out of the township of Alice Springs on stations or in bush communities. There is likely to be a close affinity to the land and a strong need to be able to make a connection with the surrounding country. For Aboriginal people it may also be necessary for certain people to avoid contact with others. It was therefore important to allow people to gain direct access to the outdoors, while ensuring that security could be maintained. The use of electronic locks to external doors was integral to the design approach to allow a range of needs to be met.

The choice of staff call system in a facility can also have a big impact on the safety and security of the environment for people with dementia. The use of reed switches on doors can allow people with dementia to come and go, but allow staff to be aware where residents are. The installation of a reed switch will mean that an alarm can be triggered on the staff call system to alert them when a particular door has been opened. Pagers can be carried by staff and used to receive messages instantly, so that staff can respond to a situation wherever they are.

Concluding thoughts

When designing environments for people with dementia we need to recognise the important role that walking can play in their lives, just as it does in many of our own lives.

How do we respond to this? There are many ways in which opportunities for movement can be created. Walking should be planned, and attention given to issues such as visual access, way-finding, orientation devices, cues, the use of familiar elements, redundant cueing and managing stimulation. Circulation routes need to take into account gradient and widths, as well as hazards, finishes, and surfaces. Safety and security is important, but the use of technology can allow creative solutions that meet these requirements while allowing for movement.

Designing for movement should be seen as an opportunity to create interesting internal and external environments for people with dementia. It is a chance to add to the range of experiences that people with dementia can enjoy, experiences that are rich and full of potential and meaning.

Reference
Judd S, Marshall M, Phippen P (eds) (1998) *Design for dementia*. London: Hawker Publications.

8.4 Going out: how assistive technology may help

by CHRISTINE CALDER

We believe that technology can be a valuable tool which helps people to maintain their independence and enhance a person's freedom without unduly increasing any risks that he or she may face, and this is to be welcomed.

Mental Welfare Commission, p1 (2004)

Assistive technology has been described as "any item, piece of equipment, product or system, whether acquired commercially, off the shelf, modified or customised, that is used to increase, maintain or improve functional capabilities of individuals with cognitive, physical or communication disabilities."

Astrid guide, p9 (2000)

Going out and keeping in touch with the local community is very important for people with dementia as for us all, but sometimes people with dementia need help. An assessment of what level of support they need and what they can still safely do for themselves should be undertaken. For example, the person may get lost easily, not dress appropriately, forget how to cross a road safely, be at risk of abuse from others or become overtired when walking too far.

All risks need to be weighed up. Some may be influenced by the community in which the person lives – how well they are known and supported by their neighbours, for example.

The term 'wandering' can have negative connotations but is usually a positive experience which provides much needed physical activity. It is well recognised that physical activity maintains and improves general health and reduces the risk of falling in the elderly. If the use of technology to manage wandering behaviour increases the opportunity of the person to use existing skills and develop new ones, then it merits serious consideration.

Mental Welfare Commission p2 (2004)

If someone tends to get lost, keeping a note of where they usually go is useful. Including the local police in putting this information together can help. Some local shopkeepers may play a key part in reminding the person how to get home. Putting small labels on clothing can help, as can an identity bracelet giving a telephone number of people who can help (but not a home address).

Any of these actions should be discussed with family and professional carers. The person with dementia should give their consent if possible.

Before using technology, other interventions should be considered, such as highly visible clocks, notices on doors reminding the person not to go out, or reminding them to put on a coat and appropriate footwear if they are going out.

Assistive technology in practice

In South Lanarkshire a project was set up, involving 10 people with dementia, to look at whether and how assistive technology could enable people with dementia to continue living at home, while reducing some of the risks identified by carers, the local community or professionals – such as fire, flood and 'inappropriate wandering'. Five of the people taking part in the project were identified as having wandered or being at risk of wandering, or it had been expressed as a concern by the family, the local community or a social worker.

Four of the participants were involved in the project from the outset and one further participant joined the project halfway through, at the request of his family and social worker. The first four were similar in that the main concern was wandering after the last person (a carer) had visited at night and before the next person (another carer) arrived in the morning. These times were generally from 10pm until 8am the next morning.

All four participants were given a community alarm unit and had magnetic door contacts fitted to the front door of their houses. The door contacts are switched on by the last carer who leaves in the evening and switched off by the first person to arrive in the morning.

Each time the door is opened from inside during these pre-set times a signal is sent to the community alarm which then contacts the response centre which operates on a 24-hour basis, and a response is provided based on the assessment.

The key is kept in a key safe box which is similar to a small safe and is accessed by a five-digit code. The key safe box is fitted to the outside of the house and is covered by a black rubber cover which makes it look like a burglar alarm. This has proved to be very successful because most of the participants have a high-level package of care and it would not be appropriate to make duplicate keys for all the people needing access to the house.

The responses vary. One of the participants has his technology, including the door contacts, call-routed to his son's mobile telephone and his son responds when the door contacts are activated. The other participants have a homecare responder who will attend on the activation of the door contacts. For some very fit people, it is more helpful if neighbours agree to respond – they can often assist in helping the person home before s/he has gone too far, and sometimes even before the official responder arrives.

Mrs A

Each of the participants was different, so a technology solution tailored to their individual need was required. Mrs A likes to look along the street in the morning to see if the milk float is on its way. She opens the door every five minutes to see if it's on the way. Because her door is monitored until 8am when the first carer arrives, each time she opens it from 7am onwards activation occurs. This meant a homecare responder was dispatched each time. The problem was resolved by fitting a time delay switch which gives her five minutes to open the door, look for the milk float and come back into the house without an activation occurring. If she does not return after five minutes, a call is raised at the control centre.

Mrs B

Two other participants had quite different patterns of 'wandering'. One of them, Mrs B, is very fit and often leaves the house during the night. She is regularly brought back by the police. In this case the usefulness of door contacts was limited. Although the control centre was alerted as soon as she left the house, Mrs B was able to cover quite a distance before the homecare responders were able to reach her and help her return home.

Mrs B had always been active and out and about with her family when her children were young. Her wish was always to remain at home. Her son, who has welfare guardianship, was keen to assist his mum to do so. The care package was reviewed and her day care increased. A request was also made for some more home support to assist her to go out on the days she did not attend day care. This all made a positive impact on her quality of life, but the 'wandering' continued.

There was an interesting twist at this stage. For unknown reasons, she began leaving the house but closing the door behind her. Since there was a five-minute time delay on the door contacts it meant that the contacts were not activated. This came to light when the police started to bring her home again.

We then contacted the supplier of technology and asked if there was any door monitoring system on the market that could alert the monitoring centre when she left the house during the night, even if she had closed the door behind her. A device, which was still under development, was provided which used a sensor alongside the door contacts.

This meant that the sensor would pick up that she had gone out of the house and when she returned whether she closed the door or not. If she did not return after five minutes an alert was sent out. This period of time allowed her to go into the garden, even at night, but only for five minutes as agreed by all involved in her care.

Mrs B remains at home but 'managing' her wandering continues to be a daily challenge. Her son and daughter are very active in their caring roles and keen to do whatever they can to continue to support their mum at home. Mrs B's general health is still good and the care package works well but whatever interventions are tried in relation to her going out at inappropriate times are only providing a very minimal reduction in the risk she continued to face.

Last year, Mrs B's son contacted the local social work manager and expressed an interest in a personal locator device, which he had seen on a documentary, that he felt might resolve the issue of his mother wandering. The personal locator is worn on the body and Global Positioning Systems (GPS) are used to find the person by tying up the signal on the device worn with the satellite signal. Some time was spent with a local company trying to develop a system which would be suitable. However, this type of device is not available yet due to difficulties such as the fact that if the person wearing a device enters a building the signal is lost. This would not have worked for Mrs B. The personal locator is still under development. If available, and with the right protocols and systems in place, it could provide that essential support to Mrs B and help to keep her at home.

Mr C

Mr C was the final person to join the project. He lives at home but is supported daily by his two daughters. Like Mrs B he is very active and enjoys walking. His daughters are keen to support him to do so. Mr C used to be a shipyard worker; during his working life he left home very early in the morning and walked to work. He followed the same route every day. Since the family had a good knowledge of where he liked to walk to they were happy to live with the 'risk' since he always came home and he generally did not go out during the night. The family began to become concerned when Mr C went missing for a whole weekend. He was spotted on the third day outside a nearby church, by a member of his family who was able to bring him back home. The immediate response from his relatives was they wanted door contacts fitted to be activated 24 hours a day so family members could be contacted any time their dad left home.

After some discussion with the social worker, the family agreed they would try out the same device as was used for Mrs B but have it programmed with a time delay of 30 minutes. This allows Mr C to get halfway along his usual route. If he is not detected by the door sensor coming back after this time, the response centre calls one of his daughters. She then sets out on the route to see how he is going and bring him back if necessary. If the daughters are not available, a responder is dispatched from the monitoring centre. This system is working out quite well for Mr C. Since its installation he has gone missing for one whole day but again was spotted by a family member making his way to 'work at the shipyard'. This family has also asked the social worker to find out more about devices such as personal locators that will allow their dad to go out without anyone having to follow or bring him back but provide the added safety measure that he could be found if he were away too long.

Peace of mind

Carers who completed project questionnaires reported that although the technology did not necessarily reduce the caring role, it provided peace of mind. They could see how the technology reduced some of the risks to the cared-for person staying at home. One carer reported that she no longer had to visit her father in the evening because the technology was in place. She felt that he was safe in the evening and during the night. She said the technology reduced the pressure she felt in her caring role. All of the carers who took part said that they would recommend technology to others.

For all of the participants, monthly 'calls histories' were produced by the 24-hour control centre which provided the project management group with a clear picture of all the activity generated by the equipment. They were able to begin to identify patterns of wandering. This enabled care managers to take a more proactive approach to the person's care package and look at what other supports might be appropriate at the key wandering times identified.

Regular monitoring of the use of the equipment is essential in order that the person's needs continue to be met and that the changes are logged with the care manager.

References

Mental Welfare Commission for Scotland (2004) *Draft principles and guidance on good practice in caring for residents with dementia and related disorders and residents with learning disabilities where consideration is being given to the use of wandering technologies in care homes and hospitals*. Edinburgh: MWCS.

Astrid (2000) *A social and technological response to meeting the needs of individuals with dementia and their carers*. London: Hawker Publications.

I remember when I first came to Britain wandering into a bookstore and being surprised to find a whole section dedicated to 'Walking Guides'. This struck me as faintly bizarre and comical – where I came from people did not as a rule require written instructions to achieve locomotion – but then gradually I learned that there are, in fact, two kinds of walking in Britain, namely the everyday kind that gets you to the pub and, all being well, back home again, and the more earnest type that involves stout boots, Ordnance Survey maps in plastic pouches, rucksacks with sandwiches and flasks of tea, and, in its terminal phase, the wearing of khaki shorts in inappropriate weather.

For years, I watched these walker types toiling off up cloud-hidden hills in wet and savage weather and presumed they were genuinely insane. And then my old friend John Price, who had grown up in Liverpool and spent his youth doing foolish things on sheer-faced crags in the Lakes, encouraged me to join him and a couple of his friends for an amble – that was the word he used – up Haystacks one weekend. I think it was the combination of those two untaxing-sounding words, 'amble' and 'Haystacks', and the promise of lots of drink afterwards, that lulled me from my natural caution.

'Are you sure it's not too hard?' I asked.

'Nah, just an amble,' John insisted.

Well, of course it was anything but an amble. We clambered for hours up vast, perpendicular slopes, over clattering scree and lumpy tussocks, round towering citadels of rock, and emerged at length into a cold, bleak, lofty nether world so remote and forbidding that even the sheep were startled to see us. Beyond it lay even greater and remoter summits that had been quite invisible from the ribbon of black highway thousands of feet below. John and his chums toyed with my will to live in the cruelest possible way; seeing me falling behind, they would lounge around on boulders, smoking and chatting and resting, but the instant I caught up with them with a view to falling at their feet, they would bound up refreshed and, with a few encouraging words, set off anew with large, manly strides, so that I had to stumble after and never got a rest. I gasped and ached and sputtered, and realized that I had never done anything remotely this unnatural before and vowed never to attempt such folly again.

And then, just as I was about to lie down and call for a stretcher, we crested a final rise and found ourselves abruptly, magically, on top of the earth, on a platform in the sky, amid an ocean of swelling summits. I had never seen anything half so beautiful before. 'Fuck me,' I said in a moment of special eloquence and realized I was hooked. Ever since then I had come back whenever they would have me, and never complained and even started tucking my trousers in my socks. I couldn't wait for the morrow.

Bryson, B. (1995) Notes from a Small Island. London: Transworld. (pp224-5)

8.5 Assistive technology to support walking

by FIONA TAYLOR

Mrs Brown, aged 78, was admitted to a residential home after being found in her gas-filled house. This had happened on several occasions and family and neighbours were very worried about both her and their own safety.

Although she had been diagnosed with dementia some years earlier, she was physically very fit and had remained in her own home with support from family and services. She regularly walked to the local shops or took a bus to a nearby town. She usually did return eventually, although sometimes it was very late.

Mrs Brown had attended day care three days per week in a day centre attached to the residential home. This meant she had good relationships with the staff providing care and some people who used the service, and was familiar with the building and surrounding area.

The admission was arranged late at night and Mrs Brown was very distressed. Despite support from her family and staff who knew her, she was clearly very unhappy at not being able to go back home in the immediate future.

Increased anxiety

During the following two weeks Mrs Brown's anxiety increased and she regularly left the building and headed into the surrounding countryside. Police returned her on several occasions. Her previously good relationships with staff and people using the service quickly declined.

Staff felt they needed to keep a close eye on her and tended to follow her. This meant they had to keep leaving other people requiring a service to run to the door every time the door alarm was activated in case Mrs Brown was leaving the building.

Other people using the service became quite angry with her too. Their freedom was restricted as previously open doors into the garden area were now alarmed so staff would know if she left the building. They began to see her as a nuisance and were becoming intolerant.

The community mental health nurse and Mrs Brown's GP suggested medication and a move to a nursing home.

Her family became so anxious that they often shouted at her when they heard she had left the building again, and their previously warm relationship began to cool.

A case conference was called and the possibility of using a 'Wanderguard bracelet' was discussed. Mrs Brown herself recognised the danger she was in but also knew that when she became upset she just needed to get out.

Following agreement with Mrs Brown, her family and key professionals from the local area team, the bracelet was purchased and the system put in place.

Procedures were drawn up locally and staff were encouraged to see the aim of this intervention as to assist her going out safely, not to stop her going out. Mrs Brown's bracelet was programmed into one staff pager. This meant that not all staff were notified every time Mrs Brown left the building and were therefore not abandoning other people who required care.

Additional resources were allocated to ensure that this staff member was not included in the core staffing levels required and so was free to walk with Mrs Brown whenever she left the building. For the first few days the staff member stayed a discreet distance behind Mrs Brown and only approached to offer assistance when she appeared tired, confused or in danger. This assistance was usually to call for a taxi to take them both back to the care home.

As the week progressed Mrs Brown would call the staff member from behind her and encourage the person to walk and chat with her. To avoid them having to rush back to the unit, the cook would often pop out with a flask of soup and two coats and arrangements were made to enable them both to return later in the day.

By the following month, Mrs Brown was starting to check out who was walking with her that day and to call that person when she was ready to go.

Happy ending

Following a further case conference it was agreed that the crisis situation had passed and that Mrs Brown no longer needed the bracelet. Staff now had a clear picture of when she was most likely to want to go out, how far she could walk without getting tired, and where she liked to walk to.

Her care plan was adjusted to coincide with the times she liked to walk and this resulted in her going out with staff at key times every day to collect the papers, deliver the mail and feed the ducks in the local pond.

Her relationship with staff, other people using the service, and her family improved significantly. Mrs Brown was now seen as someone who contributed to life in the unit and no longer a nuisance. She no longer saw staff as 'guards' and began to relate well with them.

During the next few months Mrs Brown began to learn her way to and from the shops and eventually no longer required someone to go with her. She remained in the care home until her death last year.

Therapy

9.1 George: thinking with his feet

by STEPHEN WEY

George truly looked like a man driven. Traipsing down the street in the drizzle, clothes grubby and wet, limping slightly from the blisters on his feet and the fatigue, eyes fixed ahead on a path to a place maybe more in his mind's eye than in the streets ahead. Going nowhere – simply going. He had been missing for nearly 36 hours – not for the first time either (though the longest). Though I and my colleagues had been out looking for him repeatedly, as had the police, it was blind luck that it was I who found him. I was visiting another client at the time and he was many miles from home. I managed to get him to stop and come with me for a cup of tea while I arranged for a nurse to pick him up and take him home and for a check-up with the doctor. He seemed very thankful to see a friendly face. Maybe, deep down, part of him knew he needed to stop – he just didn't know how. I think if we hadn't found him there at that point he could have kept walking and walking till he dropped.

George had only been home from hospital for little over a week. He had been admitted to a dementia assessment ward three weeks previously following a sudden and rapid deterioration at home, where previously he had been managing fairly well. He had a diagnosis of multi-infarct dementia. In hospital things got even worse; George clearly hated being cooped up and managed to escape from the ward three times, each time being brought back by the police. Hospital, it seemed, was doing nothing for him; if anything it was exacerbating the situation as he was going further afield each time, and each time he was brought back seemed to make him more anxious to get away.

Difficult decisions

It was therefore decided that George should return home for a trial period of assessment and support from my team. This was, at the time, a recently created team with the remit of working intensively and assertively with people like George who were seen to be 'on the edge' between hospital and the community – a home assessment and treatment team for people with dementia as an alternative to hospital assessment.

Now, however, it looked as if we might have no choice but to have him readmitted to hospital, probably under the Mental Health Act. He had repeatedly 'wandered' off and got lost nearly every day since returning home – and each time he'd gone in a different direction and walked for many miles before being found. Like it or not, the risks to George were clearly enormous and it seemed it would be hard to justify keeping him at home. As George's key worker, this was going to be one of the hardest decisions I'd ever had to make.

The problem was that at that point it seemed impossible to conceive of a solution that would be 'best' for George. While being at home was becoming increasingly risky we had already witnessed his disastrous reaction to hospital care. The last thing we wanted was for George to be re-admitted under these circumstances, even worse if this might mean him ending up needing to be medicated to 'manage' his 'behaviour' and in all likelihood placed for the long term in secure care. We needed to look for another alternative.

Focus on well-being

Two tools that helped us to explore what might be driving George's actions were a 'wandering' assessment process developed by the Dementia Services Development Centre at the University of Stirling (Allan 1994) and Bradford Dementia Group's 'Well-/ill-being' (WIB) profile (Bruce 2000). We were already using the WIB profile with all clients coming under our care and as we had spent time getting to know George on the ward (as much as possible under the circumstances – we tried to do this with all clients coming to us) we were able tentatively to compare WIB scores from before and after discharge.

I had used the 'wandering' assessment tool before with other clients, and from the outset it had helped to guide the questions we were asking ourselves about George's actions. We were also guided by a philosophy based on the person-centred approach which treated so-called 'challenging behaviours' such as 'wandering' as signifying something for the person experiencing dementia, rather than as aberrations of behaviour brought about as a direct consequence of neurological impairment. Therefore we used the Stirling tool and the WIB profile information to help guide us in trying to enter into George's world, to make George's actions more explicable – to help in finding what might be driving him.

Assessment on the move

Assessing George was not easy in practice, however. He was not much inclined to just sit and talk; his language was impaired as well (more expressively than receptively). Though he could give short direct answers to questions, he found protracted conversation difficult, and of course he was constantly wanting to be on the move. We felt the best approach would be to follow his lead and be on the move with him. In practice this meant trying to accompany him on his walks, at least part of the way. This was difficult, however, because he was often out before people could visit him, so it could be hard to initiate going for a walk with him (though on the occasions when this had been possible he had been perfectly amenable to having company). The solution took some discipline and some flexibility on the part of team members.

We created guidelines for people who managed to catch George out and about or go for a planned walk with him. They were not to try to guide him back home – the aim was primarily to make accompanying him a social process, one of relationship-building. We needed to win his trust; we had confidence that to be able to be with him on his terms would yield more in the long run than trying to force the process using some kind of standardised assessment or trying to achieve a short-term aim such as orienting him to returning back home. Where possible, but only if it did not conflict with the primary aim, they were to try to observe the cues he followed when out and about – things he seemed to be aiming for, patterns in the routes he took, ways he had of orienting himself such as attention to particular types of landmarks, themes emerging in things he said, evidence of awareness of risks such as road safety and so on.

From the WIB profiles conducted on the ward and back at home we could see that George's well-being had plummeted and his ill-being steadily increased during his period on the ward, and that this trend had continued on his return home. In particular, he was expressing feelings of anger and powerlessness and signs of agitation and intense tension. Although at first sight one might expect his well-being to improve once back at home, this would have been naive. It was clear from our walks with George and from listening to what he was saying, that while he was 'oriented' to his home on a practical level (he was able to find his bed, toilet etc), he was increasingly feeling it was not 'home' on an emotional level. Much of this seemed connected with feeling imposed upon by visitors such as the (three times a day) homecare package that had been set up on his discharge from hospital.

George's well-being hit a low point about 10 days after discharge when, worn out physically by the endless walking (not long after the incident described above where I found him) and emotionally by the situation he found himself in, he was beginning to show significant signs of despair and depression. He had felt trapped in hospital, but in some respects returning home had made matters worse because now home felt more like hospital, leaving him with little to hope for.

Radical steps

By the end of George's first week at home, it was looking increasingly as if things were failing badly. To avoid making use of the last resort of re-admission we decided to take a number of radical steps. First, we referred George to an advocate. We felt George was in desperate need of someone to hear his voice and fight his corner, especially if we were having to consider hospital care. Although as practitioners we all like to think we fight in our clients' corners, realistically we have to recognise that we are not free of conflicting pressures and duties of care. We also felt it would be important to have someone challenging us every step of the way to justify ourselves if we did feel we had to seek admission.

Second, we asked ourselves the question, "Are we part of the solution or part of the problem?" In other words,

we had to take a hard look at the service we were providing for George. In particular we took steps to cut down the frequency of visits, and to re-emphasise the social rather than task or goal-oriented nature of visits. As part of this we also decided to cancel homecare services completely, pending review. In practice, although he was on paper getting three visits a day, he was rarely in, so he was not receiving more than one visit most days (usually you could catch him in early morning).

All of this might seem very risky or even foolhardy given that George was going out and getting lost most days – it would at first glance seem more sensible to try to observe and monitor him as much as possible. Indeed this had been the aim of the package of care set up on discharge. However, not only was it not working, it was probably making things worse, so we felt that what was needed was to take a few steps back. It was a risk, only taken after much discussion including with George and his son and daughter, all of whom wanted to pull out all the stops to prevent their dad being admitted to hospital. We felt the risk was a justifiable one. We had to ask ourselves what the alternatives were: what would the risk be to George's well-being if he was admitted to hospital again, or to long-term care?

As well as modifying the package of care we also asked George's GP to review him medically to try to cut his medication to the bare minimum, to try to rule out any possible medical factors in his presentation and as much as feasible give him a 'holiday' from medication. This was evaluated regularly and over the subsequent few weeks medication was re-introduced or changed step-by-step to make it easier to monitor any impact.

Finally, in order to help address further the issue of George not feeling his home was his own, a family friend offered to come and spend a week or so with George, to give him some quality time at home. This meant we could cut down home care visits and thus the number of relatively unfamiliar faces arriving at his door.

Seeking a meaningful role

By this time we had begun to develop a clearer idea about the factors involved in George's drive to keep moving. We had been unable to find much of a pattern to his walks; he didn't seem to go in any particular direction, did not seem to aim for particular landmarks and did not show signs of seeking to return to previous haunts. However, we did find that if he went out for a short walk with a particular goal, such as to the local shops, he was consistently able to find his own way home again. We could see from this that his mental map of his immediate vicinity was still relatively intact; as long as he stayed within these limits he was able to find his way around. Because of his emotional distress, however, he was being driven to go beyond these limits and therefore getting lost.

We reasoned that if we could find ways to improve his well-being and reduce his level of distress, it was possible that he would stick more to his boundaries. We also found that a recurring theme in his speech (often he would talk to himself while walking) was that of his former work as an electrician. So it was possible that as well as seeking to get away from a sense of feeling disempowered and trapped, there was also a more positive motivation: seeking for occupation and a meaningful social role.

This was especially significant: contained within George's actions were clues not just to what was driving him to keep walking till he got lost, but also to factors that could potentially improve his well-being. As a practitioner influenced strongly by humanistic philosophy, I could see here evidence that people, even in severe distress and confusion, contain within them a positive striving for integration and development. Paradoxically, the seeds of George's future development were contained within actions ('behaviours') that a more simplistic model of care would seek to stop and 'manage'.

Well-being improved?

All of these changes began to bring about benefits, some almost immediately. We started to see the first improvements in George's well-being after his friend moved in with him and the frequency of homecare visits was reduced. These improvements largely took the form of greater relaxation: he smiled more, he stayed in more. Because we knew his friend was going to stay just for a week or so, we also attempted to lay the foundations of a longer-term well-being programme.

As part of this we sought to introduce George to a day centre. It was becoming clear that under the right conditions George could enjoy social contact with people he counted as friends, so we wanted to provide opportunities for this after his old friend had returned home. We also reasoned that this might help him meet his need for occupation and a sense of having a social role. However, as is often the case, it wasn't quite so simple in practice. We tried on several occasions to take George to the day centre but on each occasion he refused to go in. We thought it was possible he associated it with hospital or thought we were taking him to hospital or even to a home. So again we had to try a different approach.

As well as having been an electrician George had been a keen model maker. He still had some very detailed and beautiful hand crafted wooden models of ships and aeroplanes in his house and used to enjoy looking at them with a visitor; he was, rightly, very proud of them. I spent some time exploring ways to help George engage in a woodwork-based activity that on the one hand would not be too complex to make him feel a failure, but on the other would not be perceived as patronising. In the end we hit upon making some cut-out wooden shapes of birds and other objects – he had made similar pieces for his garden in the past. George was able to sand and paint these shapes while I did the cutting out, and he found this acceptable and enjoyable. He seemed particularly to enjoy working with me. There is an unspoken bond that forms when people share a common activity: communication flows through the activity and this sort of 'meeting' through the medium of occupation is itself a rich source of well-being.

Initially we did the model making at George's house. At the same time his potential key worker from the day centre came to visit him at home to build up a relationship with him. Luckily the day centre was within walking distance from George's house so when we felt it was appropriate I suggested to George that we continue to do the woodwork at the day centre and walked with him to the centre on several occasions. The aim was for George to begin to associate going to the day centre with having a work-like role. Because he associated it with a work activity and knew someone there, this time he was happy to go, and he continued to attend after his friend had left. Eventually he made a number of good friends at the centre and continued to attend to maintain those friendships more than 'to go to work'.

The improvements in George's well-being continued well after his old friend had returned home. Although there was a slight dip straight afterwards we ended up with a period where his WIB profile was relatively stable. As predicted, although George continued to be an active and independent person who liked to go out and to have his own space, he began to confine his walks more to his immediate locality, to limits he could handle, and the frequency of occasions when he became lost diminished to acceptable levels. He continued to attend the day centre after we discharged him from our team's care, and he was eventually offered more days there. George continued to live in the community for another two and a half years, attending the day centre throughout, until sadly he passed away following a further stroke, this time more severe.

Take a step back

I learnt a lot from George. Firstly I learnt – the hard way perhaps – that if you are standing too close you can't see the wood for the trees. You need to take a few steps back, even if sometimes that means taking a few risks. You need to let people be. On a deeper level he helped provide evidence for the theory proposed by Kitwood and other advocates of the person-centred approach that what we describe as 'challenging behaviour' is very often the only way a person can get their message across. In George's case the message was that he needed to get away from situations where he felt powerless and trapped. This is a very normal thing to do.

At the same time he was also looking for ways to make his world more meaningful by recapturing activities and roles that at one time afforded him a position in the world: status, power, self esteem, even hope. These are all things which we all need but which were being taken away from him, not just by being put in hospital – that was just one factor in a negative spiral of blows to his self-esteem and hope. These also included his own reactions to his inability to do things he had always done, to his speech disability, and the reactions of those around him.

Actions and opportunities

My own view of phenomena like walking and other such challenges is that we need to transform 'behaviour' into 'actions', and 'problems' into 'opportunities'. Firstly, people act; they don't 'behave'. People's actions are socially mediated and embodied – they not only signify something both to the actor and 'audience', but they are also a means of practically making a mark on the world, a way of understanding it and changing it to suit better our needs and wishes.

Walking, for example, is an activity rich with meaning and symbolism. It enables people to feel free to move around, even just to enjoy being an embodied person who can move. It enables people to get to places they are attached to, or get away from things they don't like. It enables people to maintain their physical and mental health, through exercise and through social contact with others. When I say we 'understand' the world through acting upon it, I think it's important to move away from too 'mentalistic' a view of understanding and cognition (including memory). We usually grasp things with our hands before we grasp them in our minds; people think and perceive through doing – through actively engaging in the world around them with their whole bodies including in social processes and occupations such as walking or working, not by just sitting passively and watching the world go by (Wertsch 2000).

Embodied cognition also includes remembering things through our actions and bodies. A walk, for example, can bring back memories of things in a way that just sitting and talking about them cannot. If I sit in a church it immediately takes me back to my childhood – my whole body contains senses that activate these memories. So for George, walking brought back memories of when he used to work, memories from a time when he probably felt more in control of his life or experienced a greater sense of well-being. Through his actions, he was attempting to provide himself with the conditions he needed to work through his feelings and the obstacles he was encountering in his life.

To me, George's need to keep going was an attempt to make sense of the world around him. He wasn't just communicating something to us; he was, more fundamentally, attempting to work through problems that had been put in his path, through action, through doing, through walking. The challenge for us was not the 'problem' set by his actions insofar as they placed him at risk, it was to create a set of conditions that would help him to work through some of these 'problems' for himself.

Transforming problems into opportunities means learning to recognise this positive striving in all such actions and to facilitate this positive process – indeed to form what I see as a therapeutic alliance with the person. For example, if we think about walking as a 'problem', we need to find ways to stop, manage or limit it. If we see that contained in this set of actions is a striving to make sense of and act on what is going on in a person's life – a life that may have drastically changed without keeping them fully 'in the loop' – we should see it as an opportunity for meaningful therapeutic contact. To seek to curtail such actions not only does a disservice to our clients by blocking emergent tendencies within the person for growth, integration and resolution, but we would also effectively be shooting ourselves in the foot by inhibiting the processes we should be aiming to engage with as therapists, practitioners and carers.

References

Allan K (1994) *Wandering*. Stirling: Dementia Services Development Centre.
Bruce E (2000) Looking after well-being – A tool for evaluation. *Journal of Dementia Care* 8(6) 25-27.
Wertsch J (2000) *Mind as action*. London: Oxford University Press.

Wandering around and restlessness is one of the by-products of Alzheimer's disease. Many people have tried to guess why Alzheimer's disease patients are so restless and want to walk around at all hours of day and night. I believe I may have a clue. When the darkness and emptiness fill my mind, it is totally terrifying. I cannot think my way out of it. It stays there, and sometimes images stay stuck in my mind. Thoughts increasingly haunt me. The only way that I can break this cycle is to move. Vigorous exercise to the point of exhaustion gets my mind out of the black hole.

Davis, R. (1993) My journey into Alzheimer's disease.
Amersham-on-the-Hill: Scripture Press Foundation. (pp108-109)

9.2 Walking: a slog or a pleasure?

by JAMES McKILLOP

Using my feet has meant differing things at different times over the years. From my first toddling steps to skipping along beside my mother, to tearing around at childhood games, to punting in the winning goal at Hampden (in dreams), to boosting my arms when swimming, to pedalling along a long highway, to chasing after the fair sex, to dancing to a rock-'n'roll melody, to paying penance for feet compressed into (then) fashionable winkle-pickers, to hiking through the hills, to marching behind a CND banner, to walking on air down the aisle, to plodding along behind a bawling pram, to chasing after my squealing children in parks, to a more sedate adult walk, and now to a hirpling, painful gait which restricts but fails to immobilise.

The list of peripatetic journeys goes on ad infinitum. Everyone will have their own favourite memories of where their feet happily wandered. Some (postmen, footballers etc) have their feet to thank for earning them a living.

Wherever I ventured, whatever I did, my feet have been there – friends in need indeed. We had a tacit agreement, I looked after them and they looked out for me. They were in symphony with my feelings and readily sprouted wings when I was in a buoyant mood and could speed me away when the going got tough.

Now, after a lifetime of use in almost every possible scenario, my feet have regrettably, though inexorably, limited my horizons and restricted my mobility, though thankfully they remain faithfully willing and ambulant. So what can my feet do now? Can they provide a mental medicinal effect? What does walking really mean to me now?

It is an axiom (among those who deal with our grey matter) that the brain will atrophy, as surely as muscles do, if unused. I have found this to be true in my case. When my feet had a month's rest when I was laid low with a back complaint, I found my short-term memory and my powers of reasoning and deduction fell away quite drastically. My feet need to keep me in community circulation so that my mind is continuously stimulated.

Apart from the obvious, as in getting from A to B, walking now also has a cathartic effect on my mind, confused with dementia, when I am wresting with a problem. Walking helps to blow away the cobwebs, leaving my subconscious clear to muse over a problem and/or to allow my creativity to come to the fore.

When song writing, where I have been stymied from finding a word to rhyme, I have gone on an amble with no clear destination in mind, and an appropriate word has come to me mid-step. The only problem is having a means of recording the word, on paper or mini-cassette etc, otherwise I will forget it, and that would never do.

Sometimes I question myself if I am the epitome of someone with dementia. I would like to think so. Years ago 'we' were segregated and not allowed to meet socially. That has changed. Now I meet people with my illness, and I am gratified to discover from them that there is an untapped reservoir of talent out there.

To my fellow travellers I commend – a simple walk.

Walking with

10

10.1 The art of walking: meeting with Edith

by CLAIRE CRAIG

Walking is a creative act, an art form. The length of stride, the movement of the body, the gait, arm swing, the pace and rhythm of each step are all unique to the individual. It is the means of joining inner to outer, a way to connect, to communicate feelings (how often have you stomped with anger?). I once asked a gentleman on a hospital ward why he spent his every waking moment walking up and down the corridor. He said simply, "It makes me feel connected to myself." Each step we take can be an expression of something deeper within, whether it is the desire to be somewhere, or to move, to gain space, to explore, to conquer, to achieve or to think.

Essentially, creative approaches to walking look beyond the mechanics of the way we walk. They seek the person and ways to uncover the meaning, the significance of each journey for that individual, whether it is spiritual, physical or emotional. In this journey with the person it may be useful to think about roles, or routines, or reminiscence. It is also useful to think about where walking takes place, since it does not occur in a void but in a context which will have meaning to the individual and will evoke unique responses and emotions.

This chapter will consider all these elements. Above all, it will describe part of my journey with a lady with dementia for whom walking had particular significance. In describing this journey it will illustrate that how we walk, why we walk and where we walk express as much about who we are as the way we look and think and breathe.

Limited horizons

When you hear the word 'walking', what images spring to mind? A favourite place, a leisure activity, a specific memory, an emotion, a feeling of being out in the fresh air with the senses engaged, spending time with friends or family members, a time for thinking?

Walking in hospital or residential care settings is often a very different experience. Wards, locked for the safety of the individuals who reside there, can be restrictive, confining. I have often heard members of staff describe individuals as 'pacing up and down', where the need to pace arises because of the limited space within the environment itself. The corridor might be the only place to walk.

Environments may be impersonal and lack stimulation; walking in such spaces can lose its sense of purpose. The difference is like that between walking on a treadmill in a dull, sterile room and walking in the countryside, around an art gallery, or even round a supermarket. On the treadmill the emphasis is very much concentrated on the physical movement, whereas the other settings engage the senses, provide a focus, create a sense of purpose and enjoyment.

The following description illustrates how, for one lady with dementia, this sense of purposefulness was at the heart of walking. As she once told me, if there is nowhere to walk to, what is the point of embarking on such a journey?

A working life

Edith was the kind of person that you wouldn't forget in a hurry. She was very striking – slender with a shock of grey hair piled on top of her head. Her eyes were of the palest blue. Everything about her seemed ordered: the way she sat, the way she placed her hands. In spite of sitting in an oversized hospital dressing gown, she still managed to carry about her an air of elegance. When she spoke, her voice almost sang, although it was clear that dementia had affected her speech. Once she had confided that she had difficulties making the words go where she wanted them to, and I understood completely what she meant.

I remember Edith for lots of reasons. She was the kind of person who inspired you just by the way she was. When I was thinking about creative approaches to walking, she particularly came to mind. I first met Edith while working on a busy assessment ward in a hospital setting, when I was asked to see her specifically with a view to engaging her in activities which would help her to move, to 'mobilise' – to walk.

Edith had initially been admitted to hospital because her physical health had deteriorated. Her chest infection was serious and, although she was receiving intensive physiotherapy, the concern was that unless she started to move complications would develop which could threaten her life. Walking for Edith in this way was not a luxury, it was a necessity.

We didn't get off to a particularly good start. I think that I was so intent on telling her about the importance of walking, conveying a sense of urgency, that I didn't really listen. In response to my request to come for a walk with me, she looked me in the eye, raised her eyebrow and said,

"Why do you want to do that? There's nothing to see."

I couldn't really respond to this. The difficulty was that Edith was right, there literally was nothing to see. The ward was like any other hospital ward, a lounge area, dining room with tables and bed bays. There was a corridor leading to the nurse's office which was adorned with a few picture postcard images, the kind that you might see on calendars or birthday cards, but nothing else.

They say that the longest of journeys can start with a single step. This was my first step in a much longer journey with Edith. Edith would not be encouraged, cajoled, or persuaded to walk for walking's sake. Over the following weeks I learned much about Edith, about myself and about creative approaches to walking.

From the very first meeting Edith made it clear in no uncertain terms that walking was not just about enjoying the process of getting from A to B. It had to have a purpose. She once tutted, pursing her lips at my suggestion of a stroll in the grounds. She rolled her eyes and said, "Strolling, idling more like, I know your sort".

Wounded, at least I knew where to start. I devised a gentle programme based around different 'tasks' as I called them. A stroll in the garden, for instance, became a gardening activity, or a walk to collect flowers for the sitting room. A meander down the corridor became a journey to collect post from reception ("collecting my pension", she called it). A trip to the kitchen was focused on selecting biscuits for the other residents on the ward.

It was all about how the walk was described. The more it sounded like work, the more eager Edith was to take part. Sometimes she would take great delight in sending me on even longer and harder journeys, relishing her sense of control.

Her daughter later told me that Edith had worked from the age of 14; that she was a lady of great principles; her work ethic ran deep. To Edith, walking was completely integral to having a role. Just because she was living temporarily in a different environment did not change who she was or what was important to her. Walking at home was about completing jobs, retaining a sense of control over what she did and ultimately who she was.

We once dusted the occupational therapy department together. Days before, I had watched Edith reluctantly taking part in chair exercises, hardly lifting her arms. Yet with a duster in her hand Edith walked the length and breadth of the department – stretching and bending in almost acrobatic poses in order to reach the tiniest specks of dust, invisible to the human eye. Her sense of accomplishment on completion of this activity was tangible, although she complained bitterly at my feeble efforts.

Responsibility and routine

I learned that Edith loved responsibility, and again tried to build this into activities based around walking and movement. We painted a frieze which ran the entire length of the ward's corridor, and with great pleasure I watched Edith walk up and down, commenting on the efforts of staff and other residents, monitoring their work. When the frieze was completed she would often walk the length of the corridor, "inspecting the work", and at times we would have conversations about the colours, about memories of her youth; the images on the frieze acted as a focus and gave her walk a sense of purpose.

I discovered other things about this remarkable lady. For instance, routine was important to her. She really enjoyed walking with me to the hospital reception first thing in the morning to collect the post and the ward's

paper. She particularly liked taking the route outside instead of the labyrinth of inner passages. At the time I was sure that it was because she enjoyed the wonderful scents and colours and sensations in the grounds, the fresh air as opposed to the sterile atmosphere of the hospital. We would often walk the route in silence, pausing to take in a view, to smell a flower or to touch a shrub, and spend time savouring the sensations. Looking back now I can't help wondering whether it was the familiarity of the route that she enjoyed – whether there was something that felt 'safe' about that walk.

I wished that I could have taken Edith on longer walks outside the hospital grounds, to places near her home which she often talked about. Her daughter brought in a photograph album; we spent time together looking at places she had visited, and I came to understand the significance of walking in her life. She described the long trek to work, rising at first light to the sound of clogs on cobbles as the miners from the night shift returned to their beds. She told me of once walking to Scarborough in search of employment. Walking had been her only form of transport. It was a way of life.

A social activity

Edith told me of the Whit walks, great religious occasions she had taken part in, dressing up, the sheer pleasure of the social gathering. Taking her lead, we organised an afternoon outing within the hospital. It was a familiar route to the canteen, but the difference was that we made it into an occasion. Everyone dressed in their 'Sunday best' and relatives joined us for tea and cake. There was a great sharing of stories.

I realised for the first time the importance that many of the individuals I worked with placed on the act of dressing up – wearing a coat and proper shoes and a hat or scarf. The occasion didn't matter – whether it was a walk in the grounds or outside the hospital, or the simple act of leaving the ward to travel the short distance to the canteen, looking one's best was central. It brought back deeper memories for me, as I remembered how my own grandmother would not leave the house unless her hair was immaculate and her dress smart.

Edith helped me to rediscover the social significance of walking. I think she enjoyed the contact, the sense of being connected. Often she would link arms and if we were accompanied by another person she would link arms with them too. At times when more people joined us we would form a kind of human chain. Walking in this way was fun. There was always the sense that you had been transported somewhere in time. Often if a record was playing in the background on the ward I would move in time to the music. Sometimes people would waltz across the floor to the dining room with me or join me in a jig. These times were precious because it was possible to catch a glimpse of who that person was simply by the way they moved.

Before I met Edith I had been very focused that any activity, whether walking or otherwise, should take place during the day. Yet Edith loved to have an evening stroll before going to bed. At this time in the peace of the grounds the scent of the flowers seemed stronger, our senses heightened. The light would cast different shadows making the garden dance. During this evening stroll Edith would tell me of her husband and how walking had been part of their courtship. Sometimes her memory and words would become 'foggy' as she called it, but during those times she would link her arm through mine and we would gently walk through the grounds as though we were old friends in a familiar garden.

Valuable lessons

To our delight, Edith finally returned home to live with her daughter. Years have passed yet she is never forgotten.

She was such an inspiring lady who taught me a number of valuable lessons. She taught me above all that creative approaches to walking begin with the person. They are about individuality and everyone will be different. For some people the importance will be on the social component, for others a sense of achievement, a way to explore an environment, to enjoy the leisure aspect and have a 'change of scenery'. Yet whatever the reason, if we can take time to understand the personal significance of walking for the person with dementia, then it becomes possible to create quite remarkable opportunities to communicate, to come alongside that person, to engage with them and, ultimately, for our worlds to overlap.

10.2 Walking with dogs: an alternative therapy

by GILLIAN McCOLGAN

Love them or hate them, dogs are a part of our society. Their behaviours and roles reflect cultural aspects back to us, some of which are more desirable than others. Our personal experiences of and attitudes towards dogs in part determine which aspects we focus upon. I make no apologies for focusing on the positive, as for me there are few greater pleasures than walking with dogs.

Dogs are widely used to help people with sensory and ambulatory impairments and can be trained to fetch and carry objects, load washing machines and alert people to dangers, alarms, telephones and doorbells. One dog in Britain has recently been trained to help a profoundly deaf client who also has failing eyesight (Menteith 2004). With the support of her dual trained dog, she can continue to live independently and go out walking again. Studies have also suggested health and therapeutic benefits from contact with dogs, for instance in increased one-year survival rates for recovering coronary care patients (Friedmann et al 1980) and in lowering of blood pressure levels when a dog is present (Katcher et al 1983; Friedmann et al 1983).

Undoubtedly, the exercise gained by walking a dog is beneficial. Dog walkers have reported taking longer walks with a dog than without one (Serpell 1991). They have also agreed that their dog has made friends for them and presented opportunities for interactions with other people (Adell-Bath et al 1979). Walking with dogs presents the opportunity to both exercise and socialise. This was confirmed in the research interviews I undertook with people in their own homes (McColgan 1996).

Six people were interviewed individually, with their dogs, to explore the relationships they had. Among the advantages they listed were companionship, security and doing more as a result of having dogs. Overwhelmingly, research participants said that by going on walks with their dogs they met other people, and that the dogs often

acted as a catalyst for conversation. For instance, one interviewee said:

> Because I live in a flat I have to take him out a lot. Sometimes before [I had a dog] I wouldn't see anyone all weekend. If I went to the town I often didn't talk to anyone. When I'm out with him in the park other people come and talk to Brand, then they notice me and talk to me as well.
> [Interview with Julie, 22 year old].

This was also my own experience of living in a village with a dog. I knew the names of most dogs I saw on a regular basis. I also learned most of the local news through talking to other dog owners while dog walking. A quotation from another interview also concerns walking:

> I can't be bothered going out myself, I know I should, the doctor said I need to for my heart. But see, the dog always wants to go, so I take him for a walk and I enjoy it when I'm out. It's like he knows I'll like it and he makes me go.
> [Interview with Bruce, 70 year old]

This same research informant provided me with a short story he had written as an obituary for his previous dog. In it, naughty antics became funny anecdotes and the storyteller described something he loved about his dog – the high regard he had for his owner: "He was something special ... I was his boss, and wherever I went he was with me. If I walked anywhere he was at my heels all the time" (Bruce's story). Later Bruce's wife developed dementia, and while she was able to remain living at home she often accompanied Bruce and Tiger on their

Dogs offer practical and emotional support to people with and without impairments, providing support to exercise and to meet other people.

walks. This appeared to offer a degree of routine in their world otherwise turned upside down by dementia.

Independence and companionship

Older people and people with dementia, even if they have owned dogs, have often given them up or failed to replace old dogs when they die because they are unable to care for them and exercise them. However, people with dementia often remain physically active and can enjoy regular walks. Rikki Fulton, the Scottish comedian who died early in 2004, had Alzheimer's disease and was fortunate in maintaining the companionship of his West Highland terrier while he remained at home with his wife. In a documentary on living with Alzheimer's disease Rikki joked that his dog often brought him home when he had forgotten the way (Wark Clements 2003).

In the course of research with older people I was told of another man with dementia who also continued to walk with his dog. He was a local man, with family living close by and was well known to neighbours. When he was out, neighbours understood that he might sometimes need help in finding his way home and were happy to walk with him or show him the way. It enabled independence and choice to be maintained and continuation of the walks he had taken for many years with his dog.

Further evidence of the therapeutic effect of contact with dogs and specifically walking with dogs can be found in an animal-assisted therapy scheme in Essex (Society for Campanion Animal Studies 2003). In the scheme, which is incorporated into service users' care plans, dogs are used

to work with people with a variety of mental health problems, including one person with a diagnosis of Alzheimer's disease. The scheme includes dog walking. Meeting the dogs, helping to take responsibility for them and then accompanying them on walks, has been greeted enthusiastically by participants. A social care development worker uses her own dogs who have been temperament-tested for suitability as therapy dogs.

For some service users it is the first time they have been outside their homes for many years; they are now exercising and socialising both with dogs and with people they meet while out. It has proved to be particularly beneficial to the service user with dementia, as before walking with the therapy dogs she had gone on walks with her spouse at a very fast pace. These rapid walks had proved to be stressful for the spouse and presumably also for his wife. Walking with the dog, the service user had adjusted her pace in line with the speed of the dog and thus reduced the stress for all accompanying walkers.

Walking with dogs is not for everyone. Some people do not like dogs, others do not like walking and would not choose to walk, and a number of people are also prevented from walking because of mobility impairments. However, for those able and choosing to walk there do appear to be clear benefits from walking with dogs. Bruce would not have gone out walking alone but did with his dog and so had exercise. Julie would have remained socially isolated if she did not go out walking with her dog. Like people on the animal-assisted therapy scheme in Essex, Julie met and talked to people through her dog.

Dogs offer practical and emotional support to people with and without impairments. When people are able and want to walk, dogs also offer support to exercise and meet other people. People with dementia are often physically fit and want to walk. Walking with dogs might offer support, focus and meaning to these walks and perhaps serve as an alternative and additional therapy for people who have dementia.

References

Adell-Bath, M Krook A, Sandqvist G, Skantze K (1979) *Do we need dogs? A study of dogs' social significance to man*. Gothenburg: University of Gothenburg Press.

Friedmann E, Katcher AH, Lynch JJ, Thomas SA (1980) Animal companions and one year survival of patients after discharge from a coronary care unit. *Public Health Reports* 95, 307-12.

Friedmann E, Katcher AH, Thomas SA, Lynch JJ and Messent PR (1983) Social interaction and blood pressure: Influence of animal companions. *Journal of Nervous and Mental Disease* 171, 461-465.

Katcher AH, Friedmann E, Beck AAM, Lynch J (1983) Looking, talking, and blood pressure: the physiological consequences of interaction with the living environment. In Katcher AH and Beck AM (eds) *New perspectives on our lives with companion animals*. Philadelphia: University of Pennsylvania Press.

McColgan GM (1996) Dogs as significant others: an exploration into the relationships between people and dogs. University of Stirling: Unpublished dissertation.

Menteith C (2004) Two minds are better than one. *Dogs Today* May publication, Chobham, Surrey: Pets Subjects.

Serpell JA (1991) Beneficial effects of pet ownership on some aspects of human health and behaviour. *Journal of the Royal Society of Medicine*, 84, 717-720.

Society for Campanion Animal Studies (2003) 'Animals assisted therapy in Essex', *Society for Companion Animal Studies Journal*, XV(4).

Wark Clements (Producers) (2003) 'Kirsty meets Kate and Rikki Fulton', in series *Lives Less Ordinary*, BBC Scotland, transmitted 3rd March 2003.

10.3 Spirited walking

by ROSALIE HUDSON

The word 'wandering' has unfortunate connotations when associated with dementia. Rather than concentrating on 'wandering' as a problem to be solved, this chapter on 'spirited walking' is intended to promote a more hopeful and helpful approach.

To begin, a brief excursion into the Judeo-Christian scriptures shows that wandering has particular significance as a spiritual journey. The Jewish liturgy of offering and response before the altar has its roots in this Old Testament passage:

> A wandering Aramean was my ancestor: he went down into Egypt and lived there as an alien, few in number, and there he became a great nation, mighty and populous. . . we cried to the Lord, the God of our ancestors: the Lord heard our voice and saw our affliction, our toil, and our oppression. The Lord brought us out of Egypt with a mighty hand and an outstretched arm . . .
>
> *(Deuteronomy 26: 5-9).*

The wandering of the Israelites is their history - their memory of who they are as a people, as a nation. As Jenson says:

> . . . in Israel's memory, Exodus was inseparable from forty years' wandering in the desert, in which the Lord figures as the dangerous leader of a journey whose final end was geographically chancy and temporally unknown, and whose possibility depended every morning on the Lord's new mercy' (Jenson 1997, p67).

This Old Testament reference and commentary may well direct our thoughts to the meaning of 'wandering' in the alien land of dementia. First, the Israelites' journey was not without danger, nor was their destination always evident. Second, they were often overcome with weariness and frustration, wondering who would redirect them. Third, although they were not always aware of it, they were not left alone and without hope. And, finally, they recognised their dependence on the transcendent God who proved forever faithful to them. Theirs was a 'spiritual wandering' whose purpose and destination were not dependent on their understanding. Whether or not we share this Judeo-Christian understanding of wandering, it may provide some useful metaphors for the care of people with dementia.

In this chapter, the term 'spirited walking' is intended to convey the association between walking and an exploration into the heart, or soul or spirit of the walker. Spirited walking also invites a companion, so the essence of spirituality in this context will be shown to reside in mutual relationships.

'Walking through' – spiritual assessment

Much that is written about spirituality in health care is now directed towards assessment tools, documented plans and quantitative outcomes. To explore this issue in relation to a person with dementia is to go deeper than the surface, to a level of insight, understanding, imagination, intuition and creativity. When spirituality is understood merely as an explicitly religious component of life, carers may be tempted to look no further than the person's religious denominational category and/or to call the chaplain. When, however, spirituality is understood as the essence of a person, other paths will open up, inviting the carer to walk beside the person who has dementia, discovering together this person's unique spirit. This focus of care is illustrated by the following personal example.

Flo's journey

I phoned the nursing home to find out how my mother-in-law was settling in to her new environment, as I was out of town for a few days. As Flo was no longer able to communicate meaningfully by phone, I was dependent on the nurse's account: "Well, I'm absolutely delighted to tell you that right now she's being accompanied on her third circuit of the nursing home. I've overheard snatches of the conversation. Florence seems to be telling Margot (the nurse) how she hates her middle name and also much prefers 'Flo' to 'Florence'. We've all been astonished because we didn't think Florence could walk or talk so well. We've also been using her full name; I'll now make sure we call her Flo. It's lovely to see her, arm in arm with Margot, chatting animatedly as though she'd known her forever."

For my own part, I was elated to have this news of Flo, whose path towards nursing home entry had been rocky, to say the least. I found when I hung up the phone that I had made no enquiries nor been given any information about her many and various medical problems. What was conveyed to me was part of Flo's journey. This was welcome news indeed.

Although the nurse in this episode may not have considered herself to be engaged in spiritual care, the idea of a spiritual sojourner springs to mind. With our propensity for fast trips and technological support for most of our movements, the image of walking along a road with another person does not appear the most efficient means of travel. Given the length of the journey into dementia,

Sue Benson/Darnall Dementia Group

Spirited walking is dependent on carers offering companionship, rather than waiting to be asked.

however, the metaphor of a sojourn may be apt. One of the meanings of sojourn is to 'tarry', not something we care for in our busy lives. This nurse had, for a few minutes at least, left the comfortable, familiar road of care plans and tasks, taking the cue from Flo's agitation and restlessness, to join her on a journey that revealed something of Flo's essential nature.

In a few minutes of spirited walking the nurse (unintentionally) invited Flo to tell her about herself. The road map may not have been precisely clear, but the sojourning together was more important than either the route or the destination. My mother-in-law probably had no idea of Margot's status as professional nurse; this excursion was spiritual because it was personal and relational. Margot was not merely fulfilling a functional role; she was offering her personal presence. Margot also conveyed some of her own spirit in this particular situation; she became for a few brief moments Flo's partner and companion and friend, not merely supervisor of Flo's safety. She did not remain on the side of the road analysing every movement, seeking a solution to every perceived problem; rather, she joined Flo on her 'road to dementia', as one human being alongside another.

Spiritual presence as communal

Orchard raises the question of "what happens when there is no presence" (Orchard 2001, p147). Looking at the flipside of presence, we may well ask what it means for the person with dementia to be left to wander or walk alone. Orchard's question arises from the belief that spiritual needs are communal, not merely individual. Spirited walking, therefore, involves the whole community of care, whether the home of the person with dementia, the day care centre, or the 24-hour residential care setting. The culture of care that is attuned to the spiritual as well as to the physical will embrace the person with dementia communally. When the spiritual dimension is included, staff and other carers' attitudes towards those who 'wander' will no longer be focused on tasks and efficiency and supervision as the only factors to consider. Such a change in culture will not frown on 'wandering'; rather it will be

taken up communally. As Seedsman says, the essence of this culture is our shared humanity:

> Any management philosophy and related practice concerned with the care of the frail aged must take total responsibility for its human consequences. As a criterion, efficiency alone has never been, nor will it ever be, the hallmark of humane care... *For those who work genuinely with and for the frail aged, the power of workplace socialization and familiarity is such that there is the constant danger of becoming a spectator rather than an active participant in the processes that sustain meaningful existence. The worth of a human life is validated when those in a position to do so make the effort to understand and work with the total person – the soma and the psyche.*
>
> *(Seedsman, 1994).*

Seedsman's call for humane care is also a call to acknowledge the essence or soul of our own community. To discover this spiritual centre is to view dementia care in a different way. This is a far cry from the custodial view of care that sees carers in the role of supervisors and protectors. While these factors have their place and the issue of safety certainly comes within every duty of care, spirited walking invites the active participation of the carer. We may say that in the context of dementia care it is more important to have a philosophy about the meaning and purpose of care than a list of interventions, recreational diversions and a costly review of physical surroundings. These factors all have their place, particularly in 24-hour residential care, but they are ultimately of secondary importance to issues of meaning and purpose. "Overzealous risk management may protect a physical body from bruising but it may also damage irreparably the already vulnerable human soul" (Nay 2002).

Risky walking

What risks are inherent in spirited walking? When walking is considered by carers as problematic behaviour to be curbed, the supervising carer is not put at risk for he or she is merely overseeing the care. Protected by a wall of power and status, backed by legislated policies, the carer takes on the role of policing, watching out for dangers, even attempting to 'cure' the problem. On the other hand, spirited walking usually involves letting go of protective behaviour in order to walk together, hand in hand, arm in arm, sharing the experience.

Duty of care and protection from harm is of course a key component in caring for the person with dementia. Risk, however, involves more than identifying physical obstacles. What of the fears and anxieties of the person with dementia? Are they not at risk if a companion is not available? Is the person with dementia not at risk of loneliness, isolation and boredom when left to walk alone, or when prevented from walking?

And what about risks for the carer? Spirited walking may involve the risk of looking ridiculous as one tries various strategies to manoeuvre the person with dementia away from inappropriate routes. It may involve the risk of one's conversation being overheard when that conversation seems like a flight into fantasy. It may involve risk when the person with dementia lets go of inhibitions and social graces. The challenge for the carer is to 'hold on' rather than to let go. Taking on an air of detachment, the carer remains aloof and untouched. Taking on a degree of risk, the carer says in both word and gesture, 'I am with you.'

Woman to woman

In the following illustration, Jan the night nurse took a risk. She would not have categorised this episode as spiritual care. She would, however, have acknowledged the frustration of trying to deal with Alice's 'spirited walking' up and down the corridor, in and out of the nurses' office, hour after hour, night after night. She had tried all the persuasive arguments to deter Alice from her constant pacing, with no effect. Finally, Jan allowed herself to listen to her own intuition, perhaps at the same time tuning in to Alice's spirit:

"Alice, come along with me. I've prepared a nice warm bath for you." With the addition of fragrant oils and some soft music, the scene was set at 2am for an extraordinary exchange as Alice's usually unintelligible speech suddenly and unexpectedly became distinct and focused. "You've got nice breasts", she said to Jan as her own body was disclosed in all its nakedness. "Mine are too big, I've never liked them", she added. Jan was immediately drawn into an intimate conversation, a path with no map, for she had never walked this territory before.

With little encouragement Alice began to talk about her past relationship with her husband, about the clothes she used to wear with pride, about the sad loss of her only daughter and no other children to replace her, touching on those areas of intimacy usually considered 'out of bounds'. All boundaries between the professional nurse and the frail nursing home resident tumbled down as Jan allowed her own inhibitions to give way. Together, for a few moments, they entered a different world – woman to woman.

To enter spiritually into another's journey may involve letting down our guard and opening ourselves to encounter new depths of companionship.

Spiritual companionship: 'walking with'

Writing from personal experience as a person with dementia, Boden describes the benefits of having someone 'walk with' her, even though she may not realise help is at hand:

Unless someone is right there beside me, I don't remember they are there, and could help... So I don't remember my neighbour is

there, and we could go for a walk together; I don't remember that I could go for a walk myself; I don't think to ask for help in so many ways, because I forget that I am surrounded by friends only too glad to help if asked. And therein lies the problem: how am I going to remember to ask!

(Boden 1998, p63)

Spirited walking is dependent on carers offering companionship, rather than waiting to be asked. Many writers have described 'wandering' in dementia as the search for security and familiarity, or merely the search for a different view of the world (Lai & Arthur 2003, p78). To walk with this person is to understand that "even when a person's memory fails, that person's social identity remains" (Kimble 2003). This recalls questions such as: "Am I still a person when I don't know my name and can't explain where I'm going? Will they want to turn me round or stop me from going on this journey or will they come with me?" The aim of this chapter is to affirm that the spirits of social identity and security are born of companionship.

This concept of spirited walking is not to be found in a prescriptive textbook for it involves mystery and ambiguity rather than discernible processes and guaranteed outcomes. We are entering unfamiliar territory when we couple 'spiritual' with other aspects of care such as 'walking' and, as Ronaldson (1997) observes, there is a dearth of literature and research regarding the spiritual care of a person with dementia. Stories from others who write from personal experience assist us on this new pathway. For example, Goldsmith sees his role as chaplain to people with dementia in the following terms:

Who are you – walking to the toilet every few minutes? Who are you – wiping bottoms, answering the same question time and time again, sitting with those who weep and absorbing the anger and the frustration of those who do not know where they are? Who am I? I am a minister of the Gospel of love, and this angry lady is my sister and this weeping man my brother.

(Goldsmith 2000).

Goldsmith challenges all carers to ask not, "What is wrong with this person?" but, "Who am I in relation to this person?" Spirited walking asks: "Who are we together? How can we make the most out of this strange and unpredictable relationship? How may we keep in step when the path is not smooth? How will we know where to go when the signs are not easy to follow?"

'Walking with' requires a different set of values from 'doing to'; it is not dependent on skills or technique but transcends both. To walk with a person on the dementia pathway is to meet on a different plane, not an ethereal, 'otherworldly' plane but walking with feet firmly planted, step by step, keeping close, sometimes traversing completely uncharted territory. There may be no clear signs of progress towards a particular destination. The journey may at times seem like a one-way street rather than a wide, open highway; it may nevertheless be a journey of discovery. The journey may not always be trouble-free, it may at times be unpleasant, and it may even be a dismal failure. The journey into dementia has its disappointments to be endured as well as its triumphs to be cherished. In all of the ambiguities and confusion there may also be signs of hope, for this is a journey with intersecting signposts; reminders of the past and pointers to the future. There are always fresh opportunities for a new walk on a new day.

Spiritual insight

Much has been written about the need for carers to approach the person with dementia in such a way that their presence will not cause fear or surprise. If we look more deeply into the interpersonal field we may ask with Bush, "What do I really see?" (1997, p91-92). We may see a person wandering without purpose, in danger of becoming hurt, getting in the way of others, not responding to logic or persuasion. Adopting the calm confident approach advocated by Bush, we may ask, "How may I meet this person?" And what does the person with dementia see in the carer? "Someone in a hurry, someone flustered and impatient, or someone who has a genuine smile, an aura of calmness and an apparent willingness to spend some time?"

It is not necessary for the person with dementia to recognise who is walking with them, or the details of the journey; it is the feeling of security and warmth of the companionship that are more important. Making contact with some early memories also enables the spirit of insight to be captured: "A man who was severely demented still remembered his boyhood task of carrying wood, and by walking with a bit of kindling in hand, his self-esteem and emotional state improved dramatically" (Post 1995, p10). These spiritual insights associated with walking are also profoundly practical; as well as addressing feelings of being lost and alone in a world no one seems to understand, spirited walking is also a very physical, bodily gesture.

The bodily spirit

To separate the spiritual from the physical is to adopt a false dualism, with the unfortunate connotation that matters of the spirit or the soul do not belong to the real world. To focus on spiritual aspects of care is not to disembody the spirit from the whole person; rather it is to reconnect the disconnected. To focus on spiritual aspects of care is therefore not an optional extra for the carer who claims to be engaged in holistic care. Neither is it to leave spiritual care to 'those who like that sort of thing'. The point has also been made at the beginning of this chapter that spiritual care is not the sole province of the chaplain. Spiritual care occurs in the ordinary, everyday encounters in which one person meets with another. It cannot be segregated to another realm or time or place; spiritual care is part of the whole.

To keep in step, or to keep pace with the person with dementia is to identify not what's lacking, but what's there. As Ignatieff says to the doctor in his moving account of a son's care for his mother: "You keep telling me what has been lost, and I keep telling you something remains" (1993, p58). There is a propensity to define people with dementia according to what they lack. This leads to the planning of care based on needs, needs usually perceived by the carers. Spiritual needs then become defined as the individual's perceived problem for which the carer is challenged to find a solution. To classify spirituality in this way is to reduce the spirit of the person to definable concepts. The spirit of walking being discussed here relies on a different discourse: the discourse of history and narrative, of listening and response.

Steps towards 'spirited walking'

Having explored a very small part of this relatively uncharted terrain of spirited walking, how may this spiritual focus be translated into practical outcomes for the care of people with dementia? The following points may act as prompts, particularly for the person requiring 24-hour residential care:

- Identify any specific religious beliefs the person with dementia may hold and whether there is a particular person, eg clergy/pastoral carer/lay visitor who may appropriately 'walk with' them? Are there associated symbols and/or rituals that may be meaningful?
- Is there other literature or poetry that may revive the person's memory as they are walking?
- Build into the daily routine of care a particular accompanied 'walking time' for enjoying the benefits of exercise.
- Be alert for those moments of lucidity and clarity that characterize the unexpected communication of the person with dementia.
- Tune in to the meaning of 'lost' for the person who seems to be looking for something. Is there something, a tangible article, a reminder from their distant past that may be restored to memory?
- Don't rely on questions that require a rational answer, such as: "Where do you think you're going?"
- Avoid admonitions such as: "You'll get hurt if you try to cross the road by yourself".
- Ask yourself what it means to be 'in step' with this particular person at this particular time.
- Identify aspects that are clearly 'out of step' with the person's feelings and orientation.
- Examine your own walking pace and style, asking whether you are 'walking with' or 'walking against' the person with dementia.

Conclusion

The focus of this chapter has been on 'spirited walking', an invitation to view 'wandering' not merely as 'challenging behaviour' but a way of seeing the spirit or essence of the person with dementia. It is also an invitation to see carers as those whose spirit makes connections, as the dementia pathway is negotiated together. How will we know whether the path has been successfully negotiated and the destination reached? Scott-Maxwell, giving voice to her thoughts about ageing, disability and death, speaks of 'the distaste for what we may become' (Scott-Maxwell 1968, p75 and p138). In similar vein we may dare to step into the shoes of the person with dementia, to see where the journey is taking them. From that perspective, the destination may look something like this:

> Spending my last days on this journey, I am able to be myself; dancing a creative tango with all my carers. I am now in a place where my 'wandering' is not considered a problem, my idiosyncrasies are acknowledged and having 'a mind of my own' is not regarded as deviant behaviour. My variant moods also are no cause for blame or shame. Though dependent on others I am not left in isolation; my family and friends are welcomed as fellow travellers on this highway. Here I need not fear abandonment; I will be cared for no matter how strange and muddled and directionless I may appear. On this road, my deepest spiritual yearnings are met through companionship, understanding and humour. Here I am known not only for what I am, but also for who I have been and who I may yet become.

References

Boden C (1998) *Who will I be when I die?* Sydney: Harper Collins.

Bush T (1997) Spirituality in care. In Ronaldson S (ed) *Spirituality: the heart of nursing*. Melbourne: Ausmed publications.

Goldsmith M. (2000). Through a glass darkly: a dialogue between dementia and faith. Paper presented at the Ageing, spirituality and pastoral care conference, Canberra, Australia.

Ignatieff M (1993). *Scar tissue*. Toronto: Viking.

Jenson RW (1997). *Systematic theology: the Triune God* (Vol. 1). Oxford: Oxford University Press.

Kimble M (2003) The whole person. In R. Hudson (Ed.), *Dementia nursing: a guide to practice* (pp. 25-32). Melbourne: Ausmed Publications.

Lai C, Arthur D (2003) Wandering. In R. Hudson (Ed.), *Dementia nursing: a guide to practice* (pp. 70-82). Melbourne: Ausmed Publications.

Nay R (2002) The dignity of risk. *Australian Nursing Journal*, 9(9) 33.

Orchard H (ed) (2001) *Spirituality in health care contexts*. London: Jessica Kingsley Publishers.

Post SG (1995) *The moral challenge of Alzheimer disease*. Baltimore: The Johns Hopkins University Press.

Ronaldson S (ed) (1997) *Spirituality: the heart of nursing*. Melbourne: Ausmed Publications.

Scott-Maxwell F (1968) *The measure of my days*. New York: Alfred Knopf.

Seedsman TA (1994) The worth of a human life: a focus on the frail aged. *Australasian Journal on Ageing*, 13(2) 90-92.

10.4 A helping hand: walking with Gordon

by PAUL BATSON

Gordon was in his sixties. He had been diagnosed with Alzheimer's disease over 10 years ago and was in a long-stay ward for patients with advanced dementia where he would remain until he died. He was a tall man, well over six feet, somewhat gaunt now having lost a lot of weight, but he was still quite a powerful man. He would sit all day on the ward with a fixed, mask-like expression on his face. He looked quite disapproving, menacing even, as if he was angry and was a brooding presence on the ward. Gordon taught me an important lesson.

Whether what I observed about Gordon was a true reflection of his feelings, I don't know, because he had not spoken for a long time and no one could get any response other than the mask-like expression. Even his remarkable wife, who came every day to care for him so lovingly, no longer felt she could reach him or sense what was going on in his mind. Gordon was no longer able to do anything for himself. He was usually co-operative with staff as they washed, dressed and fed him every day. But he would stare at them with the same unchanging expression of disapproval which at first I found quite unnerving.

Most of my work as a drama therapist is with people with early to moderate dementia so I wondered what, if anything, I could usefully do with Gordon, given the limitations caused by his advanced dementia. I was told that one role that Gordon could carry out was that of 'walker'. He had often walked around the ward and continued do so, but less often now. My response was, "OK let's start with where Gordon is, let's do what Gordon can do: let's go for a walk together, if he's agreeable."

I explained to Gordon that I hoped we could go for a walk outside together and asked him to try and let me know if he didn't want to. I suggested that if he would rather not come out with me he should remain sitting down. But when one of the nurses produced his overcoat, gloves and a scarf he was very co-operative, stood up and put them on while maintaining his usual expression. So he and I set out for a walk round the grounds of the hospital. It was February, cold with grey skies, not an ideal time of year for a pleasant stroll. The grounds weren't particularly attractive or stimulating either: the usual collection of old buildings that had once been a workhouse, plus a few trees and garden area.

A small initiative

As we walked, I pointed out and commented to Gordon about the buds on the trees, the birds in the branches and the people we passed. I spoke as if he understood every word I was saying – and sometimes he seemed to be focusing on what I had drawn his attention to, but always with the same mask-like expression. This way of walking together became a regular weekly pattern over the next three months. In all that time Gordon's expression never changed significantly, though occasionally there were brief moments when I thought perhaps he was more aware – and even looked towards me – but it was so fleeting. There was, however, one initiative Gordon took which might seem small, but which I think was quite remarkable, given his medical condition and usual patterns of behaviour.

It started on our very first walk together. Off we went, hand in hand – Gordon seemed happy enough to do this, which gave me a way of connecting with him as well as reducing the risk of him suddenly walking off on his own. He was, after all, a big man who could still walk at quite a pace. As we walked between the buildings we came across a wide pathway between two hospital buildings. In the middle of the pathway there was a large metal post, perhaps four feet high; it was there to prevent any traffic getting through.

Rather than break contact with Gordon, it seemed to me to be more convenient for us to walk either side of this post, so as we walked I lifted his hand over the post, and on we went. We hadn't gone far when I suddenly stopped – in my own mind at least – and thought, why did I do that? Why did I do for Gordon something that he might

have done for himself? Why did I lift his hands over this post? Naturally I did not want him to bang his hand against the post, but I had done it for him. I had made the classic mistake of assuming he couldn't lift his hand himself and I had denied him the opportunity to exercise any initiative by doing it for him.

We walked around the grounds for about 15 minutes or so and then I decided to return the way we had come, past the post, to see what might happen this time. When we approached the post I kept hold of Gordon's hand but didn't make any move to lift it; without any prompting Gordon, quite spontaneously, lifted my hand over the post. I turned to him and said, "Thank you very much, Gordon". He continued to look at me in the same way – there was no change of expression, nor any sign of acknowledgement from him.

Gordon and I had about 15 weekly walks, and each time we passed the post, on the way out and on the way back from our walk. Each time, without exception and without any word from me, Gordon took the initiative and lifted my hand over the post, and each time I looked at him and said, "Thank you Gordon" – and his expression never changed.

It would be lovely to say that Gordon's ability to communicate and respond to others improved, but that would not be true. In fact his health continued to decline and some months later he died, a merciful release for him and his family. But walking with him powerfully reminded me that there was something going on inside Gordon: he had some awareness and ability to recognise this one situation and act appropriately, despite all outward appearances to the contrary.

Gordon taught me never to make assumptions about people living with dementia. He reinforced my belief that if we are on the look-out and offer sensitive opportunities for interaction, then we can connect with people living with dementia, even when their illness is severe. On our walks together, Gordon gave me a helping hand, far more than he ever knew.

But walking is also praying. Solitary walking is both contemplative prayer and intercession. I'm not a contemplative walker, something in me always wants to push on too fast, but I intercede as I walk. David did both. Like the best prayers, David never hurried. He moved over the hills at a contemplative pace, seeing deeply, taking it all into himself. But walking is most profoundly a kind of intercession, because the solitary walker's mind is filled with images and faces from his own life, scraps of memory, regrets, remembered joys, loved ones. You touch them all with love and remembrance as you move on, watching the film playing in your head. Walking releases the switch and plays back to you the movie of your life.

Richard Holloway (Bishop of Edinburgh) (1996) Limping towards the sunrise, Edinburgh: Saint Andrew Press